Dear Reader:

The book you are about to read is the latest bestseller from the St. Martin's True Crime Library, the imprint *The New York Times* calls "the leader in true crime!" Each month, we offer you a fascinating account of the latest, most sensational crime that has captured the national attention. St. Martin's is the publisher of Tina Dirmann's VANISHED AT SEA, the story of a former child actor who posed as a yacht buyer in order to lure an older couple out to sea, then robbed them and threw them overboard to their deaths. John Glatt's riveting and horrifying SECRETS IN THE CELLAR shines a light on the man who shocked the world when it was revealed that he had kept his daughter locked in his hidden basement for 24 years. In the Edgar-nominated WRITTEN IN BLOOD, Diane Fanning looks at Michael Petersen, a Marine-turned-novelist found guilty of beating his wife to death and pushing her down the stairs of their home—only to reveal another similar death from his past. In the book you now hold, WICKED INTENTIONS, Kevin Flynn follows the disturbing trail of some men who went missing in New Hampshire...

St. Martin's True Crime Library gives you the stories behind the headlines. Our authors take you right to the scene of the crime and into the minds of the most notorious murderers to show you what really makes them tick. St. Martin's True Crime Library paperbacks are better than the most terrifying thriller, because it's all true! The next time you want a crackling good read, make sure it's got the St. Martin's True Crime Library logo on the spine—you'll be up all night!

Charles E. Spicer, Jr.

D0954497

Charles E. Spicer, Jr.
Executive Editor, St. Martin's True Crime Library

WICKED
INTENTIONS

THE SHEILA LABARRE MURDERS

A TRUE STORY

KEVIN FLYNN

St. Martin's Paperbacks

Published by arrangement with New Horizon Press

WICKED INTENTIONS

For information address New Horizon Press, P.O. Box 669, Far Hills, NJ 07931.

EAN: 978-0-312-57577-9

Printed in the United States of America

New Horizon Press edition published 2009
St. Martin's Paperbacks edition / January 2010

St. Martin's Paperbacks are published by St. Martin's Press, 175 Fifth Avenue, New York, NY 10010.

10 9 8 7 6 5 4 3 2 1

For Lily

AUTHOR'S NOTE

The point of view of this book is based on the investigative journalism of Kevin Flynn and reflects his perceptions of the past, present and future. The facts about the Sheila LaBarre murders recounted in this book are true to the best of his knowledge and recall. Some of the names have been changed and identifying characteristics altered to safeguard the privacy of individuals. The personalities, events, actions and conversations portrayed in this book have been taken from extensive personal interviews, police reports, court documents, including trial transcripts, letters, personal papers, research, press accounts and the memories of some participants. Quoted testimony has been taken from interviews, pre-trial and trial transcripts and other sworn statements. Some minor characters are composites. Some conversations have been reconstructed. Events involving the characters happened as described; only minor details have been altered.

TABLE OF CONTENTS

PROLOGUE

Dusk was falling on the New Hampshire town. It was around 6 P.M. The trip to the farmhouse took the officers down a long, wooded private road. The branches of the trees on either side of the path reached out to one another, touching fingers midway across. The canopy of bark and early spring buds enveloped the police cruiser and its passengers.

When Epping Police Detective Richard Cote and Sergeant Sean Gallagher pulled up to the property at 70 Red Oak Hill Lane on Friday, March 24, 2006, they noticed the wooden gate to the horse farm was closed and padlocked. Neither could remember a time the gate had been secured like that, but they knew historically the homeowner had disputes with the town road agent about plowing beyond her gate even though she herself had chained it shut on him.

The officers had come to conduct a well-being check. Not on the homeowner, but on someone who had recently moved to town.

Cote and Gallagher knew the property well. There was a farmhouse, a large barn and several outbuildings. Tonight, the house seemed quiet. There were no lights on inside. They scanned the yard and all of the owner's cars seemed to be there. They knocked on the door, assuming that someone was home, but no one answered.

There was some activity on the farm, however. As they

stood at the front door, Cote pointed out a completely burnt mattress and box spring. It was right in front of the porch entrance, about twenty feet to their right. About thirty-five feet away from the mattress was a second burn area. It was a rusty metal barrel and a pile of hay. Although there was no one on the property, both of these areas were actively burning.

Gallagher approached the pile of debris. There was an awful smell in the air.

The police officer's step stuttered with disbelief. *No. That can't be what I'm seeing,* he thought to himself. Sticking out of the burning hay pile in plain sight was a bone. The bone was only about three and a half inches long, but appeared to be jagged at the bottom. It was as if it had been cut or hacked in some sloppy way. The top of the bone sprouted into a round ball meant for some corresponding joint. It turned the cop's stomach with horror.

Immediately, Gallagher made a phone call. Cote, however, didn't hear the conversation. He had moved in for a closer look at the bone in the fire pit. When the sergeant snapped off the phone he told Cote, "We're kicking in the side door to find this kid."

Cote watched Gallagher steady himself at the door. He punched through with the heel of his foot right under the doorknob, breaking the wooden frame. Cote knew the sergeant was so deeply focused on what he was doing that Gallagher probably couldn't hear what he heard: a set of wheels, a car of some kind, making its way up the windy dirt road approaching the farm. Soon they would not be alone.

"Someone's coming," he said.

Cote turned back and looked closely at the bone, braced for the odor. On the ball at the top, he saw something he'd never forget. The bone was covered with soft tissue that looked like a burned hunk of human flesh.

PART 1

THE FARM

"'Oh, you dear children, who has brought you here? Do come in, and stay with me. No harm shall happen to you.' She took them both by the hand, and led them into her little house."

—Brothers Grimm, *Hansel and Gretel*

CHAPTER 1

ON A SECLUDED FARM . . .

Until the day he left the state prosecutor's office, Peter Odom would never really know exactly what happened on that farm. How some people could fall off the face of the earth. How some people could be directed like puppets. How some people could watch eagerly with wide-open eyes and could simultaneously look away. Odom understood the stresses that caused one to strike down another: jealousy, hatred, rage and greed. Even madness. They all bloomed from the same emotion: fear. Pushed far enough, fast enough, any human could give in to temptation. They could kill in self-defense or kill in selfish abandon.

Odom had yet to learn why some people seemed predestined to murder, why they had been born to kill. These were people in whom murder had been incubating their whole lives. They didn't kill as an impassioned powder keg, which exploded once and released its malicious tensions. They didn't attack as a bee does, stinging once, then dying. They attacked like a wasp, stinging repeatedly and easily without consequences.

Odom knew nobody would ever know *all* of what happened on that farm. Nobody except Sheila LaBarre.

The unmarked police car moved through the town of Epping, New Hampshire, without lights and siren, but with a sense of urgency, past brick buildings that house mom-and-pop restaurants and barbershops doing business out of garages. Assistant Attorney General Odom watched the March sun comfort the town in the last throes of a New England winter, spring peeking through cracks. He made a note of the date: *Sunday March 26, 2006.* The prosecutor did not know the way there, but knew the destination. Murder. That's why Odom and the homicide division had been called in. This whole mess was falling into his lap.

"I have seen more fucking shit on this job," the man in the passenger's seat said. New Hampshire State Police Lieutenant Russ Conte was talking almost to himself. But his comments were intended to ease the driver. The town's police chief had never seen anything like this and, for all Conte's world-weary expression, doubted Conte had seen anything like this either.

Odom, riding in the back, watched the little houses fall away and the country roads stretch farther and farther to the next landmark. The car's wheels squealed a little as it cut right at a fork. Odom noticed the hand-painted sign offering farm fresh eggs up ahead. He had never visited this section of Epping before. So few of the other rural New Hampshire towns still offer anything like a real working farm. Today, the only things that grow from much of those early settlers' soil are suburbs and subdivisions.

Mixed among the tiny houses sprinkled in this area are the original farms and their elderly owners who made thousands systematically selling off parts of their land in order to make ends meet. The road climbed.

"I have seen shit you wouldn't believe," Conte continued. As head of the NHSP's Major Crimes Unit, Conte could back up his claims of being witness to all kinds of depravity. The olive-skinned man was wearing a gray suit with a handgun hidden beneath its folds. Conte's shoulders took up most of the space as he stretched out in the front seat.

"We're going down here," said Police Chief Gregory Dodge as the car left the paved road and cut into the woods. A street sign marked the way as "Red Oak Hill Lane," a slight variation on the name of the road from which they had just pulled off. The crunch of rocks and gravel beneath the tires was pronounced, and the car heaved as it struck a stray root. The path was lined with maple and pine trees, which, even before the spring burst of foliage, suffocated light from the sky.

Immediately to their right was a home, set back a bit from the road. There was an antique green tractor sitting in the front yard, as if it were a monument to the land. To the left there was a slight clearing, and Odom caught a glimpse of old trucks and farm equipment. An abandoned school bus, painted a faded blue, its windshield smashed, was tangled in the weeds among the other wrecks.

"That's Gordon Winslow's place," the chief said.

"Is there anyone else on this road?" Odom asked.

"No. Just Gordon," Dodge answered. "And Sheila."

They pulled away from the Winslow farm and then there seemed to be nothing. They continued bumping over rocks and stumps in the uneven road. Trees ran along both sides and Odom could tell the road was narrow. A stone wall kept pace, first on the left, then on the right, then on both sides of the road. Barbed wire kept the wall company. A quarter-mile down, a half, and still nothing.

Odom noticed a *No Trespassing* sign on a tree. Something was written in underneath it. *You are being videotaped.*

"Do you really think there are video cameras on the property?"

Chief Dodge shrugged. "Knowing Sheila, anything's possible."

Around one more wooded bend and the dirt road straightened to lead to a wooden gate. It was swung open and a police cruiser was guarding the property's entrance. The chief slowed slightly as he pulled in.

The three got out of the car and took in the view. Red Oak Hill Lane fed directly into the courtyard of a beautiful country home. The white house with black shutters and tin roof was propped to the left, and the momentum of the road would lead one across flattened grass to a barn and several outbuildings to the right.

A grand view awaited those who stood at the home's front door. The house overlooked a sprawling pasture of grass still thin and yellow from the winter. The trees that had been lining the access road were only a few feet deep. It had created the illusion they had just traveled through some deep forest. But from here, one could see the trees had enveloped the path, creating a tunnel of bark and overhanging branches. The land surrounding on both sides was unspoiled.

"That's got to be fifty acres just over there," Odom said, gesturing to the grand pasture. Off in the distance, a tiny car passed the road that formed the land's farthest border.

"It's 115 acres altogether," Dodge said. "Some of it is woods, but a lot is just like this: rolling fields."

Conte had been focusing only on what he found in the courtyard, not the expanse to his back. "That's a lot of land," he said, his voice trailing off.

Odom asked, "How does she afford all this, Chief?"

Dodge stared not at the vista, but back at something in the yard in front of the house. Some black object. His eyes squinted deep and his nose took in a pungent smell.

"Chief . . . ?"

"She owns it outright," Dodge finally responded. "Inherited it from Doctor Wilfred LaBarre. Chiropractor. He died back in 2000."

"They were married?"

"No. She changed her name when she moved here. Changed it to Sheila LaBarre, but no, they never were married. When he died, she got the farm and some rental properties out on the seacoast. Best I can tell, that's how she makes her money."

"What's the land worth?"

"You chop it up and build houses, it's worth ten million to a developer. On the tax rolls, it's two million." Dodge added, "Not that she's paid all her taxes."

Odom looked closely at the house. Its white paint was just starting to peel, its landscaping just starting to become unkempt. He walked up to the window, cupped his eyes and tried to peer in.

Not this week, he thought. *Any other week except this one. This is not the week for me to be getting a case like* this.

"Search warrants are for the exterior of the property only," Conte reminded the prosecutor.

Odom couldn't see anything, but he knew he had to get inside the house. "Sergeant Mitchell's on his way back. The new warrant's for the entire property, including the interior."

"I think this is what you guys came for."

Dodge and Conte huddled together, but Odom took one last look inside the farmhouse. Had he seen something moving? He turned and saw the policemen standing over a burn pit. Until now, he hadn't noticed the smell in the air. It was acrid, like burning fuel.

The pit was a couple of feet wide. A rusty brown barrel was nearby. Smoke was still wafting from both of them. Odom walked closer and could finally make out what the black shape on the ground was: the charred remains of a bed mattress. The box springs had maintained their shape.

Odom peeked into the barrel. Inside were a large pair of pruning sheers and a pair of hedge shears. Both had burnt handles. He wanted to pick them up to examine them, but he didn't want to compromise any potential evidence. Also found nearby was a blue DVD case, a rental from the local video store. Its corners were blackened and covered with soot. The movie was the ultra-violent horror flick *Saw.*

Next to the burn pit was a blue plastic bag from Wal-Mart. It appeared to be full of soot and crackled in the wind.

"Take a look at this," Conte said. Odom did a deep knee bend and joined Conte on the ground next to the burn pit. Odom squinted as he followed Conte's finger pointing under the mattress. Mixed among the gray-white ash were tiny shards of white bone. *And could it be . . . ?*

Odom turned to the lieutenant. "Is that a tooth?"

Conte just stood up, brushed off his knees and walked over to Dodge. The chief waited to hear more of their takes. The three stood there, arms folded, just looking at one another.

"So," Conte began, "do you think she dismembered him

inside? Or did she drag him out here on the mattress, do it here and then burn the body?"

The order of things meant so much to his prosecution, but the answer meant little to Odom. It was savage beyond all measure. All that mattered was someone's son was dead. How long could they keep the details here under . . .

Snap!

Odom spun toward the barn. *Something stepped on a branch?* He watched, but nothing moved.

"Get some photos to Doctor Jennie Duval at the state medical examiner's office. E-mail them," Conte ordered one of the technicians. "We need to know as soon as possible if this is human or livestock."

"I'll tell you what's worse," Odom said. "Look at that." He pointed to a wooden chair out on the grass. It wasn't an outdoor chair though. It looked like it came from the kitchen and was facing the burn pit.

Dodge agreed. "She pulled up a chair so she could watch."

Odom started taking notes. *Sunday, March 26, 2006. LaBarre farm, Epping . . .* "Did you ever think she was capable of being this violent?" he asked the chief.

"Violent? No. Wild? Yes. She's more like a wild animal. She called me at the station at all hours of the night. She sent me letters, pages and pages of rants that she faxed over. Finally I had to tell her to stop calling the department."

"What were these rants about?" Conte asked.

"That we were out to get her. That I hated her. That we weren't doing enough to protect her home and property."

Odom took notes on all of it. "Where is she now?"

"Don't know. Just told her to get out while we executed the search warrant."

"And tell me again how she looked."

"She was," Dodge stated, "covered head to toe in ashes and soot."

"Great," Odom muttered. "Just beautiful."

"The crime van is ready," Conte said. "But this is going to take a while to process. Maybe even a couple of days. This place is huge. And we haven't even looked inside the house yet."

"I'll get the warrant for inside the . . ."

Odom turned again. Something caught his eye. *What the hell was that?*

This time Conte saw it too. "There it is," he said. The hulking cop in the suit stepped into the underbrush around the home. He reached into the weeds and pulled something out.

"What is that?" Odom shouted.

Conte carried it in his arms, digging his thick fingers into fur. "It's a rabbit."

"Rabbits? Shit," Dodge spat. "Sheila's got a million of them. She lets them run around free in the house."

There were some rabbit pens next to the home, but they were empty. "Do any of them get outside?" Conte asked.

"I guess so. Why?"

He held the rabbit out so Dodge and Odom could see the hocks of its feet and the fur on its belly marked chocolate brown. "Because this bunny is covered in someone's blood."

CHAPTER 2

DON'T TALK TO STRANGERS

It was the perfect day to take a walk. Not everyone is allowed to go all the way to the pet store. Not everyone has the responsibility of watching her brother. Or even better, not everyone can take care of a pet. For Amy, it was shaping up to be a perfect day.

The pet store Amy and her brother Donald were headed to is probably the biggest pet store in the city of Manchester. Its massive, barn-like store structure anchors one end of a strip mall on busy South Willow Street. The other end of the strip mall is a sporting goods store, and there's nothing in between.

The only other bit of commerce on this property is a Mexican fast food restaurant that sprang up in the parking lot.

The afternoon was slow, though Sundays are busy at the pet store. It was the perfect time for Amy to bring her brother to the store to look around and play with the animals. Both she and Donald are developmentally disabled adults, and they walked the two and a half miles to the store.

Owners are encouraged to bring their animals inside and browse the store with their pets. Amy liked to stop and scratch dogs behind their ears, but cats were her favorite. Her mother owned cats. She wanted to look at cats with Donald. But . . . where had Donald gone?

"Donald!" she called out in a voice a little too loud. It

was up to her to watch him, and that's a grown-up responsibility. Donald was always doing his own thing, driving her crazy. She knew she was not supposed to lose him in the store. Donald had epilepsy. What if he were having a seizure right now?

Amy found her brother standing at the end of one aisle talking with a woman. She was a striking figure with long blonde hair down past her shoulders, about five-foot-four, wearing a heavy black coat. They were looking at rabbit hutches.

"Donald, you know you're not supposed to talk to strangers!" she chastised her brother as if the older woman could not hear them.

"It's all right, angel. We're just talking about rabbits," the woman said. Her voice was soft and smooth, with the slightest lilt of a Southern accent. It sounded pleasant to Amy. "Have you ever taken care of a rabbit?"

The woman produced a full-sized white mottled rabbit from . . . where? . . . under her coat? Up her sleeve? Like a magician? It squirmed a little bit while being moved, like a house painter on a rickety ladder. The woman gestured for them to pet it and they did.

"He's so furry. What's his name?"

"His name's Little Satin." The siblings stepped closer to the woman as their hands ran all over the rabbit. "He likes you," the woman told them.

The girl watched as the rabbit twitched its nose, trying to catch her scent. She adjusted her thick glasses and talked "Bunny." The woman showed great patience with both the animal and the siblings.

"So, have you, darling?"

Amy looked up. "Have I what?" she said loudly.

"Ever taken care of a rabbit?"

Amy thought about it, twisting up her face to demonstrate the great attention she gave the question. "I don't think so. We've had lots of pets, but we've never had a rabbit."

The woman shifted the rabbit in the bow of her arm so it was now just out of the couple's reach. "How would you like it if I gave you this rabbit?"

Amy didn't respond; she only blinked.

"How about," she continued, "if I gave you one hundred dollars to take Little Satin for me and take care of him."

"Whoa," Amy blurted out laughing. "Why can't you take care of him anymore?"

The woman rubbed her nails through Little Satin's back. "I had a fight with my boyfriend, and I'm not going to stay with him ever again. I have to take care of myself, but I need someone to look after my babies. Someone has to look after my rabbits for a little while, darling."

"You have more rabbits?"

The woman gestured to the parking lot. "In my car. Satin's sister and brother, Sapphire and Snookster."

Amy looked at Donald, then back at the woman with the long blonde hair. She liked the way the woman talked to them. She didn't talk down to them, like some people did. She listened to what they had to say. "But we don't have a cage or anything."

The woman looked over at the hutch on the shelf. "What if I bought you this hutch? That way, all three rabbits will have a place to sleep tonight."

Amy was excited. Not only was she getting the bunny and hutch for free, but also she was getting one hundred dollars to take care of it. That was a real grown-up responsibility. Then again, another complication occurred to her. "We can't carry the hutch home." Donald asked if they could take the bus, but Amy didn't know if they even let rabbits ride the bus.

The woman smiled. "Then I'll give you a ride home, darling." They all walked out of the store together. Donald stroked Little Satin's fur as his sister held the rabbit. The woman led them through the parking lot to her awaiting car, a green sedan. It was turning out to be a perfect day.

"You are an angel, darling, for taking my baby," she told Amy.

"What's your name?" Amy asked.

And sweetly, as sunbeams for cherubs, she told them, "My name is Sheila LaBarre."

CHAPTER 3

PROOF OF MURDER?

Writers who describe crime in a small town often try to make the community seem smaller than it is. Just a wide space in the road, where nothing extraordinary happens. Communities that the evils of the world have failed to notice. As if that town were the sole repository of innocence and purity left in the Western world, then the suspect is one who not only committed a crime but also soiled an Eden.

Epping, New Hampshire, is a small town, but probably no more or less shocked by violent crime than any other. Much of New Hampshire's modern development occurred south to north, along the pathways of the two major arteries out of Massachusetts. Along Interstate 93, Salem grew into a major retail destination; Derry and Londonderry became huge bedroom communities. Up Route 3, a.k.a. the Everett Turnpike, Nashua became a fine city that was named Best Place to Live in America twice: in 1987 and 1997. Both highways shake hands in Manchester, the state's largest city and the state's center of economic activity.

Aided by demand for available and accessible land, the communities within this triangle flourished as Massachusetts expatriates settled in. But small towns outside that area remained landlocked, linked instead by a series of back roads and secondary highways that tempered sprawl. Those dozens of towns, with their New Deal-era road plans, worked to keep growth to a minimum and to preserve their perception of small town New England. Epping was just such a town.

Residents meet each March for the annual town meeting. While the town has a part-time Board of Selectmen, they're relatively powerless. It's the residents who vote Norman Rockwell-style to approve spending plans. The previous year, Police Chief Greg Dodge watched quietly as about thirteen hundred people voted on whether to approve his proposed $4.3 million operating budget for that year. Dodge asked the citizens of Epping to give him two new officers. The cost to taxpayers would be only $20,810, because a federal grant of $50,000 would cover the rest. But in true Yankee fashion, residents rose from their seats and voiced their concerns about what would happen in three years when the grant expired. By a hand vote, citizens amended the request to one officer, but the proposal still failed 527 to 811. Dodge did not go away empty-handed from the town meeting. Epping residents had okayed his request to lease a new police cruiser by a vote of 791 to 558.

Epping was experiencing growing pains, as developers finally had spotted the town and recognized its key position if further growth was to happen. Residents wryly called it "The Center of the Universe" and bumper stickers saying so can still be spotted. At one point, Epping was considered the Great Crossroads to the state, back when highways were two lanes wide. Windy, crooked Route 101 had been renovated a decade ago to be a multi-lane east-west route from Manchester to the Atlantic. That sowed a row for commercial and residential development to also blossom. Epping is roughly halfway to Portsmouth from Manchester, and State Highway 125 intersecting there offers good shortcuts to Durham and other eastern communities.

After the Wal-Mart opened off exit 7, Epping's police department felt the impact. Shoplifting calls and fender benders in the parking lot were consuming time in what once was a Mayberry-like patrol route. The extra calls, which included criminal assaults and one rape, did not sit well with Dodge.

The crimes reported at Wal-Mart were serious and sometimes violent. But as far as anyone could remember, it had been years and years since there had been a murder in the town of Epping.

I rarely had a need to go to Epping as a television reporter in New Hampshire. To me, the signpost merely meant halfway to the ocean or halfway back to the station after a live shot. But after one hour on the story, I knew it would change my life.

Sunday afternoons are deadly quiet in newsrooms everywhere, deadly for the young college graduate-cum-television producers who have to fill thirty minutes of news at 6:00. I had been blessed (and that's definitely the way we viewed it) the previous two Sundays with breaking news. A week prior there was the murder investigation in which one woman in the mountain town of Tamworth stabbed another woman to death at a party in a fight over beer money. The weekend before in the woods of Alstead, a closeted homosexual shot his roommate and chased another man through the forest with a handgun, all after smoking one-third of a marijuana cigarette. It's these examples of stupidity and tragic miscalculation that give reporters "happy feet" and make producers high-five one another.

The assignment desk had little for me and my videographer to do when our shift began at 2:00 P.M. on Sunday, March 26, 2006. Indiana Senator Evan Bayh was speaking at a campaign event for a Democratic state senator. *No one* comes to New Hampshire to speak at a political gathering who isn't running for president.

My TV station is the only network station in the state. Channel 9 wields a lot of power within New Hampshire's borders and beyond. It's the big fish, small pond dynamic that has suited it well. Dozens of television reporters have made the jump from New Hampshire to Boston (where starting salaries are tripled and anchormen and -women can still earn a million-dollar paycheck). Some station alumni have gone on to much greener pastures, such as Nannette Hanson on MSNBC or Carl Cameron on Fox News. Even Chris Wragge, former Entertainment Tonight host and former husband to Swedish model and *Playboy* playmate Victoria Silvstedt, once did the weekend shift here as a sportscaster.

I had no intention of leaving the station anytime soon. But I really wanted to get off of weekends. It was murder on my family life. I had too little time with my five-year-old daughter and the hours were fraying on my wife.

I was not the typical TV reporter. I spent ten years in radio and I never got the shtick out of my blood. I was sent to fires and blizzards and car accidents, but my niche was feature reporting. I had no problem doing funny stories. Getting clocked playing dodgeball, singing karaoke in the shower, getting sacked by the members of an all-women's football team. No stunt was off-limits for me. Viewers loved it. I loved it.

But the face of television news was changing, even in secluded New Hampshire. There were fewer reporters, but they were being asked to cover more stories in a single day. We seemed to be doing less politics, fewer stories on education or health. The greater emphasis was being placed on the sexy, the sensational. As one videographer said to me, "We used to do stories about people. Now we just do stories about victims."

I was in a funk. I considered myself a storyteller; it was why I was recruited out of radio to fill an open position at the TV station. I didn't like the direction my job was going. I needed something that was going to shake up my career.

The Evan Bayh event moved at a glacial pace. Bayh shook hands with every alderman and selectman who could someday become a presidential campaign worker. His big political blunder was, of course, not talking to me. I was the one who was going to be putting him on television and introducing him to thousands of presidential primary voters. Instead, I was standing off in the corner, sneaking mozzarella sticks from the hot buffet.

My cameraman for the day passed me his pager: Call newsroom ASAP.

Ah, holy hell, I thought. *What grief am I getting myself into now?* I sneaked outside to place a call.

"Newsroom," someone answered.

"It's Kevin. I got your page."

"Where are you guys?" the assignment editor asked.

"Still at Bayh. He's running long."

Pause. "Do you have any sound with him?"

They're rushing this. What's going on? "We're waiting for his speech to finish up before we can get a sound bite." Behind me, I could hear applause. Bayh just said something I assumed I should have been there to hear.

"Okay." I could tell she was turning over the information in her head, calculating something. "We're going to pull you out of there and send you to Epping."

Oh, fuck me up the ass. We've been standing here this long. We're this close to getting the sound bite.

"What's shaking in Epping?" I snapped.

"There's a search for a missing person," she said. "And it could be a homicide."

"Tell me about the bones. Is there enough for DNA?"

Assistant AG Peter Odom was discussing the case with State Police Lieutenant Russ Conte and Epping Police Chief Greg Dodge. They were sitting around the police department in the Epping Safety Complex, a modern building for an old town.

Peter Odom had spent more than a decade as a deputy county attorney in Strafford County before coming to the Attorney General's homicide unit. Previously, he prosecuted cases of child abuse and sexual assault. He spearheaded the prosecution against a defrocked Catholic priest in his seventies who stood trial for allegedly molesting eight children, some of them altar boys. Odom won a conviction, but the man died in jail of natural causes after serving less than a year in his forty-four-to-eighty-eight–year sentence.

Odom ran for office in 2002, seeking the Merrimack County Attorney's post on the Democratic ticket. Odom convinced presidential candidate Howard Dean to come speak at a fundraiser at his home in Bow, New Hampshire.

"I knew that we wanted to have a kickoff event for my

campaign, and I decided to try Dean," Odom later wrote in a political blog. "The county attorney's slot appears just above dog catcher on the ballot and we knew we would need someone with stature to draw a paying crowd."

Odom reported they served 100 pounds of fresh fruit, passed out seven cases of water and juice and watched Dean eat half a watermelon before giving his speech. The day was documented by the never-blinking-eye of a public affairs cable television network. But Republicans had long coattails that year and Odom was defeated.

"You want to know about DNA from *those* bones?" Lieutenant Conte responded to Odom's initial question. "That's going to be tough. DNA breaks down in heat. It melts. We're going to be sifting through ash looking for something undamaged."

Several months prior, the state police helped on another case in Rockingham County where a crematorium was accused of all types of horrible procedures. Investigators looking into improprieties by a disgraced medical examiner paid a visit to the crematory. There they were shocked to see remains mislabeled and mixed together, two bodies being cremated in the same oven and a cadaver rotting in a broken cooler.

The public outcry was enormous, especially from the families of those cremated at the facility. No one could be positive that the ashes they had truly belonged to their loved one. They begged for officials to run tests to verify identities. The county attorney went on television announcing that the cremation process destroys the DNA and positive identification would be impossible. Everyone in New Hampshire was now well aware what fire did to DNA.

Odom turned to the chief. "What about the bone Sergeant Gallagher saw? Where was it?"

"We haven't found it. She's probably burned it since."

"The DNA isn't going to be your problem, Pete. We can probably find enough to prove he's dead. The trick is going to be finding enough to prove he was murdered."

The chief sat up straight. "What do you mean? We've got

cutting tools! The burn pit! The mattress! The blood on the rabbit! Let alone what's inside the house!"

Odom rubbed his chin silently. "It doesn't prove he was killed," he said finally. "Forget about what a defense attorney could do with a jury in court. If the medical examiner can't determine the manner of death is homicide, then our case isn't very strong, is it?"

Chief Dodge fell back into the chair. There was no air for his lungs. *She couldn't actually get away with it, could she?* he thought. *All those years of angry phone calls, nuisance complaints. Threats. This crazy woman in my town finally went off and did it, did it in the most gruesome way, and there's a chance they can't prove it?*

"Tell me again about our victim, Chief."

Dodge pulled the notes from the missing persons report and handed them to Odom. "The guy's name is Kenneth Countie. He's twenty-four years old. Came from Wilmington, Massachusetts."

Odom flipped through the paperwork. "And . . . he and Sheila . . . how long have they been together?"

"Not long, according the mother. They met about a month ago."

"And this is the last time we can confirm he was alive? Last Friday, March 17?"

"The last time we can confirm it. Yes. I'll see about getting the videotapes from the store."

"For now, this is a secret. Nothing comes out of this department! Nobody makes a statement except me! Our public position is this kid is *missing*. That's what we tell the press. That's what we tell the family." With that last statement, Odom's voice turned from angry to sad.

"We gotta see what's inside the house," Conte said.

"Get your forensics crew in there, Russ. This whole case will rise and fall based on the work they do." Odom shuddered at the thought. "And the work they need to do will take days."

"I'll have some people call the airport," Conte said. "We'll have the sheriff's office looking for her to make sure she doesn't get on a plane."

"What if she shows up here?" Dodge asked.

"What do you mean?"

"It's Sunday night. Sheila pops in here all the time. If she comes home and we're still on her property, she'll come down here to give us a piece of her mind." Dodge looked back and forth between them. "Do I arrest her?"

It was decided that, no, Sunday night was not the time. For a female suspect, there were special considerations for searching her person, checking her body for wounds or evidence. Conte wanted to do it back at the state police barracks during a normal nine-to-five shift when a female crime technician could do the job. "Be nonchalant about it. If she does show up, tell her to come back tomorrow."

Being nonchalant about any encounter with Sheila was a tall order.

"You know," Conte said again. "I have seen . . ."

". . . more fucking shit on this job. And guys either write a book or they never talk about it again."

I heard these words from Lieutenant Russ Conte clear as day. Because the Epping Safety Complex, while a model of modern municipal construction, has extremely thin walls.

I was sitting in the lobby of the police department waiting for a sound bite. If this truly were a search for a missing person, where were the searchers? Why won't the police talk to us? A search and rescue means "cooperation" from authorities (they'll give us a name and a photo, make a public plea for assistance). A homicide, that was a major pain in the ass. In New Hampshire, no one except the prosecutor could publicly comment on a homicide, so cops and other sources clammed up. True, this would be my third murder in three Sundays, and all of those stories came together fairly well. But an at-large suspect, a lengthy interrogation or an unidentified victim are all things that could delay a press briefing.

And I had to have *something* to report at 6:00.

I was alone in the lobby of the Epping PD, alone except for the newspaper reporter who had wandered in on the same tip. Editors on the desk overheard a blurb on the Manchester police scanner dispatching a squad car to check on a subject "in connection with a possible homicide investigation out of Epping." Odom, who had been fielding phone calls, denied they were conducting a homicide investigation. It was a missing persons case.

The two of us sat quietly, waiting for someone to talk. My videographer was in the tiny parking lot helping the satellite truck operator find someplace to set up. It was 5:15. They had to point the dish to the south in order to hit the satellite moving in geosynchronous orbit along the equator, and a tuft of tree was blocking the line of sight.

"Do you think she burned the body before she dismembered it or after?"

The voice came through the wall and echoed in the lobby. The other journalist and I looked at each other in shock. There was no way in hell we should have been hearing this, but the wall was thin and Conte's voice was strong.

"Did you get that?" I asked the newspaper reporter. I don't know how he could have missed it. He had his back up against the wall while I stared so hard at the wall I thought I was going to burn a hole in it.

"I heard 'dismembered.' Didn't you?"

"Ya." Neither of us could believe what we were getting.

"Who is checking on that?" Conte asked someone. "Hold on to that rabbit." Then there was some mention of blood on the animal.

I looked at the notebook resting on my lap. The page was still white, crisp and blank. I should have been writing all this down. But you learn there are some things you're not going to forget, and taking the time to write them down only distracts you from hearing further details.

Someone asked Conte a question. "We've already got the file sealed," he said. "The press is going to want that bad boy big time!"

I knew three things:

There had been a homicide and the suspect was a female.

If the files were sealed and no one went on the record with me, I was royally fucked for 6:00.

I had unexpectedly found the story of my career.

On the other side of a very thin wall, Chief Dodge made notes. It was starting to get dark and it was going to be a long night ahead. He realized the calm balance of their town had been upset. "There's one more thing," he said.

"What is it, Chief?"

"There were others."

Conte and Odom looked at each other. Now there was no air in their lungs.

"What do you mean?"

At first, Dodge wouldn't make eye contact, tapping a pen on his desk as he spoke. But saying the words brought out more strength in the chief.

"There are others who've lived on that farm with her. Other young men. Other guys we've seen around town with her."

There was silence in the room. "Go on."

"And there's at least one or two that . . . I can't say I've seen in quite some time."

CHAPTER 4

ADAM

Pamela Paquin enjoyed the girl talk with her houseguest. She had been surprised as all hell when her son and daughter came home with this strange older woman and a cage full of rabbits. *Is she some kind of freaky rabbit saleswoman or something?* she first thought. She was surprised that the woman was actually offering money to her daughter to take care of the rabbits. And then she was touched.

Donald carried in the box containing the hutch. He explained how Sheila had bought it for them and how she took the two of them to dinner. *Who does that?* Paquin thought.

When Sheila LaBarre walked up to Paquin's home, the other woman felt embarrassed, because it looked dilapidated. The exterior of the building was sea foam green, sided with ruffled metal slates made of asbestos. There were bicycles on the porch. It looked like the front door frame might have been broken. Spiderwebs caulked the outline of the porch lamp fixture, its bulb bare.

Pam Paquin kept her home clean the best she could. However, she was living on disability in a house that was so rundown that she couldn't get insurance for it. She was dealing with two adult children with developmental disabilities and her own brother, who also had problems. Paquin's other brother was dying in an institution, and her mother (who emigrated from Manchester, England, to Manchester, New

Hampshire) had slowly gone insane. Colorful people were always a part of her life, so Sheila LaBarre fit right in.

Paquin had been entertaining a friend, Sandra Charpentier, when Sheila arrived. Charpentier had bounced back and forth between housing in Manchester and Worcester, Massachusetts. She looked like Paquin's younger sister, except her hair was longer and striking platinum blonde. Paquin and Charpentier were close, but nothing prepared them for the journey they were about to go on.

Immediately, Sheila worked her charm on the mother as she had on Paquin's son and daughter. Paquin listened carefully to Sheila's story about running away from her boyfriend and never inquired for further details. The guest was polite to a fault and full of flattery.

The Paquins were captivated by the affirmation the woman gave them. Sheila told them she was a multi-millionaire who had inherited a horse farm. The women never asked why a wealthy landowner like herself would seek out a place to stay from a stranger. They were too enthralled with the stories she was weaving. Paquin wanted to know more about the horses and could she come visit the farm sometime?

Sheila introduced everyone to the three rabbits who were now under the care of Paquin's children. Sapphire was the gray one, the "alpha female," as Sheila described her. She was pregnant by one of her two companions. Little Satin was white with a pink nose and very gentle. Snooky was the oldest and the one with the most character. Sheila found the male rabbit six years earlier in Hampton on land owned by Dr. LaBarre. He was brown, with white patches on his left paw, leg and ear. The little guy was suffering from pasteurellosis, the rabbit sniffles, an illness often brought on by stress in the animal.

Sheila sat with her legs curled up underneath her on the couch, watching television. Charpentier had stayed and laughed along with them. For most of the evening, the siblings had played with Snookster, Sapphire and Little Satin. The rabbits were in the cage that Sheila had them in while in the car. Paquin's brother, Charlie, couldn't take the clucking anymore, so he excused himself and went into his bedroom.

"Pam, I just don't know what I'd do without you," Sheila said to Paquin. The kindness from her voice flowed freely. "You are a true angel and a true friend." It was a steady and powerful barrage of compliments and positive attention the woman had been showering her hosts with. Paquin felt more and more at ease with Sheila as the night went on. There was no talk about where the woman would go tomorrow or what would happen to her. The talk was of horses and rabbits . . . and sometimes of racy sex. They all seemed to be enjoying the moment.

A person of sophistication might have considered Paquin *gauche*. She was overweight, missing a front tooth and had dyed her short hair an unnatural shade of red. But she was kind and hospitable and Sheila LaBarre needed a friend now more than ever.

They felt the air come out of the room at 10:59. That's when the late-night news launched the headlines of their evening news program. The sight of something on the television caused Sheila to place her hand over her mouth and tremble. Paquin didn't know what the story was about yet, but Sheila knew instantly. With one hand she pointed to the young man's photo on the screen. She covered her mouth with the other.

"That's Adam," she gasped.

Adam? Paquin thought. *Who's Adam?*

Silence fell over the room as all eyes zoomed to the television set. An anchorwoman looked sternly back at them.

"Good evening," she said to the room. "An investigation is under way tonight for a man who went missing in Epping." The words "Missing Persons Case" appeared on the screen above a photograph of a young man in a white shirt. The name listed was not Adam.

"Kenneth Countie moved to town just three weeks ago," she continued. "And tonight the Attorney General's office, along with the local police department, is actively searching for him."

The screen divided into two pictures: the anchorwoman in one box, a field reporter in the other. She asked the reporter to provide details, and he introduced a taped segment. The first shot was of a uniformed officer holding a spool of yellow crime scene tape. He unrolled it, left to right, and tied it to a wooden post. Sheila recognized it as the hinge to her front gate.

"Authorities run tape across the entrance to a secluded farmhouse in Epping," the reporter said. "It is here they hope to find clues in the disappearance of a local man . . ."

"That's my house," Sheila said, pointing to the screen. Paquin was stunned. *How could this nice woman on my couch be involved in this?*

A gentleman in a suit appeared on screen. The graphic that was superimposed over the lower third of the picture identified him as Peter Odom, an assistant Attorney General. His tone was plain, calm, almost unconcerned. "According to his family, it's curious that he has not contacted them in several days. While we do have a concern, it would be premature to talk about foul play."

The reporter's voice continued over more evening shots of the property. "Odom says this farm on Red Oak Hill Lane is Countie's last known address. Neighbors say the property owner is Sheila LaBarre . . ."

Paquin looked over at Charpentier at the mention of Sheila's name. They both gauged the other woman's reaction, which at the moment was minimal.

"Investigators," continued the reporter, "would not comment on whether she, or anyone else, is cooperating with the search."

The next shot was of New Hampshire State Police Lieutenant Russ Conte. "Certainly any information we can get on this individual—anyone who can give us any whereabouts, last sightings, any background information—we would welcome."

Last sightings of who? Paquin thought. *Kenny or Sheila? Or Adam?*

"Authorities say this farm is not a crime scene." The reporter was now standing in front of the yellow tape at the farm. "Investigators are hoping to collect any evidence that might lead them to Countie."

They watched the scenes of police cars on Sheila's property and of men cataloging items. Paquin still couldn't believe it.

"Police say the last verified sighting of Countie was at an Epping business on March 17. Although police still believe he was around town in the following days, the formal search for him did not begin until the end of last week. The Attorney General's homicide division is helping coordinate the investigation. But this remains labeled as a 'missing persons case.' And right now, the hope is some clue found here will solve the mystery of where Kenneth Countie disappeared to."

The story ended with the reporter giving the phone number to the Epping Police Department. It was a number that Sheila already knew by heart.

"Sheila, what is this all about?" Paquin finally asked. "Who's Adam?"

The woman hunched over, weeping into her hands. "I don't know where he is!" she sobbed. "And now everyone's going to think I killed him!"

The room was silent. "Go to your rooms," Paquin said to her children. Charpentier waited until it was just the three of them in the room before pressing her for more details. Sheila's eyes were wide open and dancing between the two women as they alternated questions of her.

"Who is the man from the news report? Countie?"

"That's Adam."

"Thought they said his name was Kenneth. Not Adam."

"Yes. That's his name. It *was* Kenneth Countie, but he changed it. He wanted to be called 'Adam LaBarre.'"

"Why did he change his name?"

"He wanted a new start."

"Why?"

"His mother. He told me his mother got him drunk and

molested him. And she tried to interfere with our relationship. He had to give me power of attorney over him so I could put an end to it."

"So the missing man is your boyfriend."

"No! I got rid of him. While he was staying on my farm, I discovered he was a pedophile. And a homosexual."

"He was a pedophile?" Paquin blurted.

"Yes. I have proof."

"What kind of proof?"

"His confession. On audiotape. He confessed to everything. And there's a videotape too. I don't have it, but I know exactly where it is. I tried to get it to the police but they had no interest in it! They're out to get me. I have to get it to the press."

The picture of civility and Southern charm just moments before, Sheila was now a live wire. Her hands were in constant motion. Her eyes were imploring Paquin and Charpentier to listen to just a bit more. *Don't give up on me yet . . . just a bit more and you may understand.*

"Who's out to get you? Adam?"

"No. The police," Sheila said. "They hate me. Always have. The fucking chief has been out to get me for years. Wouldn't let me get a permit for a handgun. Imagine: me alone on the big farm with no way to protect myself. There are people trespassing all the time. There's an Irishman, an immigrant, who's been through my woods looking for me. Hunters coming through with guns. That asshole chief didn't fucking want me to protect myself. That's because he fucking wanted me vulnerable, that son of a bitch."

"Why would he want that?" Paquin asked.

Sheila looked at her matter-of-factly. "Because he wants to fuck me. I can tell."

"Sheila," Charpentier asked, "where's Adam?"

"I don't know." She paused. It seemed like that was all she would say about Adam's whereabouts. "One night this week he told me he was leaving. I told him, 'Fine.' I woke up in the morning and he was gone."

"So he just vanished?"

"I guess so." Sheila stopped and scanned the two women with bionic eyes. "He had been depressed. Before I even met him he had tried to commit suicide."

"Do you think he killed himself?"

"He could have." Another scan. "He said he might kill himself by throwing himself on a fire."

Paquin and Charpentier looked at each other, this time scanning themselves. "Could he have done that?"

"I have a burn pit on my farm. It's where I burn dead animals. I burned rabbits there." All eyes unconsciously glanced at Satin and his caged playmates in the corner of the room. "It had been burning when Adam disappeared. I knew the police were coming to look for him . . . and I wanted to help them . . . so I dug around the fire pit."

"So . . . ?"

"So I found a tooth."

Paquin gasped. *Is this a joke? Is this some kind of prank on us?*

"What did you do with it?"

"I gave it to the police. I don't know if it's a human tooth or not. Or if it's Adam's. I just wanted them to have it."

Despite the incredible details, the story seemed to run out of steam. Or at least Sheila ran out of steam telling it. There was another uneasy quiet hanging over the room. The silence was ended by Sheila's sudden sobs.

"Everyone is going to think I did it. They're going to think I'm guilty and I'm going to hell. But I'm not." The crying got harder. "I didn't do anything. I'm innocent. I'm innocent."

Paquin and Charpentier watched in silence while Sheila LaBarre kept crying. Sympathetic, Paquin put a hand on the woman's shoulder to calm her weeping. She rubbed Sheila's back and cooed in her ear.

"We believe you," she said sincerely. "We believe you."

CHAPTER 5

TALK AROUND TOWN

When daylight broke Monday morning on Red Oak Lane, I returned with a camera crew to the little Epping neighborhood. The assignment was easy: get some sound bites from neighbors about Sheila LaBarre. It ended up being much harder than we thought.

In every television story about a homicide, a reporter is always able to locate someone who will stand in the frame of their screen door and say something about the people involved.

I can't believe it.

They never were any trouble.

It always seemed so quiet over there.

Canvassing the neighborhood around Red Oak Hill Lane, things were very different. It was unlike any story we'd been on before. Neighbors opened their doors warmly to us, recognizing a familiar face from television. Then when they heard the story had to do with the woman down the street, they blanched and quietly closed the door. Some said "No comment," as if that were a magical talisman that would send us away. They were all afraid to talk, too afraid to even explain why they wouldn't talk. One woman whispered something reporters weren't meant to hear as she closed the door.

"She's evil."

Some of the neighbors made their way to the spot where

the dirt road leading to the farm forked off from Red Oak
Lane. Their homes were modern, comfortable inside. Their
land had grown something years ago, but now its loam and
lawn are cushion for small feet and soccer balls in the
backyard.

I made my way to a small ranch-style house on a hill. The
name on the mailbox said Harvey, but so had some of the
other mailboxes on the street. The videographer kept back,
so as not to spook the already-jittery citizenry. An old man
opened the door and didn't wait for me to introduce myself.
He returned my smile and sized me up as a "friendly."

"Why don't you come in out of the rain?" he offered.
With it being a perfectly sunshiny, early spring morning, I
found this salutation to be the most charming I'd ever received. So I went inside the home with the sense of being
greeted by a long-lost friend.

Rumors are the only things that sprout year-round in a farm
town like Epping. There had been a time when people didn't
believe the catty talk about Dr. LaBarre's live-in lover. The
rumors just seemed so wild, so plentiful, that they could
only be the product of a region that gave the world writers
like Stephen King, Grace Metalious and even Nathaniel
Hawthorne. They seemed like tall tales, the kind of stories
that rise from the crags of mist at dawn on cold pastureland.

Sheila LaBarre came to Epping from Alabama after answering a personal advertisement Wilfred "Bill" LaBarre
had placed in a magazine. Her hair was too long, her lipstick
too red for the tiny town. Sheila drove around in either her
pickup truck or her luxury car, both paid for by Dr. LaBarre.
She was warm as pie to strangers, but could turn quickly on
acquaintances. She was like a fist full of bees. Few people
got a second chance with her.

Sheila had been in her late twenties when she shacked up
with the sixty-year-old chiropractor. She paraded around
town in a pair of skin-tight leopard-print pants. Men watched,
and her radar for detecting their stares was infallible. She
took up flying lessons, but never stuck with it long enough to

get a license. Around the airfield, the men dubbed her "Sheila the Peeler" in hopes she'd shimmy right out of her form-fitting ensembles.

There were stories about Sheila's temper. They all had to do with some imagined slight done to Sheila followed by a gross overreaction. But residents of Epping got the message: if you had to deal with her, stay on her good side.

Dog walkers on Red Oak Lane made it a point to wave and smile at those coming and going, including Sheila. Sometimes Sheila acknowledged the wave. Other times it appeared the driver was so focused on her own thoughts she probably couldn't even see the road. Usually she was accompanied by a man who did work on her farm.

Sheila had always been flirtatious, but things escalated after Dr. LaBarre died. When deliverymen knocked, she often came to the door dressed in nothing but her mink coat (or nothing at all). As her figure became more Ruben-esque, it did not slow her down or increase her modesty. It *did* slow the number of workingmen who would take advantage of a free fling with the housewife. Eventually, some companies stopped delivering to the door or making service calls.

Sheila had unusual taste in men. She seemed to fancy adults who were developmentally disabled—semi-retarded. They were grown men living at home whom Sheila drove to her farm to work the land. She paid them in beer and ciga-rettes. Perhaps, some hypothesized, she paid them with some-thing else—some of the men went home with bruises or fire engine red slap marks on their faces.

The Harveys' home was modest. For all the McMansions that were popping up around them, it seemed like little of the new money made its way to their homestead. Daniel Webster Harvey knew his land was worth so much more as someone else's backyard than as a vegetable patch. But the Harveys were farmers going back three centuries and one's eighties are not a good time to change careers.

"We've got company," Harvey called to his wife in the

kitchen. She adjusted her glasses and bobbed the tight curls of her white hair.

"I'll put some coffee on," she said, ducking back into the kitchen.

"I sold Bill LaBarre that land," he told me, his New England accent as thick as clam chowder. "He and Leone bought it in 1962, I think i'twas. Leone was Bill's first wife. We all just got together for her eighty-second birthday last month. Ah-yep. She's still livin' with her son on the seacoast. Portsmouth, I think."

Harvey and I sat in the living room. There was a large picture window overlooking the crest of the hill on Red Oak Lane. A few bud-less, gnarly apple trees appeared like witches casting spells. The farmer's wife came out with a cup of something hot to drink, then returned to the kitchen.

"That land had been in my family . . . oh . . . I don't know how long. And for the longest time people just called it the Old Harvey farm. Then Sheila came along and renamed it, 'The Silver Leopard Farm.'" Harvey sipped from his mug. "Ah-yep. Drew quite a few chuckles, it did."

"When did Sheila come to town anyway?"

Harvey thought back to the spring of 1987. "It had been a tough few years for the doc. He and Leone had been split up for a while, nearly ten years. But he had remarried a beautiful young woman. Her name was Edwina Kolacz. She got cancer and passed on in 1983. Doc was crushed. Walked around like there was no life in him. That's when he placed the ad."

"A personals ad?"

"Can't recollect how many letters he got, but there musta been something about Sheila's that Doc found appealing. In no time 'tall she had moved up here from down South and was livin' on the farm."

"So Sheila was the doctor's wife?"

"Nope. Started calling herself 'Sheila LaBarre' instead of 'Sheila Bailey.' She just took his name. And eventually . . . his farm. That didn't sit well with the rest of Doc's family. Nor the government."

Dr. LaBarre had given Sheila power of attorney over him in 1990. LaBarre's ex-wife and adult children were not pleased with the move. He also declared Sheila executrix of his will. Over the next decade, that status never changed, even though Sheila had from time to time moved out, taken new lovers and even married.

When Dr. LaBarre died in December of 2000, Sheila used her position as trustee to transfer property to herself. This included not only the Epping farm, but also LaBarre's clinic in Hampton and a house and duplex in Somersworth that they had rented out for extra revenue.

Three months after Dr. LaBarre's death, Sheila received a bill from the New Hampshire Department of Revenue Administration. It said she owed $120,580 in legacy and succession taxes to the state. Sheila claimed LaBarre as her common law husband, but the audit supervisor did not have any documentation of that. This sparked an immediate flurry of letters of protestation from Sheila, tapped out with angry fingers on her manual typewriter. At issue was more than money; it was also pride.

In May of 2001, Sheila fired off a letter to the state Commissioner of Revenue requesting a hearing. It summed up everything that the Sheila LaBarre experience was: intelligent, enraged, obstinate and sprinkled with details so bizarre they must be true.

> My late husband, by common law, placed this real estate in these INTER VIVOS years ago with the legal intent to avoid probate. He even asked Bea Marcotte, now deceased, and Cheryl Oikle, alive and in the navy in Spain at the writing of this notice, to witness the trusts . . . I am struggling as it is and to receive a tax notice for property when none is due is distressing to me . . . I was told by Rockingham County Probate when I relinquished his will to them that I DID NOT HAVE TO BE APPOINTED BECAUSE I DID NOT HAVE ANYTHING TO PROBATE. I agree with this.

The audit supervisor for the Estate of Wilfred LaBarre figured she was on strong legal ground to deny Sheila's petition and request payment. The property wouldn't be taxed if it passed to a decedent's spouse (Sheila didn't dispute she was not married to the doctor). State law required a couple to have been "cohabiting and acknowledging each other as husband and wife . . . for the period of three years." Here, Sheila was on shaky ground, as she had been still married to a man named Wayne Ennis about two years before LaBarre died.

"Nope," said Harvey drawing deep on his cup of coffee. "That was a fight that poor civil servant didn't want. Sheila took it real personal and went after her with everything she had. You don't cross Sheila."

"She sounds like a colorful character," I said.

Harvey looked back at me incredulously. "She's not colored. She's white."

I swallowed the laugh that was pushing out the corners of my mouth. I didn't want to be disrespectful. "Are you friends with her?" I asked, raising my voice in hopes of better clarity.

Harvey didn't answer for a moment, but not because he hadn't heard the question. "Oh, I don't suppose anyone's that close to Sheila. But she comes by and says hello to me and the missus. When she colored her hair blonde she said she looked like she could be my daughter. So she started sayin' she was one of my kids."

"How would you describe her?"

"Sheila," he chuckled. "Some people'd say she's crazy."

Years later, one neighbor explained to me why she shut the door on me that day and didn't comment about Sheila. She was afraid of what Sheila would do to her if Sheila heard the neighbor commenting negatively about her on TV or in the newspaper. It didn't matter if Sheila was in custody or sentenced to jail or given the electric chair. If there was the slightest chance that Sheila would be able to come back around, the neighbor was sure Sheila would make it a priority to get her.

This woman and her husband often walked past the entrance to Red Oak Hill Lane, glanced down the wooden lane and joked about the nasty, sexual things Sheila must have been doing to those men. They joked about it being a "stud farm." They also giggled that she was doing "Jeffrey Dahmer things" down there.

"I suppose Gordon would be able to say more about her," Harvey told me in his home. He was referring to Gordon Winslow. His farm along the dirt road was visible from the street and, at three-quarters of a mile, was the closest neighbor Sheila had.

"They didn't get along?"

"Ah-yep."

Harvey knew the Winslows shed no tears for Sheila La-Barre's current predicament. The two farmers had talked over the fence post many an afternoon. Winslow had seen things. And he had questions about the men he knew had lived there. *Where were they? Where was Wayne? Where was Jimmy? Where was Mikey? Now Kenny?*

"Sheila could be a bad hostess to those boys," Harvey went on. "Even to Dr. LaBarre. There were quite a few nights she ran Doc off the farm and he slept on my couch. One of the boys told me she waved a gun at him. So he ran off and spent the night in my orchard. I think he slept in a tree," Harvey winked.

Like a skilled car salesman, I sensed now would be a good time to ask if I could invite the cameraman in and ask some questions. Harvey agreed. We chatted for a few minutes more on camera. I had my sound bite, but my questions about who Sheila LaBarre was were still largely unanswered.

When I finished my cup of coffee, the old man brought it to the sink and walked me to the door. Harvey had been a selectman in the small town for years. And although retired from service, a New Englander is never retired from politics. He still followed all action and remained plugged in.

"Did you know they have to have a special meeting later

this month?" Harvey was referring to the Board of Select-men. There had been a fight between a male and female member and a complaint was filed. "He called her a 'camel's foot.' Have you ever heard of such a thing?"

Again, I stifled the laughter. "Have never heard of anything quite like that."

"Darn fool," he swore.

I left the Harvey home and breathed in the morning air. I had to pass that dirt road again and caught a glimpse of the Winslow farm. Looking at it, I remembered one of the stories Dan Harvey had told me and it brought a chill to my spine.

It had happened about two years earlier. It was winter and a snow had just covered the ground. One of the young studs from the farm—he thought it was the one named "Michael"—came stumbling down the dirt road. Gordon Winslow was out and working near the fence. As the man came closer, he noticed he was on a slow run. There was a gash on his head that was bleeding. Drops of red fell into the snow. It looked like his ear was ripped. And his skin tone was odd. His complexion was no longer a healthy pink, but not the shocking pale a winter wind does to an uncovered face.

He limped by Winslow and caught his eye. The man opened his mouth, but no sound came out. Then like an old hinge, he croaked out a single word.

"Sheila," he said.

The man's eyes glanced back into the woods, toward the Silver Leopard Farm, his trail of blood and footprints and the mysteries too bizarre to be real. He looked back, but his feet kept him moving forward, past the stunned farmer. In my mind, I could hear him speak one last time.

"Sheila."

CHAPTER 6

HIS FIRST LOVE

On February 14, 2006, about six weeks before police would scour an Epping farmhouse in search of Kenneth Countie, the young man could be found sitting alone in the barroom of a seaside hotel. It was a ritzy restaurant on Hampton Beach, with staterooms that overlooked the Atlantic Ocean. The orange plastic snow fence was still wrapped around the beach and large patches of white snow lay on the eroding sandbars.

The lounge was moderately filled for Valentine's Day. The mood was upbeat with a deejay spinning tunes to keep it that way. The manager came to the bartender, Tony Thibeault, with a request.

"Keep an eye on him," he said pointing to a young man who had wandered in from a very cold night. The man hadn't requested a table nor asked for something to drink. "I think he's a transient."

Thibeault asked the young man what he was doing at the Ashworth. He responded that he was waiting for his girlfriend, so Thibeault told him he could sit at the bar while he waited. The young man said his name was "Kenny."

Thibeault noticed Kenny had a hard time making conversation and maintaining eye contact. He assumed the kid had some kind of learning disability and checked on him frequently.

An hour passed and no one showed up. Most people who

spent that much time alone in the bar—on Valentine's Day—usually got the hint and left. But Kenny stayed, patiently. He wanted a relationship, thought this could be a turning point in his life.

Thibeault noticed a woman breeze into the barroom and scan the place. She was bleached blonde and stocky, and she wore a denim coat, cut at the hip like an Eisenhower-style jacket. She faced the bar as Kenny came up from behind her and tapped her on the shoulder.

What do you know, the bartender thought. *He really did have someone coming for him.* But Thibeault didn't believe the woman was Kenny's girlfriend. He was quite sure, by the way they looked at each other, that they had never seen each other before that moment. Thibeault wondered if the woman was a call girl.

The couple sat down at the bar, their backs to the picture windows overlooking the street and the beach. She ordered a bourbon on the rocks; he got a soda. It was obvious she controlled the conversation.

The woman hailed the bartender. "The music is too loud. Will you tell the disc jockey to turn it down?"

Thibeault went to Dan Guy, who had been deejaying at the Ashworth for nearly twenty years. Guy was also one of the most sought-after radio engineers in New Hampshire. He could keep his own counsel on the acoustics of the L-shaped room. He knew damn well the music wasn't too loud and there were still couples trying to dance, but Guy agreed to bring the volume down a bit.

"The music is still too loud," the woman complained.

"I'm sorry," Thibeault said, "but that's as far as the disc jockey wants to go on the volume."

"That," she replied, "will be reflected in your tip."

"I can live with that," he deadpanned.

The couple chatted some more. Kenny mostly listened, nodded his head in agreement. The woman paid the tab and, true to her word, left Thibeault only two dollars for a tip. They went outside to her car, started the engine, but didn't drive away.

Back inside, Thibeault and Guy laughed and laughed about Thibeault's quick comeback. It really wasn't like him to mouth off to customers, not unless his blood pressure was up. Guy, who, as a morning radio disc jockey, once convinced gullible listeners that a moose on an ice drift was floating down the Merrimack River, liked a good laugh himself.

The pair noticed that the mismatched couple had gotten in the car but not left the parking space. Watching through the great picture window of the lounge, Thibeault and Guy looked at each other and cracked up some more. They knew the young man and the brash woman were having sex in the black car under the streetlights.

If Kenny had thought this would be a turning point in his life, he was correct. But not one of joy. One of horror and unspeakable pain. A turning point that would soon lead to the end of his life in a manner of evil design and of wicked intention.

Had he left the restaurant five minutes sooner, he might never have met Sheila LaBarre.

By all accounts, Kenny was a sweet, unassuming young man. He grew up with his parents in Tewksbury, Massachusetts, not far from Boston. He graduated from a technical high school as a mason. He was best known for his talents on the ice hockey team and as someone who walked the school wearing his purple team jersey with pride.

Kenny loved many of the things normal boys growing up in New England loved. His family was drawn to the ice. His mother, Carolynn, was a figure skater. Kenneth Sr. was a youth hockey coach and Kenny picked up both the passion and the skill for the game from him. He loved music and sang with an enthusiasm that surpassed his pitch.

"You can't wear that hat," his mother told him of the Yankees ball cap he owned. She knew little about sports, only vaguely aware when she said it that the Red Sox and Yankees were in some kind of death struggle for a championship. "You live in Boston, Kenny. People are going to give you trouble for it."

"Don't worry, Ma," he told her. He knew she worried about him dearly.

That's because Kenny Countie was not a normal boy growing up in New England. He was never formally diagnosed with a handicap; teachers said he was "a tad slow." Kids were crueler. They called him "stupid" or "retard." But he was neither. Kenny had a developmental disability. The experts told his mother his mental capacity was around that of a twelve-year-old.

His mother suspected Kenny might have a form of autism. He had an exuberant smile, but he wasn't overly affectionate. He had trouble reading others' social cues.

"Come here and give your mum a hug," she often said.

"Oh, Ma!" he moaned as she tried to put an arm around him. He wouldn't cuddle or hug or offer an unsolicited "I love you."

His mother was the most formidable presence in Kenneth Countie's life. Carolynn Countie remarried and moved to Billerica, Massachusetts. Gerald Lodge, her new husband, was born in the United Kingdom and moved to the States. After a few years of living together, Carolynn Lodge started speaking with a British accent herself.

Years before, Carolynn had gotten into a terrible car accident that left her in a coma. She was left unable to walk or talk, with both a hole in her head and a hole in her throat. Two-year-old Kenny was temporarily left without a mother. Through therapy and sheer will, Carolynn was able to recover and eventually return to her new husband. When she became pregnant again the doctors were dead set against her carrying to term. They feared for both her life and the life of the child. She'd have none of their protestations. She gave birth to her second son, who was physically and mentally strong. But for years, doubts nagged her about Kenny's development during her recovery. "Two years old is when a child bonds with his mother," she said, worried the boy's reluctance for affection was a result of her car accident.

Like any parent struggling to let their firstborn go free in the world can attest, Carolynn and Gerald and Kenneth Sr.

had ambivalent feelings about Kenny's desire for independence. Kenny's special needs had to be addressed, the balance found between holding a hand and gripping it.

"Kenny, you gotta be careful," Carolynn pleaded with him. "There are crazy people out there who will eat you alive."

"Mom, don't worry about me. I can do it."

"No, honey. You can't."

It was Kenny's idea to join the Army. Carolynn put her foot down, yelled and screamed at her son. But Kenny wouldn't listen to her.

She invited the recruiter over to her house. "Are you bloody mad?!" she railed at him. "You signed him up for four years? He won't last a week."

The man in the green uniform and gold buttons simply said, "I don't think you know what you're talking about."

Kenny shipped off for Basic Combat Training. Carolynn and her husband made the trip to Georgia for Family Day. The separation seemed more like months than weeks to his mother.

Several buses pulled up to the gathered relatives, and dozens of uniformed trainees poured out. They all looked the same in their black berets, blue shirts and polished boots. People started darting left and right, seeking a familiar face. Amid the happy chaos, Carolynn Lodge could not find her son and began to panic. She tapped the first solider who walked her way.

"Do you know Kenneth Countie?" she asked.

"Yeah."

"Do you know where he is?"

The soldier stared back. "Ma. It's me."

She was breathless. She peered deep into the eyes of the man standing in front of her. "No, it's not."

Kenneth Countie was standing up straight, making eye contact. He had bulked up and his thin face looked fuller. He had a presence that was undeniable. *He looks wonderful,* his mother thought.

Gerald and Carolynn took Kenny to a restaurant. The young man did something he'd never done before. He reached out and opened the door for his mother. She thought it was some kind of joke.

"Are you going to close it on me?" she pried wryly.

"No, ma'am," he replied. Then he waited for his mother and stepfather to sit at the table before he took his own seat. Mrs. Lodge realized the Army had made a man out her boy.

Kenny's graduation from Basic was to be a major family event. Carolynn had paid for in-laws in Great Britain to fly to Georgia and attend. It was only two days before the ceremony when the phone rang in her Massachusetts home.

"Is this Carolynn Countie?"

Responding to the name from her previous marriage, she knew instinctively the call was about Kenny. "What's wrong?"

The man identified himself as Captain Pasquale, a commander in Kenny's training unit. "Your son won't be graduating with the class." She yelled, pleaded and demanded to know why. The captain refused to say.

With their pre-paid tickets in hand, Carolynn dragged her husband to the airport and flew down to Georgia. They sat in their rental car outside the main gate, watching people come and go. Finally, with the precision of a ranger sniper, Lodge got out of the car and approached a military man walking out of the base.

"You there," she said. "What's that decoration on your uniform? What does that signify?"

"That means I'm a captain," the officer said, referring to his silver bars.

"What's your name?"

"Captain Pasquale, ma'am."

Considering there were over 100,000 soldiers, civilian workers and family members who lived and worked at the fort, this was quite a coincidence. "You're just the bloke I'm looking for."

The Lodges accompanied Pasquale into the base and found an empty room. "Tell me why my son will not be graduating with his class."

"In all honesty," the captain started, "he can run the two

miles in full gear. That's a requirement. He can do all the push-ups. That's a requirement. But he can't do the sit-ups."

"What?" Her son had never excelled academically, but he did well in sports. She was incredulous that the boy couldn't do seventy-five sit-ups.

"If you want," Pasquale offered, "come out to the parade field at five o'clock tomorrow when the unit is taking PT. You can see for yourself and decide whether he passes." The parents looked at each other and agreed they'd show up. "And ma'am, that's five A.M., not P.M., in case you didn't know."

The next morning, with the grass still wet, and orange streaks in the sky, Kenny trotted out to the field. He was wearing sneakers, shorts and a gray T-shirt that said "Army." The first exercise was a run around the track. From a distance, Carolyn Lodge watched her son glide effortlessly. He was nearly done when he slowed down and doubled back.

What's wrong? Lodge thought.

Kenny pulled alongside one of his fellow trainees who was lagging. He began clapping and shouting encouragement to him, wishing him forward to the end.

What a wonderful thing my son just did.

After the run, the unit dropped down for push-ups. Again, Kenny had no problem. He looked even stronger than he had at Family Day. Then, the young recruit began his sit-ups and Carolynn Lodge saw the problem right away. Kenny began the sit-up flat on his back, level with the ground.

"No, Kenny. Not like that. You'll never be able to get up and do a sit-up like that." An exercise instructor herself, Carolynn Lodge knew the proper technique required, going back only part of the way and pulling the torso forward. She watched as her son struggled to pull himself off the ground and make it to his knees, flopping and failing. *He'll never do seventy-five like that.*

Later that day, while the rest of his class was graduating, Kenneth Countie was directing traffic on the base. His mother caught a glimpse of him before they left. The shoulders that were once straight sagged. The eyes that met others now avoided contact and searched the ground. The confident smile had disappeared, his chin pinned to his chest.

It looks like he sank one million feet under the ground, she thought. Everything the Army had done for him seemed to vanish all at once.

Back home in Massachusetts, Kenny attempted to gain as much independence as he could. In January 2006, he moved to Wilmington, Massachusetts, with a friend. It was the first time, aside from the Army, that Kenny Countie lived away from home. He got a job at a car wash. His co-workers liked him because he was pleasant and dedicated to the job. He showed up for work a half-hour early every day. However, his colleagues noticed Kenny had trouble filling out his W-4 and the other paperwork needed on the job.

Carolynn Lodge appeared frequently at the car wash, checking on her son. On the days she didn't show up there, Kenny came to the health club where she worked. He'd beg her for something sweet to eat. She'd oblige by giving him the candies she carried in her pocketbook in case he asked.

Kenny had a cellular phone, pre-paid by his mother. He called every day, sometimes more than once. "Yes, love. Yes, love." To some of Carolynn Lodge's friends the calls seemed excessive, but she was determined to prove her devotion as a mother and nurture him.

Kenny called his little brother, too. Sometimes it irked the teen to get a call from his older brother, asking stupid questions, passing on lame observations. It was hard enough finding his way in high school (girls, sports, studies, friends) and being attentive to two sets of parents wanting to know his business. He didn't want to have to deal with his older brother.

In February 2006, a depressed twenty-four-year-old Kenneth Countie attempted suicide. For all the talking he did on the phone, he didn't share many of his inner demons. The thought of losing her oldest son unnerved Lodge. She pledged to redouble her efforts to watch over Kenny.

The young man had a hard time meeting women. He

wasn't the most confident and approaching a woman face-to-face seemed frightening. He rang up a dating service and got a voice mailbox. After punching a few numbers to set up his profile ("Press one if you are playful; press two if you are shy . . ."), he recorded a message about himself and listened to the other postings. He exchanged voicemails with a woman with a Southern accent. She liked the sound of his voice. It reminded her of someone. Dinner on the seacoast was her idea. She would pay.

Four days later, Kenny's roommate, Eric, was awakened by a truck that pulled up in his driveway and tooted the horn. He heard his roommate banging around in the other room, so he knew the ride wasn't there for him.

"Kenny, what's going on?"

"I'm leaving with Sheila," he said.

"What the fuck are you talking about?" Eric stammered back, still half asleep.

"I'm going to spend the weekend on her farm in New Hampshire. She has horses and rabbits, and I'm going to help her take care of them."

"Yeah? When you think you'll be back?" Outside, the horn honked again.

"Tomorrow. Sunday." Then Kenny squealed in the little-boy voice that reminded his roommate he was mentally deficient. "We're going to be so happy together!"

Kenny bounded down the stairs, grabbed his overcoat and jumped into the waiting truck. Sheila LaBarre never got out or acknowledged Eric, and after they left he realized Kenny hadn't packed any personal belongings. His van was still in the driveway.

On Monday, February 20, Carolynn Lodge got a call from her son.

"Yes, love," she began in Anglican tones.

"Mommy . . ."

Kenny was crying. Still reeling from the recent suicide attempt, Lodge started to panic. "Kenny! What is it? What's wrong?"

"Eric's brother called Sheila a bad name."

"Who? *Susan?*"

"No. Sheila."

Now Lodge was confused. Surely this wasn't a life-or-death situation, but her son was upset about *something*. "What do you mean?"

Kenny had not returned to his Wilmington apartment on Sunday as expected. And not on Monday either. His roommate was worried; he and his brother called Kenny's cell phone. The young man was meeting their inquiries about when he might be home with some indecision. Sheila, sensing the problem, took the phone and started arguing with the men. When Kenny took the phone back, the brothers were calling Sheila a "bitch" and a "cunt" and every other name they could think of.

In between sobs, Lodge was having trouble piecing together most of this. She had no idea from where Kenny was calling. Lodge tried to press her son for more information when she heard Sheila in the background.

"Kenny, give me the phone," she ordered. From the tone of her voice, it sounded as if she was unaware he'd made a call.

Who are you and what are you doing with my son? was what Lodge wanted to say when a lightning bolt of rage came out of the earpiece of the telephone.

"He is fucking twenty-four years old. Leave him the fuck alone!"

Lodge was stunned. Then indignant. Who was this woman Kenny had gotten himself entangled with?

Sheila went on. "We're fucking happy!"

"I am Kenny's mother . . ." she began, but heard the cell phone click off. *Bloody hell*, she thought.

On Tuesday the twenty-first, Kenny was not answering his cell phone. Lodge called the car wash looking for her son. They told her Kenny hadn't been in to work and they were worried about him. It wasn't like him not to show up, not to call.

Kenny's roommate told Kenneth Countie Sr. that this

woman had taken him to a farm in New Hampshire. *At least now we know where he is,* Lodge thought. By Friday, when Kenny still hadn't called his mother and his van and belongings were still at his apartment, Lodge decided she had waited long enough and decided to call police to report him missing.

Epping Police Sergeant Sean Gallagher took Lodge's call. The mother explained, very calmly, that her son had been staying on a farm with Sheila LaBarre. She said her son had a mental deficiency and had recently tried to kill himself. Gallagher took the information, promised to touch base with the Wilmington Police Department and said he would go to the farm to check on her son's well-being.

Gallagher was one of only two sergeants on the Epping Police Department. A Navy reservist for six years, he joined the force in 1995 looking for a career in which he could serve others. Chief Dodge was able to expand the size of his little police force by one more man by taking advantage of a grant from the U.S. Department of Justice. It covered 70 percent of Gallagher's salary for the first three years of service. The grant dictated that Gallagher's role would be as a community-oriented patrolman. And though he didn't walk a beat pulling on locked doors in urban neighborhoods, he found a way to make the philosophy of community-oriented policing fit with Epping. That meant meeting people, chatting them up, looking ahead to the potential trouble spots. Sheila LaBarre came across his path often, officially and unofficially.

Gallagher didn't need to do a lot of research before heading out to Sheila's home. She was a frequent filer, and her case file was filled with minor complaints and petty annoyances. She stormed into the station with letters of complaint—some directed at citizens, some directed at officers. She used her personal fax machine to transmit even more rants to the Epping Police Department after hours.

Some thought the feud (which was mostly one-sided) began after Sheila had been pulled over for speeding and charged with marijuana possession. It took an expensive lawyer and a pound of flesh, but the charge was expunged. Her lawyer urged her to watch out for the Epping cops from then on, advice she took too readily to heart. It was to be a jihad for the indignity they put her through.

Gallagher drove out to the farm later that day with Detective Richard Cote. The department had a standing policy when dealing with Sheila: always go with backup. The policy hadn't been instituted because they thought Sheila would become violent with a patrolman; it was put in place after one encounter when "Sheila the Peeler" became inappropriate with an officer. She started to come on to him. The sexual nature of the incident so disturbed Chief Dodge he ordered that none of his men was to approach her alone again.

Gallagher and Cote rolled up past the open wooden gate and exited the police cruiser. The sergeant stood tall and straight in his dark blue uniform and cap, knocking on the front door. A dog barked inside. Someone appeared in the window, eyes through a curtain that looked like a ghost.

"What do you want?" Sheila yelled out the window.

"Is Kenneth Countie here?"

She paused. "He's here."

"Sheila, could you come to the door, please? So we can talk?"

She refused.

"I need to speak with Kenneth Countie," Gallagher said patiently.

"Why?"

"He's been reported as missing. I need to check on his welfare."

"You can't speak with him."

"Why not?"

Sheila stared at the officer, knives in her eyes.

"Sheila, I must speak with him."

"You can't."

"Why not?"

"He's naked in the bathtub."

"Well, get him out of the bathtub. I need to see him."

Sheila moved away from the window and then reappeared.

"I'm going to check with the Wilmington Police to make sure you're not lying."

Cote watched as Gallagher stood at the door in the late February air. The farm was silent except for the police car's running engine. The more he thought about it, the more he didn't like the situation. Not coming to the door was just par for Sheila. *Why wouldn't she bring him out if he's truly in there? Is she hiding something?* They seemed to be waiting there an awfully long time.

The bolt on the door clicked open. Gallagher's hand was resting nonchalantly on his holster, his eyes fixed to the widening entranceway. He saw Sheila there, lips pursed. Standing about five feet behind the door, a man wearing only a pair of blue jeans appeared.

"Kenneth Countie?" the cop asked.

"Yes."

"Are you okay?"

"Yes." Kenny stood meekly, arms folded in front of him. Cote noticed the kid was thin, but looking at his bare chest and back, could see there were no bruises, marks or other signs of injury on him.

"Your mother's worried about you. Give her a call right away, won't you?"

"Okay," he said.

"Get the fuck off my property, right now!" Sheila said to the police officers, pointing the way back down the darkened dirt road for them.

CHAPTER 7

INSIDE THE HOUSE

Sergeant Robert Estabrook of the New Hampshire State Police had been to the LaBarre farm the day before, along with Lieutenant Conte, and had spent a great deal of time just looking at the charred mattress box spring. Conte had asked him to take over the case and become the lead investigator in the field. It was understood that this was going to be particularly challenging. Now, on Monday morning, the 27th, he found himself again staring into the rotten embers of that fire pit.

Just as the morning sun shone a warm yellow glow on the scene, Estabrook noticed a television camera on a tripod at the main gate. One had been here the night before, as he and Conte and some others had been walking the property. They decided to use the protective cover of the horse barn as a workplace and had set up some lights inside when it had become night. He had seen the piercing light of the camera cut through the darkness, though at first he thought it had been coming from the spotlight on the cruiser standing post at the entrance. Estabrook had seen the pictures on the news and was relieved that all that were usable were shots of the main house and the crime van in the yard.

But now, from that same vantage point, the burn pile was clearly visible. The cover of night had bought them time. There were details to this crime scene (though publicly they would not classify it as such) that Estabrook felt needed to remain confidential. He approached the camera crew.

The officer was in plainclothes, a tan overcoat on. Estabrook looked more bookish than the other state police, with his glasses and blond hair neatly combed. His demeanor was always very serious, very official.

The TV reporter and cameraman exchanged casual "hellos" with Estabrook. They were calm, comfortable, indicating some previous acquaintance with him.

"I need you to leave. You're too close to the scene."

The journalists looked at each other, then to the yellow tape across the gate that separated them. "The chief said the public road ends here."

"My scene extends back a half mile. You have to go."

The cameraman huffed. "This is bullshit," he said to himself. The fact that Estabrook didn't even appear to be nice about the ejection rubbed him the wrong way.

Estabrook turned away from the pair, cutting off further debate, knowing they would now follow his command. *It wasn't bullshit,* he thought. *We're going to have to search every inch of these woods before this is all over.*

By the time NHSP Lieutenant Mark Mudgett returned to the LaBarre farm, he noticed a fresh line of yellow tape strung between two trees at some seemingly random point on the dirt road. He shook his head in amusement, inching his police cruiser underneath the sagging Mylar barrier. *Estabrook must have kicked out some reporters,* he thought.

Mudgett parked along the end of the dirt road and walked in the yard. He found Estabrook overseeing the examination of the burn pit.

"You ready to go in?" the lead investigator asked him.

"Okay, Bob, let's do it."

They found the front door unlocked and walked in slowly. The interior of the beautiful cape-style house was rustic. A lot of exposed wood, uncarpeted floors. There were boxes thrown haphazardly around the place. Mudgett led a small cadre of technicians, decked out in white disposable jumpsuits and paper booties, deeper into the residence. They needed to search, photograph and catalogue an infinite number of items, all or none of which might be helpful to the investigation. They were prepared to invest several days to this crime scene. The group was stone quiet, except for the regular *pop* of a flashbulb and *click* of a camera shutter.

There's something both somber and horrifying about walking through a home where a murder has occurred. Even police with court orders can't help but feel like they're intruding in someone else's living room, thumbing through photographs and bank statements. Each step is taken as delicately as a boot camp recruit in a minefield. Every scratch on a floor, every smudge on a window, every bit of lint beneath a sofa holds the potential secret to a crime.

Beyond the puzzle of atoms lies the puzzle of the soul. What happened here to cause the ultimate in violence? Such things don't stick to counter surfaces or appear under bichromatic latent powder. But they don't escape through open windows or vanish down drains. Dust may be witness to crime, but energy is witness to rage. And that energy haunts a room or a building that remains quiet and undisturbed while judges ponder their intrusion. That energy is sometimes called "evil," and it screams in the quiet of that room until someone can exorcise it.

Mudgett could always feel the energy at a crime scene, and things like blood spatter, bullet holes and dead bodies only amplified the passive energy coursing through walls.

There was something extra creepy about the home. The deep, dark woods setting, the smell of putridity and death in the air. Peter Odom would later say that walking through the home, especially at night, reminded him of a scene from *The Blair Witch Project*, the unsettled feeling that something dangerous and undreamt was still lurking in the darkness.

Other than a mess of boxes and furniture, there didn't seem to be any obvious signs of trauma in the house. Dismemberment of a body would cause a great amount of blood loss, even if it was done postmortem. The mattress's previous location was the first place they checked.

Mudgett already knew there was a first-floor bedroom, but that Countie had slept in the living room and that the mattress was kept on the floor. They inched their way toward the living room via the kitchen. Mudgett noticed something on the cabinets. Brownish spots, tiny like spray.

He turned to a technician. "Blood?"

State Police Forensics Crime Lab Technician Tim Jackson squinted and scanned the cabinet door, which was close to the kitchen sink. He found what he thought was the largest droplet. Jackson then swabbed it with a piece of filter paper and added a drop of phenolphthalein.

"Presumptive positive for human blood," he said.

In the living room, they found more brown droplets. There was an empty space where the mattress had been. Mudgett noted brownish drops along the wall. They were about three feet off the floor and ran in an area about six feet long.

Lab Technician Kim Rumrill pointed a blue latex finger toward the wall. "Cast-off," she said. The size, shape and color were all consistent with blood. Then she followed the droplets along the floor in the walkway area of the dining room and back into the kitchen. This time, Rumrill noticed additional cast-off blood on the ceiling by the cabinet. There was a wood stove in the kitchen and more tiny spots of coffee-colored blood were on the floor.

"Here's a little something," she said. A heel print, in blood, on the floor by the stove. So far, it was the largest bit of blood they'd seen.

With his feet firmly planted in one spot, Mudgett looked around the home. He could smell something odd. *Could it be a decomposing body part?* It smelled putrid.

The lieutenant kneeled down at a heating vent on the floor. The vent was right next to where the mattress had lain. It was forced hot air, and the smell was definitely coming from the register. He could see more small drops of blood on the metal plate and in the ductwork, but there was something more pungent than that. It smelled like vomit.

Jackson looked through the first-floor bedroom and found

it in shambles. There were cardboard boxes containing letters, greeting cards and other mementoes. He could see what looked like two brown stains on the boxes. *More blood?* he asked himself.

Among the papers was a single-spaced typed document labeled "Power of Attorney." Jackson scanned it quickly. It began:

> I, Kenneth Michael Countie, DOB-JULY 18, 1981 SS# 029-XX-XXXX do hereby grant and give complete and total FULL POWER OF ATTORNEY to SHEILA LaBARRE, ESQUIRE of P.O. BOX XX, RAYMOND NH 03077 to talk to Social Services, any and all police departments, or to anyone regarding any and all business pertaining to me.

It gave Sheila the power to receive Countie's mail, sign his checks, speak for him in court and deal with virtually any business or personal matter on his behalf. Then it went on to say:

> Additionally, I only TRUST Sheila LaBarre and do completely feel safe and secure in her presence. She had helped me to relocate to New Hampshire. She had helped me by giving me employment and a nice place in which to reside. She had added my name to her address . . .

It finished with something Jackson considered odd, certainly not something one would normally put in a power of attorney:

> Sheila LaBarre has a legally taped recording of me, having informed me throughout the tape that New Hampshire is a two party consent to tape statement and I did grant permission under free will to be tape recorded. This tape is my second sworn statement regarding additional information which Social Services in the

State of MA should hear. Please listen to the tape when it is typed and faxed, please take it seriously . . .

Although the paper was written in the first person as if Kenneth Countie had composed it, it was obvious Sheila had put the whole thing together. Clearly, the "please take it seriously . . ." line indicated this was something important to her. At the bottom, both signed (Countie, in tiny letters like a grade-schooler; LaBarre, in sweeping arcs) and dated ("3/10/06," about two weeks earlier) the document.

Jackson was ready to make his way up to the second floor when he noticed a chair at the foot of the stairwell. He saw red-brown flecks on the arm, but the seat cushion was missing.

Rumrill asked Mudgett to come into the kitchen. He took a gaze at the heel print. "First impressions?" he asked her.

"Not what I thought we'd find," she confessed. "We still have to hit it with the LCV, but I'm surprised at the lack of concentration of blood. No pools yet. No puddles or big stains. So far, it's all tiny amounts."

"But there's cast-off everywhere," Mudgett said. "What did she do? Chase him through the fucking house with an ax, like in *Misery*?"

"Let's go in here." Rumrill pointed to a room off the kitchen. It was a laundry room. *We're not going to be that lucky,* Mudgett thought as he put his hand on the washing machine.

He opened the top. To his surprise, there still was something inside. He peeked in, but leaned back after a smell got into his nostrils again. There was a musty, putrefied odor again. Holding his breath, Mudgett reached in and poked around. There were some wet clothes inside, but taking up most of the well was a comforter. The detective pulled it out and it smelled even worse. It reeked of puke and decomposition.

On the second floor of the house, Jackson and Rumrill sprayed Leuco Crystal Violet throughout the bathroom. Unlike the one downstairs, it was a full bath, with a ceramic tub and tiled wall. Cast-off was found on the tiles as well as on the ceiling. *What went on in this room?*

Jackson put the LCV on the sink and in the tub using a wash bottle. The pre-mixed concentration was mostly hydrogen peroxide and 5-sulfasalicylic acid. The sink and tub looked clean, until the chemical hit them. The LCV began to react with the hemoglobin in the invisible red blood cells still clinging to the fixtures. It came alive in a vivid purple. There were dilute stains over the entirety of both surfaces.

Back downstairs, just off the laundry room, was a half-bath. Mudgett looked around and found a half-gallon jug of laundry bleach. He picked it up and shook it. Mostly empty. *Smart cookie*, he thought. *First she burned the DNA on the body. Then she destroyed what was left inside the house with bleach.*

He gave a heavy sigh. They were going to be here a while.

Estabrook and Conte were outside the farmhouse waiting patiently for Mudgett and the others to emerge with details. The sun was bright and the view was beautiful. Every now and then, a stray rabbit moved in the underbrush, startling one of them. The two cops decided to take stock of some other things found near the burn pit.

In the back of Sheila's green pickup truck were a couple of yellow fuel containers. Estabrook noted the license plate number started with "AG," the code that indicated agricultural equipment. The containers were all empty and they smelled of diesel fuel. He already knew the containers were new and knew where and when Sheila got them.

"What on this farm runs on diesel fuel?" Estabrook asked Conte.

"Not this pickup." He made note of the other vehicles on the land. There was a black luxury car, a silver luxury car and another pickup truck. None of them used diesel.

The silver car had a vanity plate. It read, "CAYCE."

There was one tractor, an old rusted jalopy of a thing. It ran on diesel, but its engine had given up the ghost a long time ago.

Conte's cell phone rang. It was the deputy state medical examiner.

"Doctor Duval just got a second opinion on the bone photos we sent her," Conte explained to Estabrook. "She consulted with a forensic anthropologist in Maine. They both agree the bones look human."

"They're going to want to see the actual bones though, right?"

"Yes," Conte said. They started making arrangements to bring some of the tagged samples from the van up to the medical examiner in Concord. It occurred to them both that they could be collecting all that remained, and all that might ever be found, of Kenneth Countie.

The lieutenant pointed across the yard to the blue Wal-Mart bag blowing in the breeze. "Make sure," Conte said, "you bring that, too."

CHAPTER 8

YOU KNOW WHO I AM

When they woke up on the morning of Monday, March 27, Paquin and Charpentier put their heads together on how to help their new friend, Sheila LaBarre. But the buxom blonde who spent the night in Donald's bedroom (Donald volunteered to sleep on the recliner in the living room) had already been formulating a plan on how to proceed. Sheila had been running her finger through the yellow pages seeking an attorney. She spotted one running a full-page ad and she made a note of the number and address.

"Angel," Sheila addressed Paquin that morning, "whatever will I do with my beloved animals?"

"Your rabbits? Amy can watch them for you."

"No, dear. Not just the rabbits. My horses. I have three of them and two ponies. And my dog, Demetrius. He's a faithful Dalmatian that comes from champion blood, a registered pedigree. They're all on my farm and those barbarians will mistreat them. They won't even feed them, I'm sure."

Paquin didn't understand what Sheila was talking about. It was early and she hadn't had breakfast yet.

"I will sell them to you."

"What?"

"My animals. I trust you and only you. You can take my horses and my dog."

"Horses, Mama?" Pam's daughter sprinted into the room. "Can we have them? Can we?"

Pamela Paquin thought it over. There was no place in her city neighborhood for horses. The costs of caring for such animals were more than her family could afford. And taking possession of such a thing in the middle of a murder investigation seemed an impossible task. Sheila sensed Paquin's thoughts.

"I'll provide you with a notarized bill of sale. And I know some places you can board them. I'll help you with money for hay."

Paquin felt there was no way she could turn Sheila down. She was sorry for this woman who didn't seem to have a friend in the world. Paquin thought she was doing a good thing by agreeing to take care of the animals.

Charlie agreed to take Sheila to the Wal-Mart in Manchester. Sheila bought new, more modest clothes for her visit to the lawyer's. She chose a black blouse, sweater and skirt and a fresh pair of underwear. She grabbed a bottle of hair dye. She also purchased a cellular telephone and a pre-paid calling card. Before they left the store, Sheila went into the ladies' room and put on the new clothes.

Charlie brought Sheila back to Pam's home. Sheila seemed nervous and started to complain of an upset stomach. Sandra and Pam agreed to go with Sheila to the attorney's office. They took Pam's car and left Sheila's parked on the street in front of the house.

The three women drove to Manchester's North End. That part of the Queen City is filled with Victorian homes that had belonged to mill owners and the well-heeled at the turn of the twentieth century. By the turn of this century, many of those burnt brick homes had been changed into quaint office spaces for professionals of every ilk.

Next, Sheila went to the law office of the attorney she found in the phone book. It was another sunny day in New Hampshire. Sure to be cold in the morning, comfortably mild by midday, then brisk again at dusk. A day when the heater knob in the car starts in the red, travels to the blue and then gets twisted back to the red before bedtime. Paquin and Charpentier waited in the car as Sheila made her way inside the building.

"What do you think he's saying to her?" Paquin asked.

"I don't know."

"Do you think Adam is dead?"

"I don't know!" Charpentier snapped as if she'd just been accused of something. "Do you?!"

"I don't know!"

"Well I don't know."

Pam paused. "What if he is?"

"What if he's what?"

"What if he's dead?"

"I don't know!"

"The lawyer's going to ask her if she murdered him," Pam mused.

"Maybe. I would."

"You'd murder him?"

"Hell no! I'd ask her the same question. If I was a lawyer."

Another pause. "I don't think she did it," Pam eventually said.

"Me neither."

"She just seems so sweet and nice. She doesn't seem the type."

"How would you know the type?"

"Shut up! I don't know!"

"She was in your house. You let her sleep in Donald's bed," Sandra accused.

"You think I'd let a murderer in my house?"

"I don't know."

"What do you mean, you don't know? You think I'd let someone who I know committed murder into my house?"

"That's not what I said."

"What do you mean then?"

"*She* let a child molester in *her* house," Charpentier said, referring to Sheila. "Who knows about anybody?"

Paquin and Charpentier looked out opposite windows for a moment. Neither watched the clock, so they weren't sure how long Sheila had been inside. But when her meeting was over, she burst out from the heavy, windowed door of the law office and jumped in the back seat.

"Let's go," she said.

"Where?"

"Anywhere. Go." Sheila's hands were twitching. She had seemed nervous before, but now her anxiety was amplified.

They drove in silence for a moment. "What did he say?" Paquin finally asked.

Sheila said they had talked about a retainer and the possibility of bail for different murder charges. She said the attorney wanted $60,000 and she wasn't going to pay that. The lawyer told her she should not talk to the police.

"Is there a bank around here?" Sheila asked. Paquin said there was one downtown. They parked and Charpentier waited in the car while the other two went in the branch together.

"Your name is Lucky," Sheila said, pointing to the teller's nameplate. She took it as a good omen. Sheila asked Lucky to close out her account and withdraw all her money. The teller asked if she'd like it in the form of a bank check. No, Sheila said she wanted it in cash. Such a large withdrawal caused a stir on the other side of the counter, as all hands suddenly were on deck to round up available cash. Paquin saw the withdrawal slip. It was for $85,778.21. To facilitate the transaction, Sheila agreed to take some of the money in cash, some in a check. The women walked out of the bank with roughly $35,000 in bills and $50,000 in a banker's check. Sheila also asked Lucky for an envelope to mail a letter. Paquin saw someone pick up a telephone, and she assumed they were calling the police.

"What will you do?" Charpentier asked when they got back in the car.

"I need to find a lawyer who's not a thief. That's the first thing." They all nodded. Neither Charpentier nor Paquin could imagine spending $60,000 for anything. Sheila's tone of voice dipped. "I'm being set up for this. I'm being set up for murder and I didn't do it."

"We believe you, Sheila. Don't we, Sandy?"

"Yes."

Sheila breathed in the love deeply. "You two are angels."

"Where to now?"

"I have to avoid the police. They may know I was at the bank. We have to keep moving."

Paquin drove faster. In the back of the car, Sheila flipped open the pre-paid phone card and began punching code numbers into the cell phone to redeem her air minutes.

"We need to feed my horses," she said.

"What do you mean?" Pam asked. "The horses at the farm? Where the cops are?"

"Yes."

"But they'll feed the horses. They're right there. They've got to."

Sheila began to cry. This show of emotion took the women aback. "No! They don't know how to take care of horses. They can't get to me, so they'll let them starve. Or worse! We have to rescue them."

"How are we freaking going to do that?" Charpentier blurted out.

Sheila stopped crying. "We need to take care of a few things first."

Paquin prepared to point the car east, back along Route 101 from Manchester to Epping. She stopped at a gas station to fuel up and they all got out to stretch their legs and buy some hot dogs for lunch. When the three women with loud voices tumbled out of the silver sedan, heads turned. The other people pumping gas stared. Sheila defiantly met their gazes.

"Oh, yeah. That's right. You know who I am," she said. Although at this point her name had only been mentioned in passing in connection with Kenneth Countie's disappearance and her picture had yet to be broadcast, she acted like everyone recognized her. "That's right. It's me. And I'm innocent."

Before Pam Paquin, Sandy Charpentier and Sheila LaBarre arrived in Epping, they stopped in the town of Raymond.

They looked for a bank in hopes of finding a notary. Sheila directed Pam to pull into a supermarket on their right. She said it had a small bank window near the checkout. She chose not to go to the full-sized, full-service bank that was on the other side of the street.

A young bank employee dressed in a clean blue shirt and necktie was the only male working among a handful of female tellers. They were busy giving away water bottles and fanny packs in an effort to drum up business for their line of checking products. The guy spotted them walking through the automatic doors.

"I need someone to notarize this document for me," the lady with the blonde hair and Southern accent said. It was handwritten on one sheet of lined paper. Its words and phrases were mysteries to Paquin and Charpentier, but the two were endlessly impressed that Sheila could compose such a thing off the top of her head.

The top read "State of New Hampshire, Rental Management Agreement." It listed the addresses of three apartments Sheila owned in Somersworth and gave authority to Sandra Charpentier to manage them and collect rent. Like the other quasi-legal documents Sheila drew up in her life, it was over the top and interspersed with pointed personal notations:

> ... it is agreed that Sandra will manage these two properties to rent by Tenancy At Will, 30 day notice either party no reason require, pro bono, as a favor to her friend Sheila. ... Keys are inside green 1995 pickup truck in Barn at 70 Red Oak Hill Lane, Epping, NH. Sandra is also to receive <u>any other keys inside farmhouse</u> to cars, trucks, anything belonging to Sheila LaBarre.

It was also noted that the agreement was revocable in written form by Sheila. It was a document she knew would be read and challenged, just like the bill of sale for the horses she presented Paquin.

They made one more stop before heading to the farm. Sheila's nerves had turned into a full-blown case of diarrhea.

The three took back roads through Epping, winding their way toward the LaBarre farm. Paquin and Charpentier weren't sure what they were going to do when they pulled up to the yellow taped gate they had seen on TV. It occurred to Paquin (who was beginning to feel like a fugitive herself) that this visit to the farm seemed like a risky move. Perhaps Sheila wasn't thinking clearly anymore. *She's nervous as hell. Are we going to get there and they pull their guns out on us? I don't want to get shot for this woman!*

Sheila said there were five horses on the farm. The Shetland ponies were named Shehasta and Whinny. The caramel-colored gelding, quite appropriately named St. Serious, was quiet and smart. Truth, a dark brown standardbred female, was the prettiest of the herd. The oldest had been on the farm for as long as Sheila had been living there. Caldonia, a huge draft horse that her late husband Bill LaBarre had bought at auction, was now scared and gimpy. The chiropractor always massaged and manipulated the horse to relieve her pain. He used to say the horses were proof that chiropractic techniques were real medicine, for with horses the placebo effect is eliminated.

Being with the horses, feeding them, brushing them, watering them, always had brought back warm memories of the man who took her in. Tears filled her eyes as she thought about returning home to the animals she loved so much.

The car began to climb the lane. Paquin regarded the farms, the same fields that Assistant Attorney General Peter Odom had seen the day before. A city girl herself, she paid no mind to the horse trailers coming the other way. But Sheila leaned forward in her seat, grabbed hold of the door in preparation to spin to the left as the trailer passed them.

"Those are my horses!"

"What?"

"Those sons of bitches! They're taking my horses! Turn around!"

Paquin and Charpentier looked at each other. Charpentier

shrugged her shoulders and Paquin stopped the car. She took five points to make her three-point turn, then shot off after the trailer.

"What do we do?" Paquin asked.

"Make them pull over. They can't take my horses."

Charpentier asked, "What if they're cops?"

She paused. "Those are no longer my horses." There was a lump in her throat. Tears rolled down her cheeks. "They belong to Pam. She's got a bill of sale."

Paquin pulled their car alongside the truck pulling the trailer. She honked the horn; Charpentier motioned for the driver to pull over. They all stopped on the side of the road. Sheila waited in the car, crouched down in the backseat.

"Go talk to them," Sheila said to Paquin.

"I'm not going! She's going," she said pointing to Charpentier.

"I'm not going! You're going!"

"You're going with me!"

"They're your horses now, Pammy!"

"Stop it!" Sheila verbally separated them. "You both go. And don't let them see me."

Paquin and Charpentier got out of the car and walked back to the truck. Their nervous energy started fueling their courage. "Where are you taking those horses?" Paquin asked the driver.

"They're going to Stratham, to the SPCA."

"Those are my horses." Paquin now was convinced they were hers.

"Are you," he looked down at a clipboard for a name, "Sheila LaBarre?"

"No. She sold me those horses. I have a bill of sale. They're mine."

"You can't have them."

"Why not?!" Charpentier joined in. "They're hers!"

"They've been seized by the police. If you want them, you've got to go talk to them."

"Epping police?" They had both heard Sheila rail against the department and the chief who had it in for her.

"I've got to bring the rest of them to the shelter in Stratham. If you talk to the police, I'm sure you can work something out."

The two women looked at each other, unsure of their next step. They knew Sheila would not want to go to the police station, but she was damn set on getting those horses.

"Are they okay? The horses?"

"They're old. But I think they're going to be fine. We'll give them a checkup, give them some hay and groom them."

Paquin and Charpentier shuffled back to the car and got in. Sheila remained low behind the backseat bench, waiting for some kind of report. None came.

"What did he say?" she finally blurted.

"If we want the horses, we have to go talk to the police."

"The police? Why?"

"They've seized them. But he thinks if we show them the bill of sale, we might be able to get them back."

"What do you want us to do, Sheila?"

She thought some more. "You're going to get those horses. Let's go."

The car pulled back into traffic and disappeared down the twisting road. In the cab of the pickup, the animal rescue worker was on his cell phone. The 911 operator had put him in touch with the Epping dispatch center.

"There are two women inside the car. It's a New Hampshire license plate, number . . ."

CHAPTER 9

WAL-MART

On the evening of Saturday March 11, two weeks before the police investigation of the Silver Leopard Farm began, Sheila turned up at the Wal-Mart customer service desk with Kenneth Countie. Although it had lost its holiday season battle with Chief Dodge over twenty-four-hour service, Wal-Mart was still one of the only businesses open late in Epping.

"I need you!" Sheila was rapping her hand on the counter. The younger of the two women behind the desk approached her, but Sheila put up a hand. "No, *you*," she said pointing to the older woman. "I need you!"

"Can I help you?" Brigit Pearson asked. She wore the familiar blue Wal-Mart vest with her first name on a tag. Sheila stood in front of her wearing a fashionable brown leather coat.

"There's a woman, a customer in this store, who just grabbed him by the arm and pushed him out of the way!"

The anger and determination in the customer's voice at first took Pearson by surprise. She glanced at the young man standing next to the woman. He was wearing blue jeans and a red sweatshirt. Although he would not return the look, keeping his head down the whole time, Pearson could see there was an age difference between the two customers. She looked closer and could see there were cuts and scratches all over the man's face.

"She did that?" Pearson asked.

"Yes!" Then Sheila said, "Well, no. This is all from a car accident. A really bad car accident, and he was burned on his arm and all up in here."

Sheila grabbed Kenny's arm and spun him around. The young man made no attempt to resist. Sheila grabbed his sweatshirt and pulled it up over his head, revealing a large burn on Kenny's back. Pearson was both shocked and embarrassed, but she noted that there was no blood on the inside of the sweatshirt. Pearson noticed something else while looking at his bare torso: his skin color was odd.

The customer service desk was in the center portion of the enormous store, right in front of the checkout lines. Shoppers passing by started to stare. Kenny did not look up. Pearson wasn't sure whose gaze he was avoiding: hers or Sheila's.

"He's in a lot of pain," Sheila continued. "I want something done right now! I want the head of security and the manager here now! Do you hear me?"

I've got to defuse this situation somehow, Pearson thought. Other employees were gathering at the customer service desk or watching from afar.

"I want that woman thrown out! I want something done now! I have friends who work at Wal-Mart, this Wal-Mart, and I want something done now or I'll have your job!"

Pearson tried to explain that they did not have a security team at their store. "Would you like to call the police?"

"No. I don't need the police. I'm a lawyer and I can do it myself."

Pearson dialed the extension for the management office. One of the store's co-managers, Dan O'Neil, said he'd be right down. Another associate, who had witnessed the tirade, found co-manager Patsy Lynn on the floor.

"There's a woman flipping out at the service desk," he told her.

O'Neil and Lynn both approached Sheila with smiles and politely asked how they could help. Sheila's anger shifted to them as she explained how a woman near the posters in the stationery aisle had assaulted her "husband." The managers explained they did not have a security team and again offered to call the Epping police.

Sheila tugged on Kenny's arm and dragged him back through the store. The employees all noticed he winced in pain as she did this. "I'll have your job! I have friends that work for Wal-Mart in Bentonville. Don't you hear my Southern accent?!"

Another customer, who had been standing in line at customer service, pulled Lynn aside. "I saw the incident," he said. "The other woman barely brushed against the man and even said, 'Excuse me.' That lady started screaming at the customer in the aisle."

Minutes later, O'Neil's walkie-talkie squawked for a co-manager to get over to the electronics department. Sheila was standing in front of a yellow smiley face sign, her own face twisted into a terrible frown. She was yelling that her husband had been assaulted in the store. Again, she pulled on the red sweatshirt and tugged it over Kenny's head.

"Please don't do that," O'Neil requested. "That's not necessary."

"You're all being unprofessional," Sheila spat. "Don't you know your own job description?"

"There's no need to turn this into a personal attack," he countered.

"I'm going to sue Wal-Mart for millions of dollars! And I'm going to have you all fired!"

"Since you have mentioned suing," O'Neil said, "we no longer have anything to say to you." The employees all walked away, hoping this would calm things. Sheila grabbed Kenny and left the store.

A half-hour later, store co-manager Hank Linton was asked to take a call from an angry customer. The associate said the caller specifically said she didn't want to talk to Dan or Patsy.

After punching up the line, Linton got an earful from a woman who said she had had a run-in with two assistant managers and that her husband had been assaulted in the store.

"My husband is home with me and he's crying, because he is in so much pain from the assault," she said. The caller then asked about the security cameras positioned around the store. "Do they have audio attached to them?"

"Security is not my job title, and I really can't answer your questions about it."

The caller said she was looking up flights online to Bentonville, Arkansas, where Wal-Mart's home office is located. She said she wanted to present her case directly to the company president.

"I have family that work at the home office," she said. "I also have a family member that does polygraphs for the FBI. I'm going to call my polygraph person and my husband and I will take one. I want the store managers to take one, too."

Linton endured much of the rant with professional courtesy. The caller threatened to sue for millions. Then she began asking about Dan O'Neil's history at the store. The caller was sure she'd had a confrontation with him at another store over dog biscuits or something. Linton provided the woman with phone numbers to the district manager and to corporate offices. He ended the conversation by wishing the caller "a great night," although by now he didn't really mean it.

Within the hour, Linton got a page to dial the service desk extension. The associate said there was a strange woman on the phone asking about the managers and talking in what sounded like a fake Chinese accent.

The arrival of the Epping Wal-Mart Supercenter in January of 2004 had been greeted with the typical mix of feelings: great for the consumer, bad for the competitor. Forcing out the tiny shops and storefronts meant altering the character of the town. But for "The Center of the Universe," the "Great Crossroads," the gravitational pull of modern American commerce was too strong to escape.

Jumping off of Route 101 at the junction of Route 125, there were already the universal commercial offerings of fast-food restaurants. There was a coffee and donut shop, as ubiquitous in New England as gourmet coffee is everywhere else.

Not long after Wal-Mart went in at the junction, a who's who of franchise labels sprouted nearby. Within a half-mile, there was also a home improvement store, a deli, a family restaurant, a drug store and a second coffee and donut shop (this one on the opposite side of the road, for the apparent convenience of commuters driving the opposite way).

There were those who saw the construction of the Wal-Mart as the *Beginning of the End* for their town. A cataclysmic event. They tossed at night, counting their fears like sheep. But others were rocked to sleep by the convenience and the lighting, the crowds and the prices. To them, it made no difference. The character of a town is what one makes of it. It didn't matter if the clerks and store owners knew their names, asked about their aging parents. They could walk inside with their winter jackets unzipped and go from the nail salon to the portrait place to the fast-food restaurant *inside* the store. They felt plugged in, not to the local community of delis and hardware stores, but to the national community of shoppers who were browsing from sea to shining sea. They could buy armfuls of stuff and go back to the country homes they took pride in.

Four months after it opened, a cashier and a worker in the tire and lube center got married in the Wal-Mart garden center, with a reception in the break room. The department store finally had become a town square. In the battle for the soul of Epping, Wal-Mart wasn't the enemy. Like Walt Kelly said, "We have met the enemy and he is us."

On the evening of Tuesday, March 14, Wal-Mart cashier Jodee Hook was working the register when a customer with blondish hair and a brown leather coat began slamming her groceries down on the belt.

"Hi," Hook said with as much saccharine enthusiasm as she could muster. "How are you tonight?"

"Fuck this store. The fucking door lady said that I need to fucking put more clothes on."

The comment didn't sound like something a Wal-Mart

people greeter would say. "I'm very sorry. Is there anything I can do?"

"No. There isn't a fucking thing you can do! I hate this fucking store!"

Hook quickly scanned the grocery items, not wanting to tangle with the customer.

"My fucking family fucking owns this fucking business!" the woman continued. "So I'm going to fucking sue this fucking place! I'm a fucking multi-millionaire and a fucking lawyer!"

Thinking she could calm the customer down by changing the subject, Hook asked what kind of lawyer the woman was. Then Hook apologized when the customer told her it wasn't any of her fucking business.

"I'm fucking calling my fucking family up and fucking talking to them about this store and getting all you guys fucking fired! You're all fucking nosey and fucking rude!"

The cashier scanned the last of the groceries and bagged them. The customer handed Hook a fifty-dollar bill, which she proceeded to mark with the counterfeit detector pen.

"You don't need to fucking check out my fucking money. I'm a fucking multi-millionaire and a fucking lawyer!"

"I'm sorry, but I have to check every customer's money." The woman took her change by ripping it out of Hook's hands, then threw her bags in the carriage.

During her break, Hook asked the door greeter if she had said anything about a customer needing to put more clothes on. The greeter said only that she told one woman it was chilly outside.

Sheila LaBarre returned to the Wal-Mart with Kenneth Countie on Friday, March 17. This time, she was pushing Countie in a store wheelchair. The couple stopped in front of cosmetics and talked to store co-manager Priscilla Burch. Sheila introduced herself, then began telling Burch how management was negligent by not scouring the store for her husband's attacker.

"I am an attorney-in-fact and a notary. I can sign my own arrest warrant for her," Sheila said.

"When customers mention being assaulted, we need to contact the police," the co-manager replied.

"I would have followed this woman to her car to get her license plate number. I own a horse farm and I'm a multi-millionaire. I can shop for designer clothing, but the clothes you sell are good enough for me, because they're good enough for Sam Walton."

Burch got a good look at Countie's face. His skin was wan and peppered with bruises and scrapes in various stages of healing. Sheila asked him several times if he was going to faint.

"My late husband was a medical doctor," Sheila informed the employee. "And I have a medical background. I can treat his wounds."

You have got *to be kidding me,* Burch thought. *That guy looks like he belongs in a hospital.*

Sheila told Burch that she had paid $700 that day for a professional polygraph and her "husband" had passed it with flying colors.

The manager followed Sheila to the seasonal aisle, where she planned to reconstruct the incident. Sheila pushed Kenny around, paying no mind to the shoppers around them. The man's head was down, as if in defeat. He didn't seem concerned in the least which direction she pushed him. At one point, Sheila touched Kenny's shoulder. The man jumped in pain. Again, Burch offered the customer some corporate phone numbers and excused herself to get back to work.

Sheila continued shopping, grabbing a disposable camera. She pushed Kenny past hardware and into the automotive section. They passed dozens of yellow smiley faces, faces that now seemed joyless. Sheila made a sharp right around a corner. Her eyes quickly scanned the shelves. They were there, just beyond the car jacks and cans of automotive oil. There were two rows of them. One whole row of red for gasoline. A couple in blue, meant for kerosene. Next to them, the five-gallon containers in yellow. Those were for diesel fuel.

They cost $11.64 apiece. She took two and piled the yellow plastic jugs on Kenny's lap in the wheelchair. Then she pushed the broken man and the fuel containers to the checkout aisle. All alongside of them, the malevolent smiley faces peered down like some Lewis Carroll nightmare.

She rolled Kenny with the containers in his arms. Her plan for them was lodged in her own wicked mind.

Burch was paged to electronics. When the manager got there, she saw Sheila taking pictures of the security camera domes mounted in the ceilings.

"Is everything okay?" she asked as nicely as she could.

Sheila gave her a look, like an animal regarding a flea. "Yes," she said rudely and walked away.

At 8:45 P.M., the report came over the Epping police radio for a suspicious person at Wal-Mart, and Detective Richard Cote got the call. Cops in other towns were cracking heads with St. Patrick's Day revelers stumbling out of bars. It seemed it wouldn't be a night patrolling Epping if the cops didn't have to stop by Wal-Mart for something.

Burch flagged down Cote when he arrived at the store. The officer asked what the story was and the manager explained what had been going on.

"Do you have a name?" Cote asked.

"Sheila LaBarre."

Cote's reaction was immediate and evincive. Cote was both a football coach and the head of the department's police union, so he wasn't afraid of getting into a tumble. But he was smart enough not to approach "Sheila the Peeler" without at least one other officer with him. This call was going to require backup. He radioed for Sergeant Sean Gallagher to meet him at the store.

On February 26, two days after Gallagher and Cote had knocked on the farmhouse door looking for Kenny, Sheila made three phone calls to the chief's office within a few minutes of each other. She was in a lather about the well-being check and threatened to sue if the cops came back to her home for the same purpose. She also requested a copy of the National Crime Information Center report that listed Countie as a missing person.

"This woman has a history with the Epping Police Department," Cote told Burch. "We need to be careful about how we handle things."

Gallagher entered the store and met Burch and Cote at the customer service desk. He asked Burch how she wanted to proceed and she said she wanted Sheila removed from the store and told not to return.

Sheila's eyes were drawn tight and beady when she saw the two officers approaching her. She and Kenny were in the frozen food section, and Sheila was using a disposable camera to take snapshots of the security cameras. The sergeant explained that management wanted her out of the store.

"Can I pay for my merchandise first?" The cops looked over at the Wal-Mart employees, who nodded that it would be okay.

While Gallagher talked to Sheila, Detective Cote tried to get a private word in with Kenny. The kid was wearing a goofy kind of top hat and a fur jacket that seemed too big for him. It had been only a few weeks since the well-being check at the farm, but he was taken back by how badly Kenny had deteriorated.

"Are you all right?" he asked Countie.

Sheila LaBarre, who seemed to have a wicked radar about such things, turned away from Gallagher and yelled at Countie before the wheelchair-bound man could speak.

"Don't fucking answer that question!" she exploded. "You don't have to answer any fucking question they ask you."

Kenny dropped his head. He said nothing.

Sheila pushed the non-responsive Kenny toward the self-checkout kiosk. She scanned a box of crackers and some other things, then stuffed them in a blue plastic bag. She had two yellow plastic fuel cans that she didn't scan, so the associates asked her about them. In a huff, Sheila produced a receipt for the diesel cans and the disposable camera that she had paid for earlier that evening.

Kenneth Countie tried to get out of the wheelchair, but he

strained, moving gingerly. Sheila grabbed hold of him and pulled him out. The man had been hunched over in the chair and looked like he couldn't lift himself. The store managers, seeing the injured man attempting to steady himself with the shopping cart, offered to let Sheila take the wheelchair out to the parking lot.

"No," she said coolly. "You have harassed me enough. I'm all set."

Gallagher took a good look at the man stumbling along next to the cart. *It is him. It is Countie,* he thought. But Countie looked nothing like he did on February 24, standing in the farmhouse door. His skin color was ashen. He had cuts on his face. He had cuts on his hands, and one of them appeared to be swollen.

"Are you all right?" Gallagher asked Kenny as he got into Sheila's car. Kenny did not have a chance to respond as the woman he had fallen in love with shut the door on them. Gallagher stood there outside the passenger door, but Kenny never looked up, never looked out the window. Sheila drove out of the parking lot and the two of them went north toward the farm.

Later that night, Gallagher filled out the report for police call number 06-1468. He wrote how he told Sheila not to return to the store. "Sheila was removed from the store without incident," the report's narrative said. Nothing was said in reference to any concern about Kenny or how he looked.

Kenneth Countie was never seen in public again.

CHAPTER 10

A CALL IN THE NIGHT

Police Sergeant Sean Gallagher couldn't shake the uneasy feeling he got when he saw Kenneth Countie with Sheila LaBarre that night at the Wal-Mart. He told himself, *Countie is an adult; it wasn't like I could take him into protective custody.* So much could account for the way Countie appeared. Bad diet. Rough sex. Humiliation. All were medications townsfolk assumed were served on that horse farm to the boys who moved there. Nevertheless, he still felt apprehensive.

Some people thought of the Silver Leopard Farm as Hansel and Gretel's house. A sweet gingerbread home in the woods where a young man walked in expecting candy, only to find a witch. *A witch who'd suck your dick then beat you like a dog,* they laughed, *but a gingerbread house witch nonetheless.*

It was Thursday night, March 23, nearly a week since Gallagher responded to the manager of Wal-Mart and kicked Sheila and Kenny out of the store. There was paperwork on his desk, all of it had to do with Sheila LaBarre.

One report filled out by a patrolman on March 8 said that Sheila had called requesting police contact a man living in Somersworth. He was a tenant living at one of the properties Sheila still owned. She wanted the officer to tell the man not to come onto her property. The report said the tenant had come to the farm and left a note for Sheila on the windshield of one of her vehicles. The tenant readily admitted he came on the property to leave the note, saying it was the only way he was able to contact Sheila. He agreed not to come back to the farm.

Under that paper was a report taken on March 10. Sheila called the police station to report a harassing phone call. The number came back to a listing in Buffalo, New York. She said at 12:15 P.M. someone called, breathed heavy into the phone and hung up. Sheila advised the cop taking the report that she had taped the phone call with a handheld recorder.

Somewhere beneath that report and the one from the Wal-Mart encounter was an incident report taken on behalf of Sheila's neighbor, Gordon Winslow. It was unclear in the narrative if Winslow contacted the police or the other way around. On March 21, Winslow notified Police Lieutenant Michael Wallace that he was blocking a passageway between his farm and Sheila's land. The farmer said he was blocking it with cow manure. Winslow informed the cop he was "doing it as a preventative measure, so Sheila LaBarre will not go onto his property."

What had caught Gallagher's attention was a report taken earlier in the day by the police station's secretary. Unlike other administrative assistants, the station's secretary had a background in law enforcement. She had worked as a police officer in the tiny town of Milton, New Hampshire, as well as a public safety officer for a university. She no longer wanted to be a cop, so she sought a way to put her associate's degree in paralegal studies to practice. She had a good balance of street smarts and book smarts. It was one of the reasons she rose to the top in a field of more than fifty applicants when the secretary's job came open.

The Epping police station's secretary was also friendly and kind, someone who was easy to talk to. It was a quality that was appealing to Sheila LaBarre. The secretary took Sheila's phone calls long after Chief Dodge decided he'd had enough. She let the high-strung LaBarre blow off steam

in her ear while her hands were busy typing or filing. When
Sheila couldn't get the chief to take her calls, she resorted to
long rambling letters written in poison pen ink that were
transmitted to the police department from her home fax
machine. The secretary would be on the other end to inter-
cept the letters; it's unclear how many of the faxes actually
made it to Dodge. The station's secretary was loyal to the
chief, but she did not make a show of taking Sheila's calls.
She'd learned Dodge's moods and knew he didn't approve of
her indulging Sheila.

On Thursday the 23rd, Sheila called the secretary at the
police station around noon. The secretary looked to her left,
into the chief's office, then let Sheila vent. Sheila called to
discuss her removal from Wal-Mart on the previous Friday.
Of course, she complained about her treatment at the hands
of Gallagher and Detective Cote. She ranted about her rights,
both legal and moral, and the station's secretary listened
with a sympathetic ear. Occasionally, she had to put Sheila
on hold to pick up the other phone line, but the interruptions
did little to kill the momentum of a LaBarre tirade. This conversation lasted about twenty-five minutes, much of it driven
by Sheila.

At some point in the conversation, the talk turned to
Kenneth Countie. The police secretary knew of Carolynn
Lodge's previous missing persons report to the station and
heard from the officers how the young man looked like hell
when they saw him at Wal-Mart.

"How is your relationship going?" she asked.

"What relationship?"

"Your relationship with Kenny? How is it going?"

"He's gone," she said.

"What do you mean, 'He's gone'?"

"He left me."

There was something in this statement that seemed oddly
out of character for Sheila. The woman who was so indignant about *any* confrontation with law enforcement, who
would not be crossed by neighbor or stranger, could she really be this at ease with a man walking out on her?

"Where did he go?" the secretary asked.

"He told me that he was leaving in the middle of the night. I asked him how he was getting home and he told me not to worry about it. And when I woke up this morning, he was gone."

"Where is he now?" she asked her.

"He's back in Massachusetts," Sheila said. She added that his departure was all right with her because he "didn't do anything anyway."

Her tone was calm and her demeanor was dismissive, but the secretary felt that Sheila was going to say more. The police station's secretary wanted to press her with additional questions, but the phones started to light up. She had to hang up with Sheila.

Gallagher was standing at the secretary's desk looking at a phrase in her notes . . . *didn't do anything anyway* . . . tapping it with the end of a pen, when the telephone rang. It was Carolynn Lodge, Countie's mother. Gallagher said he'd take the call.

"I want to file another missing persons report," she said.

Gallagher had taken Lodge's original complaint one month earlier. She seemed even more worried this time. He decided to say nothing of Sheila's call to the station that afternoon. "What makes you think Kenneth's missing, Mrs. Lodge?"

Lodge said she had spoken with Sheila LaBarre on the telephone. Sheila said that Kenny had left her farm, left Epping, and was heading back to Massachusetts. "Kenny is unable to take care of himself, Sergeant. If he left he would have contacted me. Or his father."

Gallagher was taking furious notes. "Are you sure he's not staying with someone else? A friend or former roommate who might have picked him up?"

"No. My ex-husband and I have contacted everyone we know, everyone Kenny knows. Nobody has seen him. No one can get hold of him."

"Does he have a cell phone?" Lodge gave Gallagher the number.

"Before he moved in with her," Lodge began slowly, "Kenny called me almost daily. He's twenty-four, but he just moved from home for the first time in January. He cannot care for himself if he's left alone."

The woman now seemed anxious, but collected. The police officer promised he'd file the report and look into it personally. Lodge didn't want to get off the phone, break the connection from someone who might be able to do something and go back to the loneliness of waiting.

Gallagher did not like the way things were falling into place. He went back into his office, called Kenneth Countie's cell phone and got no answer. He tried to trace the phone; it was pre-paid and the minutes had expired. He made calls to friends that Lodge had suggested. He tried everything, except dialing Sheila directly. Gallagher wanted to check everything he could think of before taking that route.

It was well past midnight, past the end of Gallagher's shift, and he was still making notes and writing reports. At 1:00 A.M., the phone rang. It startled him, ripping through the silence of the darkened office. On the phone was Sheila La-Barre.

"Sheila, where is Kenny?" Gallagher pressed her.

The sergeant was ready for verbal spears, but was surprised by what he heard. Sheila began to cry. It started as a whimper, but quickly elevated to maddening, uncontrollable sobs.

"Sheila, calm down." He knew he'd get nowhere if she couldn't stop crying and focus on his questions. "Where is Kenny?"

"I don't know!" she yelled. "And I don't care!"

"How can you not know? You drove him to your farm."

"I woke up one morning and he was gone. Just gone."

"When was this?" Gallagher asked.

"I don't know. Couple of days ago. Maybe two or three days ago. I don't really care. I don't ever want to see him again."

"You don't? Why not?"

"He's a pervert." It seemed a strange statement coming

from "Sheila the Peeler," the town flirt who brought young men to her farm to be her playthings.

"What do you mean?"

"He's a child molester."

Gallagher wasn't quite sure where she was going to go with this. Kenneth Countie, the mollycoddled mama's boy, didn't fit the traditional profile of a child molester. "How do you know that? He tell you that?"

The tears stopped. "You don't believe me, do you Sergeant Gallagher?"

"I didn't say I did or I didn't," he replied.

"I can prove it to you. Right now."

There was a low bass-toned clunk of the handset as Sheila put it down momentarily. Gallagher could hear her reach for something, then the handset be repositioned. The mouthpiece bumped up against something. Then there was a click and the up-cut "whoop" of an audiotape coming up to speed. The police officer could hear Sheila's voice again, but the extreme high and low ends of the sound were gone. It was her voice on tape.

"I, Sheila LaBarre, am a justice of the peace. And I am legally recording this conversation with Kenneth Michael Countie, also known as Adam Olympia LaBarre. Is that correct?"

"Yes." There was a soft mumbled voice. Gallagher remembered it as Kenneth Countie's.

"And are you speaking to me in my official capacity as justice of the peace and a notary?"

"Yes."

"And you are aware that New Hampshire is a two-party consent-to-tape state?"

"Yes."

"And you have granted me permission under free will to be tape recorded? Is this true?"

The answer was but a mumble, hard for Gallagher to make out.

"Talk right!" Sheila ordered. The shout startled Gallagher and must have terrified Kenny. "Is this true?"

"Yes," Kenny replied a bit clearer but none the louder.

"Is it true that you are a child molester?"

"Yes."

"Is it true that you raped many children?!"

"Yes."

"Including members of your family?!"

"Yes." The cross-examination by Sheila was growing more heated, but Kenny's answers remained weak. Gallagher thought his voice was muffled in some way.

Sheila listed names of people: young children, step-siblings and nieces. Everyone "in the family." She got Kenny to admit to raping them for as long as he could remember. She asked him if he had ever videotaped these rapes and whether that videotape could be found in the left-hand side of the top dresser drawer of the Wilmington home he previously shared with a roommate. But each admission was a simple, defeated "Yes" after a question was screamed at him. Sheila was in the background screaming hysterically, "Why? Why?" It was bone-chilling.

"Talk right!" the tape-recorded Sheila shouted over and over again.

Kenny finally made a noise other than a capitulating "Yes." It sounded like a gag. Then Kenny started to vomit.

"He's faking," recorded Sheila said to no one. "You're faking throwing up! Kenneth Countie is faking throwing up." But it didn't sound like he'd been faking it to Gallagher.

The tape was near its end. Sheila pressed Kenny some more, but the man stopped answering. There was another indistinguishable noise.

"You didn't faint!" Sheila said. "Stop faking that you fainted. Kenneth Countie is now faking that he fainted."

Gallagher could picture Kenny passed out on the floor, next to a puddle of his own vomit, with Sheila standing over him. There was a hard click as a button was pressed and the magnetic heads pulled away from the 1/8-inch thin strip of acetone audiotape. The horrible radio-play was over, but the cop could not erase the macabre theater of the mind. For years they had laughed at Sheila LaBarre. They had seen her as an unlikely character to be living in their town. Part whore, part lioness and part Tasmanian devil. No one had truly suspected she was capable of this level of real violence.

She came back on the phone and resumed crying.

"Sheila," Gallagher asked calmly, "where is Kenny?"

"I do not know."

"Sheila, you must know."

"He's not around here."

"Where did he go, Sheila?"

"The tape, it's all true! Every bit of it," she blurted out between sobs. "I don't care where he is! I never want to see him again."

Sergeant Gallagher did not sleep well that night. He wanted to go to the Silver Leopard Farm and check on Kenneth Countie himself. Sheila's phone call came in after midnight on March 24, so he felt going there so late in the evening would be fruitless. He and Detective Richard Cote made plans to do the well-being check when they got in for second shift later that day.

The police car made the drive up Red Oak Hill Lane, over the tree root bumps and past the stone walls. It was around 6:00 P.M. on the 24th, and there was still some daylight left on this Friday.

The two found the wooden gate to the property closed and padlocked. That was unusual for Sheila.

They parked outside the gate, slipped between the cross beams of the fence and walked to the house.

All of Sheila's cars were parked in the yard. They assumed she'd be home, but the lights were off inside the quickly darkening home. They knocked, no answer.

That's when they noticed the smell of something horrible in the air. Sheila had been burning something on the property. There was a mattress box spring blacked from fire. There was a barrel filled with hay. Although Sheila had not been around, the areas were still actively burning, so she couldn't have

been away that long. The yellow diesel fuel containers they'd
seen Sheila make Kenny carry were in the back of her pickup
truck nearby.

Sticking out of a burn pile was the jagged length of bone.
But it was not the clean white bone of an anatomist's skeleton. The severed body part was covered in the meat of human flesh, still roasting in the diesel-fueled fire. Cote
reached in and picked it up. It felt heavy, about five pounds.
It was moist. He dropped it back on to the smoldering pile
with a look of disgust and horror.

They had come to check on Kenneth Countie, take him
away from this home if it was necessary. Now, they feared
they were too late.

PART 2

SOMETHING WICKED
THIS WAY COMES

"No notice is taken of a little evil, but when it increases it strikes the eye."

—Aristotle

CHAPTER 11

THE STRAIGHT MAN

Wilfred "Bill" LaBarre sat alone in the waiting area at Boston's Logan International Airport.

The man sitting next to him had the newspaper flipped to the sports section on the back page. The night before, the Boston Red Sox dropped a 3-2 decision to the Milwaukee Brewers at County Stadium. The Sox were 0-2 to start the '87 season after coming within one out of finally winning the World Series against the New York Mets some six months earlier. There was anticipation the team would resume its winning ways and redeem itself. (In fact, the Sox were about to go down 12-11 again to the Brewers that night and would never be one game above .500 that whole season.) But New England baseball fans are Calvinistic like their colonial ancestors. They believe in predestination, that they are meant to suffer and that glory is reserved for the few. And that maybe this was finally their time for such glory.

LaBarre did not read the sports section that day, although there was a new season of redemption about to begin in his life too. He did not bring a paper or a magazine to browse. He had a postcard in his pocket, but he dared not remove it from its hiding place. Nor would he take out the racy photo of a bare-breasted woman, her face obscured by the flash bouncing off the mirror she posed in front of. His mind would not focus on newsprint this afternoon. Instead he'd read his wristwatch, waiting for the springs to maneuver the hands to 3:42. His ears remained open for any news about flight 5340 from Atlanta.

Bill LaBarre caught a glimpse of his reflection in the shiny façades that surrounded him. For a moment, his heart sank. He wasn't tall and never had an athletic build. His thinning, graying hair came to an untamable tuft at his widow's peak. His blue eyes were kind, but his large nose and thick mustache made him look like an older Groucho Marx. *I'm going to be sixty-one years old next week,* he reminded himself. *What am I doing here?*

LaBarre had never missed a day of work at his successful chiropractic clinic in Hampton, New Hampshire, just a mile and a half from the ocean. That day, he hopped into his car and left the clinic for Boston at lunchtime. LaBarre was regarded as kind and cheerful, but he was deeply lonely. The past couple of years had been almost more lonely than he could bear. A widower, he longed for companionship. LaBarre hoped so badly that this woman who was flying from down South would bring him happiness.

Wilfred Joseph LaBarre was born on April 23, 1926 in Norwich, Connecticut. He was the only son of Wilfred LaBarre Sr. and Emma Fink LaBarre. He gave himself the name "Bill" when he was fifteen years old, growing up in southern New England. He joined the Navy during World War II, trained at the Aviation Technical School in Putnam, Connecticut, then was sent into combat. He earned his wings as an aerial gunner specialist.

After the war, LaBarre came home to a nation of expanding possibilities. But the young man was unsure of what direction to take.

LaBarre was close to his cousin, Edward Charron. Three years his senior, Charron was bold and strong. At age sixteen, he was the New England gymnastics champion. A natural athlete, Charron excelled at any sport he tried. He had an unusual combination of strength and balance. Boxing built his upper body. As a young man, he joined The Eriksons, a world famous hand-balancing group. He even toured the country with the act as part of the Siebrand Circus. LaBarre couldn't help but look up to him as he would an older brother.

It was Charron who noticed an advertisement in the back pages of a weightlifting magazine. "Take a look," he told LaBarre. *Become a Doctor of Chiropractic*, it promised. *GI's Accepted.*

The ad sounded promising to both of them. Charron had served in the Army rehabilitating wounded soldiers. LaBarre had been seeking a school to attend. They made a pledge to go to the Palmer School of Chiropractic together.

Aldea Charron was Wilfred LaBarre Sr.'s sister. She thought the possible career sounded promising. "I've been to a chiropractor. He pushed on my back and it felt better."

LaBarre's mother, Emma, was less enthusiastic about the possibilities. "I give them three weeks," she said. Emma predicted it would take the boys a week to get to Iowa by train, a week to flunk out and a week to get back to Connecticut.

Dressed in new suits and sharp-looking hats, the pair hopped a train in New London and made a transfer at Penn Station in New York to Davenport, Iowa. En route, the boys met a chiropractor on the train. They were filled with questions about the mysterious practice and the clinician was eager to advocate for the profession.

The chiropractor discussed the premise of spinal misalignment, also known as subluxation. The theory was that the body had its own ability to heal itself through the nervous system. "If a single organ is sick," he told them, "it must not be receiving its normal nerve supply." Through adjustments of the spine, the chiropractor believed he could relieve pain and cure disease. D. D. Palmer, the nineteenth century founder of the college to which they were traveling, is said to have cured one man of deafness and another of heart trouble with his first adjustment.

Their discussions in the club car went on late and even included some demonstrations on their backs. Upon arriving in Iowa, LaBarre immediately wrote to his mother and begged her to seek chiropractic care. Emma LaBarre was often described as "ailing," a common label used in the 1940s. But soon after her reluctant visit to a local chiropractor, the woman's health miraculously turned around. At that point, Emma gave her full endorsement to the career path chosen by her son and nephew. Shortly thereafter, Bill LaBarre and Ed Charron graduated from the Palmer School of Chiropractic.

While he and Charron were studying at Palmer in Iowa, LaBarre married his girlfriend from back East. Leone LaBarre took his name and moved to Davenport to be with her husband. While there, she gave birth to their first child, a daughter. The young family returned to New England in search of establishing a practice.

Legal trouble and regulatory problems faced many chiropractors, as few states at the time recognized chiropractic as a legitimate medical treatment. LaBarre's first practice was an illegal clinic set up in Springfield, Massachusetts. The sign on his door listed only his name. "I was lucky," he'd tell people years later. "I never got thrown in jail. My friends did."

The state of New Hampshire was the first to grant Bill LaBarre a license. He persuaded his cousin to join him and opened a clinic in the Granite State. They soon had a steady stream of clientele willing to try this new kind of physical manipulation for their aches and pains.

Bill and Leone LaBarre purchased a large tract of land in Epping from Dan Harvey. By now the couple also had a son, and this is where they decided to bring up their two children. The house wasn't too big. It was tastefully but sparsely decorated. The pastureland was just right for raising horses, the doctor's new passion.

During the next decade, LaBarre got involved in the political movement to recognize chiropractic medicine and to strengthen the profession. He was unprepared for the bitter divisions that festered among his fellow chiropractors. Most, like LaBarre, practiced "straight" chiropractic. Practitioners focused solely on manipulating vertebral subluxations to relieve pain. This school of treatment is considered non-therapeutic, an alternative to conventional medicine.

But a growing number of practitioners claimed they could not only relieve pain, but also cure disease by mixing spinal manipulations with acupuncture or ultrasound, nutritional counseling or using it in conjunction with a medical doctor's drug prescriptions. The "mixers," as colleagues dubbed them, posed a threat to those who believed in the purity of the chiropractic principle. LaBarre helped found the New Hampshire Cooperative Chiropractic Society and, while serving as president, brought together practitioners from both camps for the good of the profession. He was crushed a few years later when he watched that unity dissolve over a spat as to which one properly defined what chiropractic was. The "mixers" were reluctant to limit possible new methods or treatments, to box themselves in.

"How can we be unified without definition?" he implored his colleagues. The failure of the group taught LaBarre it was important to stick to one's principles, even at the expense of professional unity.

Though many patients and neighbors considered LaBarre to be warm and approachable, the man had trouble expressing himself with his family. His marriage hit some rough spots. The couple's son, who had learning problems, was a stress inside the marriage. Their daughter felt the pressure of living up to her father's expectations, and the two drifted emotionally. By 1972, Leone and Bill LaBarre finally filed for divorce. The decree cited "irreconcilable differences."

The country doctor turned his life around in 1976 when he met Edwina Kolacz. She was tall and pretty, and friends prodded that she was way out of LaBarre's league. The second Mrs. LaBarre was at least a decade younger than her husband. But the relationship was a good one. Bill LaBarre was transformed. He became more demonstrative, more affectionate with Edwina. He reconciled with his daughter, and she joined the clinic to run the office. He was happy and satisfied with life. He was truly in love.

In 1983, the Sherman College of Straight Chiropractic in

Spartanburg, South Carolina, named LaBarre *Chiropractor of the Year.* He had been serving as a regent to the college, founded by one of his Palmer professors. The honor was not only in recognition of his successful practice or his years fighting for the profession. Standing for the ceremony in a light blue suit with a matching striped necktie, LaBarre was also praised for living the beliefs of "straight" chiropractic. Simple. Straightforward. True. It would seem to be a high point of his personal and professional lives.

When Edwina LaBarre was diagnosed with cancer, it devastated Bill. She died in Georgia in 1983. First a divorcé, now a widower, all the light had left LaBarre's life. He slipped into depression. He wandered the hundred plus acres of his horse farm, unable to clear his head. Sitting alone in his house overlooking the expanse of woods and high grass, LaBarre realized he needed someone to share his life with.

In early 1987, he composed a personals advertisement asking for someone who wasn't too tall and placed it in the national tabloid, *The Globe.* "Doctor, widower," was the heading. It was his distress call placed in a bottle and set to sea.

Bill LaBarre received some replies from his advertisement, but one struck him. It came from Fort Payne, a small town in Alabama. Written in blue ink on one sheet of stationery paper, it had curving embellishments on all the capital letters. The signature was underlined with a flourish.

Dear Special Man,

I am 28, 5' 5" and weigh 117. I do not smoke. I have a <u>great</u> sense of humor and I <u>love</u> life! I judge a person from <u>inside</u> the mind and heart. As you requested, a photograph is enclosed.

If you wish to know more about me, you may call. The number is (205) XXX-XXXX. I would like to have a conversation with you. You could tell me all about New Hampshire. I hear it is lovely.

                              Good luck with your ad.

                              Sheila

As promised, a photograph taken the previous week with the date handwritten on the back was tucked into the envelope. The picture was that of a woman nude but for the pink panties she wore. The model had posed in front of a mirror and taken the shot herself. On a bedroom bureau behind her, a keen eye could make out the open box of instant film she just loaded into the camera. A rumple of white clothing sat on the floor, presumably the outfit she had just shed. The woman was bronzed and even her breasts showed no tan lines. The shutter mechanism of the camera required her to squeeze with her right hand, so her arm was perfectly level and bent at the elbow to allow her to peer through the viewfinder. She had to know that the camera would hide her face, but the exploding flash obscured her head and hair in a flare of white light coming back off the mirror. Regardless of how much of her face she was willing to share, the subject was obviously not shy about showing off her other features.

LaBarre called and chatted with Sheila Jennings. A two-time divorcée herself, a fast relationship grew. She was receptive to his affections and seemed ready to take him on as a lover. He did not question why a woman half his age would be willing to move one thousand miles and start a new life on his farm. On some level, he was merely grateful.

The couple made arrangements to meet. LaBarre mailed her a check for expenses and enclosed a heartfelt note about this new chapter in his life. Sheila sent back a postcard listing flight numbers and arrival times. She wrote that his note was "real sweet" and informed her new lover that she'd be getting one more tanning session before a photo session planned for three days before she left.

Bill LaBarre stood up when they announced the arrival of

flight 5340 from Atlanta to Boston. When Sheila passed through the gate she recognized LaBarre immediately. He took a deep breath when he caught sight of the woman. She was as she described in her letter: petite and trim. Her dark hair was straight and unusually long, reaching past her breasts. She had brown eyes and apple-shaped cheeks. Her lips were painted red, which framed a charming smile. The pair kissed, then hugged, then left in his car for Epping, New Hampshire.

Sheila Jennings did not return to Atlanta. She loved the horses LaBarre kept. The first few months were like a real honeymoon. Sheila stayed home and groomed the horses. She felt isolated in the woods, but also felt free. Sheila would run naked through the tall grass, the warm sun kissing her skin. She assumed no one could see her, but a treetop deer-hunting station on the edge of Gordon Winslow's property provided a covert view of the Southern belle. Loose talk soon followed.

She began referring to herself as "Sheila LaBarre." She had been using combinations of given and married surnames, signing her name as "Sheila Jennings" or "Sheila Bailey" or even using "Bailey Jennings" as a *nom de plume* for some poems she tried to have published. The name "Sheila La-Barre" first turned up on her driver's license in 1990, although she had been known to all by that name for some time. Although it implied the couple had some sort of matrimonial tie, they did not seem to be in a rush to make it official.

Bill LaBarre had redrawn his will following the death of his second wife, Edwina, and before placing his classified ad. A neatly typeset document, it provided that upon his death the business assets would go to his cousin, Dr. Edward G. Charron. Also, Charron could live at the clinic's apartment rent-free for one year. The remainder of LaBarre's wealth was to be divided equally between his children. La-Barre's attorney drew up the will.

In 1988, a new will for Dr. Wilfred Joseph LaBarre was filed with the county. In verbiage, it mimicked LaBarre's previous will. But there were some stark changes. First off, it named "Sheila Kaye Jennings LaBarre" executrix of his estate. In the second paragraph, it ordered Charron to vacate the upstairs apartment upon LaBarre's death. The third paragraph was suspiciously sentimental given the harsh treatment to the doctor's longtime partner:

> During my life I grew to love and trust a very special lady known as Sheila Kaye Jennings LaBarre. Because of my love and trust I conveyed or transferred various real estate, cash, stocks and bonds, and personal property into trust for Sheila. I further give, bequeath and devise all of my estate, real, personal and mixed, of every kind and nature whatsoever situated to Sheila Kaye Jennings LaBarre, if she survives me.

At the time the document was drawn up, Sheila had been living with LaBarre for about a year.

Finally, in July of 1990, LaBarre filed the last of his last will and testaments. Unlike the professionally typeset document four years earlier, this single-spaced composition was pecked out on Sheila's typewriter. In a companion document, LaBarre had given power of attorney to Sheila and had placed much of his property in a trust to be managed by her.

In this final copy of the will, the first six paragraphs dealt with Sheila's powers and privileges as executrix. Paragraph seven began rather dispassionately:

> I have not forgotten my children . . .

The will indicated the office would be placed in trust for the benefit of the children and this trust would be run by Dr. Charron, who would distribute money as he saw fit.

LaBarre continued, if one assumes he was truly the one who drew up the document:

> I specifically do not want either of my children . . . to initiate or participate in any legal contest regarding the

trusts I have signed. It is my desire that the farm and all land become the property of Sheila Kaye J. LaBarre.

Almost two years later, paperwork was filed to delete Edward Charron's name from that trust and replace it with Sheila's.

It took less than four years after leaving Alabama. At that point, Sheila not only had long-term financial control over Bill LaBarre, but she also had legally eliminated the only other people who could stake a claim to the wealth he had amassed.

Sheila LaBarre was now in control. She was free to live the way she wanted to. That included bringing new men into the home that Bill LaBarre had opened to her. That included violent behavior focused toward everyone, including the doctor.

There were times when Bill LaBarre thought about that day in Logan Airport. The Red Sox were never able to redeem themselves, despite the promise that seemed so fresh that April afternoon. Some days LaBarre wondered how his life would have been different if he had stared longer at himself in the mirror that day and left the airport before that plane arrived.

CHAPTER 12

RABBITS

Sergeant Sean Gallagher stood outside the white farmhouse on the end of Red Oak Hill Lane, looking at his wristwatch. He wasn't checking the time per se. He was watching the minutes tick off. The hands seemed to move slower than normal along the springs and over the face.

He and his partner, Detective Richard Cote, had just discovered severed human remains in a burn pile on Sheila LaBarre's farm. The Sergeant had summoned another Epping officer, Bradley Jardis, to the farm. He had pulled his cruiser behind Gallagher's, outside the locked gate, and climbed through carrying his AR-15 service rifle.

Gallagher had a cell phone pressed hard to his ear, his knuckles white and fingertips firm against the object. A dog barked in the background. The smell of flesh still polluted the air and wafted around his head. He tried to keep his eyes focused on the horizon and not on the bone sticking out of the burn pile.

Gallagher was on the phone with the Rockingham County Attorney's office. Each prosecutor is required to take duty calls after hours. On Friday, March 24, Assistant County Attorney Patricia Conway fielded Gallagher's call. The cop explained about Countie's missing persons report and about what he and Detective Cote could see on the exterior of the property.

"Can we go in?" he asked. They didn't want to leave the farm and hunt down a judge. It was already past six o'clock and the weekend had begun. "If he's inside, we want to go in."

Conway must have been thinking the same things as Gallagher and Cote. The evidence was still—literally—smoking and the property owner wasn't around yet. Time was of the essence. She authorized a well-being check for the interior of the LaBarre farmhouse. They were to check the welfare of Kenneth Countie, Sheila LaBarre and any other potential occupants.

There was also an understanding that this was an incredibly delicate scene. There were legal pitfalls hotter and deeper than the burn barrels. Conway didn't have to read the sergeant the riot act, because he was already telling it to himself. *Do not screw this up!*

Gallagher, who had already tried the front door, went to the door on the side porch. By then they had been on the property for more than an hour and the sun was down. Someone held a flashlight so Gallagher could aim squarely. With a heavy firm shot, he kicked the door in. Cote's gaze was turned not towards the entryway, but down the dusk-dampened roadway that led to the courtyard.

"Sean, there's someone driving up the road."

Gallagher took a quick inventory of the cars. Sheila's car was still there. In the carport by the barn was the silver luxury car, license plate "CAYCE." *Who's this coming?*

Casually, but instinctively, palms rested on holsters. The car slowed at the bottom of a short hill before making its last climb up to the wooden gate. The headlights were on and bounced radically as the car found some rocks and other gouges in the dirt road.

The car stopped on the road outside of the property and idled for a moment. The driver's side door opened and Sheila LaBarre stepped outside. She was calm, but her mouth was pursed with intensity.

"What's the meaning of all this?" she asked Gallagher.

"Sheila, we're here to look for Kenny."

"Do you have a warrant?" she demanded.

"We don't need one," Gallagher responded. "We called the Attorney General, and she told us to kick the door in to get inside the house."

"Let us inside to look for Kenny," Cote said. "Where have you been?"

"I don't have to answer you," Sheila said. Then, turning back to Gallagher, she added sweetly, "Of course I'll consent to a search of my home."

Sheila LaBarre led Sergeant Gallagher, Detective Cote and Officer Jardis into the house. Sheila was a gracious host, completely at ease with giving a tour. Inside, the officers found the house was in disarray. Cote noticed the wallpaper was peeling and the paint was chipping. With slow, patient footsteps, the officers looked around. In one of the rooms, Dr. LaBarre's certificates still hung on the wall, a massage table he must have used pushed carefully into the corner. A sudden movement and scratch on the wooden floor grabbed their attention. It was a rabbit scampering free in the house, making an escape.

There were rabbit droppings everywhere inside the house. They found a pile of them in the center of the master bedroom. There was other matter that they couldn't quite identify. The house smelled like shit and rotten food. There was a spoiled steak in the kitchen sink. When the officers checked both bathrooms, they noticed neither toilet had a seat.

There were bags of clothes strewn throughout the home. But to the officers, walking through the halls, there was no sign of Kenneth Countie that they could see.

"Where's Kenny, Sheila?"

"He's not here."

"Where did he go?"

"He left."

"When?"

"Yesterday morning." Thursday the twenty-third.

The officers went down the stairs into the home's basement and turned on the light. Sheila followed them down. The cellar had a dirt floor, not uncommon for New England homes of its age. Friday had been the warmest day of the week, topping off near fifty degrees (infinitely warmer than the Monday night cold snap). Still, the basement was frigid and forbidding. It was like a crypt.

"Whose are those?"

The officers pointed to a pair of bright, white men's sneakers on the floor. They looked relatively new. Detective Cote immediately recognized them as the sneakers Countie had been wearing when Sheila pushed him through the department store.

"Those are Kenny's. I bought them for him."

"He left without his shoes?" Cote asked.

"I hate Kenny," Sheila offered without much venom. "Those are my shoes. I bought them."

Gallagher and Cote glanced at each other, then back to the shoes. "We'd like to take those sneakers with us."

Sheila remained deadly calm. "You need my permission to take anything from my home." The statement was half-question. The officers nodded. "You may not take them," she said.

It's going to be like that, then. The cops knew they would have to get a search warrant from a judge. "Sheila, we don't want you to touch those sneakers. You must leave them right there for now." The woman said nothing.

The investigators asked Sheila to come outside with them. On the way out of the home, they noted she owned a rifle. It was a .22 caliber long gun, perfect for hunting.

The group made its way to the burn area. Sheila's Dalmatian, Demetrius, continued barking. At random intervals, rabbits hopped freely across the yard. The officers passed the burned-out mattress and box spring, stood around the barrel and Gallagher pointed to the three-and-a-half-inch bone sticking out. Blackened flesh remained fused to it.

"Sheila, what's that?"

The woman paused a moment.

Thoughts careened through Gallagher's mind. *It's about to fall apart for her. It's like any unpleasant conflict, the mind will cycle through stages. It could take seconds or years to complete. The first stage is denial, then anger.*

"I don't know," she said dismissively. *Denial.*

"You don't know what that is?" the officer replied firmly.

"I don't!" *Anger.*

"Look at it. You know exactly what it is. It's a bone."

At that moment, a white bunny hopped forward from out of the darkness. It stopped and looked at the woman who was its caretaker. Sheila's eyes flashed at it momentarily, then back to her accusers. "That bone? It's from a rabbit."

Bargaining, the third stage. A form of denial, searching for a way to change the inevitable path. "A rabbit?"

"When my rabbits die, I cremate them. I cremated one of them about a week ago."

Cote reached in and picked up the bone with two hands and showed it to Sheila. She offered no reaction.

"This bone is too big to be a rabbit," Cote said. "What is it, really?"

Sheila's body language became stiff, uncomfortable. The demeanor of the friendly host she displayed inside had vanished. Her throat tightened up. She was growing tired of the questioning and was getting agitated. Her cool was slipping.

"Well, it's either a rabbit," she said, "or a pedophile."

The declaration stunned the cops. Remembering the taped phone conversation, Gallagher knew immediately to whom and to what the statement referred. They needed Sheila to say more. "Why would you say it's from a pedophile?" he asked.

"I didn't say that," she shot back.

"You did say that. You said it was from a pedophile."

"No, I didn't. You must have misunderstood what I said."

"I didn't misunderstand anything," Gallagher countered. "And there's a big difference between a rabbit and a pedophile."

To this, Sheila did not respond. She just looked at the bone and the burned meat starting to fall off of it.

Gallagher swung his flashlight down at the rabbit that had joined their interrogation. He saw it had snow-white fur.

There was something else. The fur was matted in spots with red-brown stains.

"That rabbit," he asked, "why is it covered in blood?"

Sheila's eyes, once kind to the animal, bore through it like a laser. "That female rabbit had sex with a male. And the blood came from the male rabbit's bloody penis."

Cote asked gently, "Could we take the bone with us? If it's just a rabbit . . ."

"No." Sheila folded her arms. "I don't want you to take it. I want you to leave."

From a legal point of view, the officers were finished. They had no further authority to stay or to seize evidence. As they walked back to their car, they were planning their next moves. Chief Dodge would have to be in on this. More warrants obtained. The state police and the medical examiner's office would have to examine the remains.

"Sheila, you are not to touch anything on this property. Do you understand?" The sergeant pointed a firm finger at her. His only chance for preserving the evidence was to convince LaBarre not to tamper with things. "That goes for the fires too. Touch nothing."

"I won't touch anything," said Sheila, a pleasant, victorious smile on her face. The grin never faded as the officers turned around in her front yard and darted back down the dirt road.

Gallagher looked at his watch again. Not really making note of the time; just watching the hands move even slower across the face and the springs.

CHAPTER 13

BAG JOB

When Police Chief Greg Dodge accompanied his officers on Saturday morning, March 25, to 70 Red Oak Hill Lane, he decided he wanted to be the one to present the search warrant to Sheila LaBarre. He hadn't slept well the night before, troubled by the horror story Sean Gallagher told him about finding the bone sticking out of the burn pit.

Dodge had crossed swords with Sheila numerous times in the past. There had been the traffic stop years before that resulted in her arrest for marijuana possession. Then, after the death of Dr. LaBarre, Sheila applied for a firearms permit. She claimed to be fearful, living alone on a secluded farmhouse. Dodge opposed the permit, fearing she was just as likely to use a gun on him or one of his officers. Sheila eventually got the permit.

Her violence against Kenneth Countie was especially unsettling to the chief. For many years, Dodge had personally supported the Special Olympics, handing out medals and guiding the torch run. Dodge and police chiefs from some of the neighboring towns even raised money for the Special Olympics by doing the "Penguin Plunge," taking a February morning dip in the Atlantic Ocean at Hampton Beach. Exeter Police Chief Richard Kane wore a tuxedo into the thirty-five-degree surf, and Dodge had threatened to dress as Cupid.

Dodge got lost in his thoughts while one of his officers ran the 8:15 A.M. briefing before their morning operation. Gallagher had attempted to get a warrant immediately after being kicked off Sheila's farm the night before, but the county attorney turned down the request. Gallagher then went to Judge Laurence Cullen of the Exeter District Court seeking another warrant. It was for the exterior of the property, and it authorized them to look for human remains, including "blood, tissue, bone, hair, teeth, weapons, clothing and other items pertaining to the disappearance of Kenneth Countie."

Until this point, the biggest unsolved crime Dodge's department was dealing with was a truck with 3,000 gallons of heating oil stolen from an oil company. Since it had been taken the previous November, ghost sightings of the giant yellow tanker had been phoned in from all over New England. Some swore *Al Qaeda* was behind the heist; others suspected it was some clever Yankee who got tired of paying an arm and a leg per gallon.

Dodge wondered what would happen in the town when word got out about this homicide. In his twenty-five years on the Epping police force, there was never a crime that came close to this one in sheer depravity.

When Gregory Dodge got his badge at age twenty-two, after a stint as an Army MP, the biggest problem the two-man police department faced was breaking up the massive keg parties that shut down Main Street on Saturday nights. Then-Chief Robert Denyou decided policing wasn't for him, so he quit and joined the post office (where he worked for three decades). In 1981, Epping residents simultaneously elected Dodge chief and voted to do away with elections as the method of hiring their top cop. The twenty-four-year-old Dodge then hired his opponent, Denny Wood, to work for him, and the two patrolled the town together.

Since that time, the department had grown from two cops to eleven. The station moved from quarters crammed into the town hall to a modern multi-million-dollar facility. But this was the first big-time crime they had to deal with.

The eight-person team consisted of Dodge's best people, including Lieutenant Mike Wallace, the department's second highest ranking official. Several members of the New Hampshire State Police assisted the officer and a police dog named Gunther. Standing by, with one phone call, was a whole phalanx of evidence gatherers and analysts.

The avant-garde pierced Red Oak Hill Lane around 8:50 A.M., driving closer to the LaBarre residence. They found the wooden gate to the Silver Leopard Farm was open. Dodge and Wallace got out of their car, getting their first look at the brutal courtyard. They saw the remains of the mattress and a kitchen chair that had been pulled near it. The fires in the barrel and pit were still going. Dodge didn't want to think about what was fueling them. Next to one of the burn areas was a blue plastic Wal-Mart bag.

Sheila LaBarre was outside the house, walking in the yard near the barn. She wore jeans and a jacket. Suddenly her face twisted in shock and horror, genuinely surprised to see the police officers there at that moment. Sheila was covered from head-to-toe in ashes and soot. She turned, ran into the house and locked the screen door behind her.

Dodge and Wallace strode to the door and called to Sheila. After a moment, she returned to the entrance. She began to cry.

"Oh, no," she mumbled as Dodge walked toward her. "I've been expecting you." The mighty woman began to collapse on herself. Tears immediately rolled through blackened cheeks, making canals of filth on her face. "Are you going to arrest me?"

"Shhh. It's okay." The chief was rather calming and compassionate considering the situation. Sheila reached out a dusty hand and steadied herself on the doorframe. "Don't cry," he said softly. "We only want to talk."

"No, sir." Sheila said. Her white eyes grew broad and wild. "Shoot me," she whispered.

"What?"

"Shoot me," she repeated.

"No, Sheila. We can work this out."

"Shoot me. Shoot me, Chief. You have to shoot me," she hunched over.

"No one is going to shoot you, Sheila. We have a warrant here to search your yard and the exterior of your home. Will you allow us to do so?"

The woman calmed down. She steeled herself and stood erect once again. Sheila invited Dodge and Wallace to come into the house, but only them. Dodge signaled for the other eight officers to wait inside their vehicles. As Sheila opened the screen door for Dodge and Wallace, she instead stepped outside. The chief and his lieutenant followed her.

"I've been up all night," she said. "I've been burning a rabbit and some clothes."

Sheila led them to the burn piles on her front lawn. They quickly appraised the two burn pits they heard about and spotted a third. Three burn sites in all. In addition to the smoldering pits, the investigators saw some luggage and other personal belongings piled near the fires. There were also several crucifixes strewn across the grass.

"I knew that you would return, so I wanted to help you," Sheila said. "I've been sifting through the ashes and removing the bones. I can do this because I've had radiological training. I've been putting them in that Wal-Mart bag."

"What kind of bones are they, Sheila?"

"I cremated a rabbit. But . . . I don't know. There are too many bones in the burn pile for it to be a rabbit."

Dodge went with the soot-covered woman back into the house. Lt. Wallace followed his chief inside and to the kitchen. The room was a mess. There were bits of ash scattered in places. Feces from the free-range rabbits were on the floor. Sheila was jittery. Dodge noticed that one of the burners on the stovetop was turned on high, the coil glowing a bright red. Sheila turned to brush something off the range with her bare hand, oblivious to the danger.

"Whoa! Sheila!" he warned. "That's hot! You'll burn yourself." The chief guided her to a chair at the kitchen table.

"What's all this?" Wallace motioned to the black bits of ash piled on the range she seemed to be trying to wipe away.

Sheila said she was burning her notes from the telephone dating service she had used to hook up with Countie.

The three of them sat down at the kitchen table and said nothing for a minute. Wallace took out a tape recorder. He asked Sheila's permission to record their conversation, and she agreed. Wallace tried to get right to the missing man and asked her what all the burn pits were for, but they couldn't get her to focus on their questions.

"Jeffery Schultz is pissed at me," Sheila said, apropos of nothing. Sheila then turned the conversation to Wal-Mart and the parti pris of management against her.

"Don't get on a Wal-Mart kick," Dodge said, raising his voice. The last fucking thing he was going to hear about today was Sheila's opinions about the service at the store.

Sheila began rambling about dog biotics, the double CAT-scan she had the previous month and some "idiot tenants" she had in her Somersworth apartments who were stealing cable TV.

The tangent went to a Doctor Meinrad, a physician she'd gone to see. "I heard that he abuses little boys."

"Yeah. I heard that too," Wallace mentioned. Sheila then turned to him and said conspiratorially, "Really?" Wallace had kept his voice very low and monotone, refusing to match hers in intensity. It was a technique he hoped would work.

Sheila confided that recently she had been afraid for her life. Not from Kenny, but from an immigrant from Ireland. "An Irish nut," she called him. His name was Mr. DePartee and Sheila told the lieutenant, "Mr. DePartee raped someone's mother."

It seemed impossible to keep her focused. Wallace tried to turn Sheila's attention to the makeshift fire pits in her front yard. "You said there were too many bones for there to be a rabbit. What are you burning in them?"

"I burned a pedophile," she replied. She said it clearly and matter-of-factly.

Dodge took over. He looked the woman square on. "Sheila," he coolly demanded. "Where is Kenny?"

The woman pointed a finger out the window, beyond the billowing smoke from flames here and there, and aimed it at the plastic sack from Wal-Mart.

"He's in the bag," she said.

"You mentioned to Officers Cote and Gallagher that you burn rabbits on your property," Lieutenant Wallace questioned. The three had been sitting quietly around the table in Sheila's kitchen.

"Maybe," Sheila offered, "Kenny is in that burn pile."

"Why do you say that?"

"Because," she said, "there are too many bones to be a rabbit." The investigators thought they were on the verge of a confession. The logic of her own evidence was slowly computing with her. *What is she turning over in her mind?* Dodge thought. *Is she coming to terms with what she's done? Or is she plotting a new way to explain the situation?*

"Those bones in the Wal-Mart bag," Wallace asked, "are they from a rabbit?"

Sheila paused. Then, she began to laugh. "No."

"Are they bones from a horse?!"

"No!"

"Are they bones from a pig?!"

"No!"

Questions came faster. Sheila laughed harder.

"Are they bones from a goat?!"

"No!"

"Are the bones Kenneth Countie?"

Sheila stopped laughing. She answered seriously, as if giving the question great thought. "I don't know."

Dodge and Wallace knew it was time to move this questioning to another venue, one where they had the advantage. The three of them stood up from the table and Sheila prepared to follow them.

"I know this," she told them. "It's going to take a DNA specialist to find out if that's him in the bag. I have been sifting through it and I found human teeth."

As the chief escorted Sheila out of her home, the woman

stuck out her hip as if to offer him something in her jacket pocket. "You might want this," she said. Dodge reached in and felt something heavy and cold. It was a fully loaded Smith & Wesson .38 revolver. The same gun she purchased after finally getting her firearms permit. It had been in her pocket the entire time and, to his surprise, now she was handing it over.

Wallace directed that Sheila LaBarre be taken back to the Epping Police Department for further questioning. He followed her outside and asked if she wanted to take her own vehicle or ride in a squad car. She opted to ride in the backseat of the cruiser. She was not under arrest and required no handcuffs, but having questioned her for as long as they did without discovering that handgun was sloppy.

"Before we go," Wallace asked, "do you have any other weapons on you we should know about?"

Sheila turned to the lieutenant and pulled her top up, exposing her bare breasts. Then she started unbuttoning her jeans, ready to drop them in the middle of the courtyard.

"Stop." Wallace was even more stunned than when she produced the .38. "That's not necessary."

They moved toward the car. Sheila stood still a minute before getting into the cruiser. She explained she was concerned about being away from her animals and asked if she could take her rabbits with her. Wallace resisted rolling his eyes. *Every rabbit?* he thought. *We'll spend the next ten hours trying to wrangle* all *these wild rabbits if we agree to that.* He compromised and said she could take one of them. Sheila took Snooky from his pen, placed him in a carrier and got in a marked police cruiser.

Although she had tantalized the officers with provocative statements about burning pedophiles, it wasn't enough to charge her. It wasn't even enough to hold her, as New Hampshire has no "suspicion of murder" statute.

The state police investigators were letting their superiors know the Epping crime scene was vast and was going to be challenging. The physical evidence was whittled down to

almost nothing and fine-tooth-combs were required. Though
the burn sites were right there on the front lawn, they could
not rule out a deeper, grander search of the Silver Leopard
Farm's 115 acres.

While the chief spent twenty minutes talking with Sheila in
the kitchen, the other state and local police officers sat patiently in their cars. It wasn't until Wallace and Dodge escorted Sheila LaBarre off the property that they examined
the burn pits.

The cops noted that one of the piles was still actively
burning and that another pile was warm. They peered into
the fire barrel and could see some tools. There was a pair of
pruning shears in there, the kind used to clip tree branches.
There was also a set of long-handled hedge shears. The
handles on both sets of cutters were slightly burned. There
was also a silver piece of metal, presumably from a knife,
which had melted from the heat.

The investigators started taking photos of the burn piles
before sifting through them. They could make out tiny bits
of bone fragments among the ash. Nothing more.

The cops assembled around the burn station where Sean
Gallagher had seen the flesh- and hair-covered bone. The
three-inch length of marrow that Sheila promised not to touch
was no longer in the pile. Or, it could be still be there, pulver-
ized into ash by a day's worth of fires.

Next to the burn pit were two yellow diesel fuel containers. They were empty. There were also some empty diesel
fuel containers in the back of Sheila's green pickup. Detective Marc Turner got in touch with an employee of the gas
station on Route 125. He learned that twice in the past week,
Sheila filled the five-gallon containers with diesel fuel. The
first time was on Friday, March 17, right after she and Kenny
left Wal-Mart. The second time was earlier that morning,
March 25.

The investigators took a peek inside the plastic Wal-Mart
bag next to the burn pile. This was the bag Sheila indicated

Countie was "in." Mixed with the other particulates, they could make out shards of what appeared be bone.

Saturday was Jill Rockey's day off from the Troop A detective bureau of the New Hampshire State Police. Rockey got a call from her sergeant asking her to report to the Epping Police Department as soon as possible and to be prepared to interview a woman in connection with a possible homicide. She got to the town safety complex around 11:30, got a quick debriefing from her supervisor, then entered the conference room to question the suspect. Sheila had been waiting there for about two hours, just sitting with her rabbit and waiting for the state police. She still looked like hell, her hair a mess, her clothes disheveled, her body still covered in black soot. Wallace had offered her coffee, but she refused.

Rockey went in, then closed the door because the building was getting loud on this particular Saturday. Her partner, a twenty-year-veteran of the state police, joined her. Sergeant Richard Mitchell was known for his short haircuts, his impish grin and his love of golf. Mitchell had mentored many young detectives, but he took a real shine to Rockey. He called her "Rocket," in part because she was such a go-getter. He playfully insulted her and pestered her, a sign of his respect for her. The young woman gave it back to him; she could take his barbs like one of the guys.

After introducing herself and explaining to Sheila she could leave whenever she chose, Rockey asked if she could record their conversation. "I have to ask, because New Hampshire is a two-party consent-to-record state."

"You don't have to explain that to me," Sheila said pleasantly enough. "I'm a notary and a justice of the peace. I record people quite frequently and I'm very familiar with the two-party consent law."

Sheila sat at the head of the desk in the conference room, Rockey across from her. Mitchell sat close to the suspect, but off a bit to the side. He hoped his face didn't betray his amusement at LaBarre's legal self-confidence.

"What happened to Kenny?" Trooper Rockey asked.

"Adam," Sheila corrected.

"Who?"

"Adam Olympia LaBarre," she said. "That's what he wanted to be called. 'Adam.' He took my last name too. That's how he wished to be referred to."

"Okay then," Rockey said. "*Adam.* Where is he?"

"I don't know." Sheila began to cry.

"What was your relationship like with Adam?"

As soon as the next question was asked, Sheila immediately stopped crying and answered as if she had been sitting there calmly the whole time. The abrupt plug she could jam into her sobbing was almost comical.

Sheila described a sexual relationship with the man, but said it ended when she learned "Adam" was a pedophile. She said "Adam" confessed to molesting several children in his home state of Massachusetts. "Adam" told her of his homosexual encounters, and "Adam" confided he had been sexually abused by his mother.

"I have a tape," Sheila told them. "A confession that Adam made. He admits to all of it. The years of molestation. Everything. It's at my house."

"How do you know it was true? What he said?"

"I hired a polygraphist to come to the house," she said plainly. "He gave Adam a polygraph. I wanted to know if he was telling the truth about his mother molesting him. He passed."

"If he's not here with you, where is he? When did he go?"

"I can't remember. It was either on Tuesday or Wednesday. I went to sleep and when I woke up the next day, Adam was gone."

"What have you been burning on your property?"

"Trash and some other things. I haven't been home for much of the last few days. I've only been back to restart the fires. And take care of my animals."

"Why did you burn the mattress?"

"I slept on it with a pedophile! I had to burn it!" Then

Sheila added, "Adam could have fallen into the fire. But I'm not sure."

"Did you harm Adam and burn his body?"

"No. I did not."

"Did you perhaps discover Adam was dead and then burn his remains?"

"I don't know if anyone returned to my property while I wasn't there and placed human remains into the fire."

"Why did you tell the police you might have burned a pedophile?"

Sheila was not able to explain the statement. Instead she offered, "I did not harm Adam. But I don't feel bad that he's gone." She sobbed.

"I thought the two of you got along."

Suddenly, she stopped sobbing again. "Adam loved it here. He wanted to stay here with me on the farm. He wanted to distance himself from his family in Massachusetts. I have power of attorney over Adam. I have some tapes back at the farm that prove it."

The questioning about "Adam" and about Sheila's life kept snaking down unexpected paths. Sheila said she might be in danger from a stalker who had been in the woods. Her caution to avoid the stalker caused her to park her car on Cilley Road in Nottingham, New Hampshire. This road runs along the northern boundary of the LaBarre estate, and a path over hills and through trees can lead one to the back entrance to the farmhouse. It's a path Sheila had used when she wanted to avoid the eyes of Gordon Winslow and his family.

"I began walking through the woods and I became lost. There was no light. I took off my coat. I'm not sure what I did with it. By the time I got home, I was plum exhausted. I nearly passed out, I was so tired. But I decided I had to burn all my clothes. So I made a fire and burned them. And I burned Adam's sneakers, too."

"The ones the officers saw in your basement?"

"Yes. I burned those. And my own shoes, too. Burned them all. I went on a Cherokee burning rage."

"How'd you get those cuts on your hands?"

Sheila looked at her hands and knuckles. The cuts were fresh and very noticeable. "I've been picking up broken glass. I didn't want my rabbits to step on any of it. That's how I cut myself."

After two hours of questioning by Rockey, punctuated by crying jags that lasted just long enough for the next question, Mitchell asked Sheila if they could return to her home, have another look around and get the woman's recordings of Kenneth Countie. The sergeant had filled out the standard state police Consent to Search form. After showing Sheila the document she made some edits.

Part of the document said the investigators "are authorized to remove any letters, papers, materials or other property they may desire." Above this line, she wrote, "Sheila to keep copies of same." There was also a standard clause saying, "I understand that anything discovered may be used against me in a criminal proceeding." Not liking this part of the form, Sheila crossed the sentence out and wrote above it, "meaning to strike that which has line drawn through and initial." Both LaBarre and Mitchell signed the document and initialed the changes.

The investigators took Sheila back to her home after the interview. They had no luck getting a confession or learning more about what really happened to Kenneth Countie. The property was to be secured for the evening, meaning Sheila would not be allowed to stay and rummage through any more evidence. When asked again what she meant by "burning a pedophile," Sheila claimed she never made such a comment.

Rockey escorted Sheila into her home and allowed her to gather a minimum of essentials. The woman showed the female trooper one of her suitcases that had already been packed. There was also a neatly folded letter placed nearby.

Sheila picked up the letter next to her luggage. "This is my suicide note," she told Rockey. The trooper glanced at it, but refused to read the note all the way through. Rockey asked Sheila if she could take it, and the woman did not refuse.

Later at the station, the investigators took turns passing the letter around. In it, Sheila included these statements:

that on approximately Wednesday, March 22, she had cremated "a very large rabbit . . . close to the front ash can" . . .

that she believed "Adam" killed the rabbit . . .

that "Adam" left either on foot or with someone on approximately Tuesday, March 21 . . .

that "Adam" was a pedophile and she had taped confessions from him . . .

that "Adam" had "threatened to kill himself, jump in the Merrimack River, or set himself on fire" if Sheila played his taped confession for anyone . . .

that "Adam" would rather die than go to prison . . .

that she did not hurt him . . .

that at some point a glass pot exploded, cutting and scalding "Adam," but he refused to go to the hospital and Sheila cared for his wounds . . .

that she was being framed . . .

and *that her house was haunted.*

"Sheila," Rockey asked, still watching her gather her belongings, "do you have any other tapes with Adam on it?"

Sheila pointed to a box that contained dozens and dozens of cassette tapes. Dozens more of micro-cassettes. They numbered more than 300 and were filled with bits of Sheila talking, singing and recording phone calls. And they dated back to the early 1990s. None of the cassettes was labeled.

There's over 1,000 hours of audio here, Rockey later admitted thinking. *It seems like she recorded every conversation she's had in the past fifteen years.*

It was a lot to take in, a lot to decipher. The officer strongly felt that Sheila somehow killed Kenneth Countie, cut up his body with knives and gardening tools and systematically burned the pieces in fires set with diesel fuel.

But what if there was more? Chief Dodge thought about the letter, about what he saw on that horse farm and about Sheila. Over the years, there had been a succession of men from that farm, men whom no one seemed to care about or keep track of. They didn't seem all that different from Kenny.

Could there be other bodies hidden on that farm? he asked himself.

Dodge rubbed the gathering stubble on his cheeks. The Attorney General's office would be coming in now and prosecutor Peter Odom would be in charge of the investigation. Tomorrow, on Sunday the twenty-sixth, he'd drive Odom and State Police Lieutenant Russ Conte out to Red Oak Hill Lane and hope they would be able to determine there was enough evidence for an arrest warrant. At that moment, officers were drawing up three additional search warrants for that day. It would allow them to properly search the interior of the house, barn and outbuildings. Additionally, it would allow them to search Sheila LaBarre's person for cuts and bruises, bodily fluids and DNA evidence.

He was amazed at the violent drama they were piecing together. Twenty-five years as police chief and nothing like this had ever come to his attention. He truly wondered what would happen in town when word got out about Epping's homicide.

CHAPTER 14

SOUTHERN CHARM

Six officers from the Manchester Police Department were moving quickly down the street toward the sea foam green home on Hayward Street. They were not SERT (Special Emergency Response Team), but moved like a tactical unit.

"Right there," one of the plainclothes detectives said, pointing to a patrolman to go to the front door. Another pair of cops went around back. The detective noticed the green sedan parked on the street.

"That's her car."

The detective banged a hard fist against the door, causing the windowpane to rattle inside its frame. He announced himself, then put his hand on the knob and felt it turn. The front door was unlocked. He went in, the patrolmen following.

"Put your hands up!"

"What?" said Charlie Paquin.

"Hands up!" the detective shouted.

Charlie was in the kitchen making a late lunch. He saw the guns and his eyes bulged.

"Where is she? Where is she?"

It was a blur. *Where is who?* he thought. "Pam's not here! Pam's not here!" he said haltingly.

"Not her!"

"Who then?"

"Sheila! Where's Sheila?! Her car's outside!"

The disabled adult felt helpless. The officers looked angry with him, but he had done nothing. He couldn't answer their question.

"She's with my sister," he said. "But I don't know where they are."

Pam Paquin's car rolled into the Epping Safety Complex around 2:15 P.M. on Tuesday, March 28. There was a large satellite truck parked in front of the police station. Cables were strung all over the lot, but there were no people to be seen. Paquin recognized the brick building from last night's 11:00 newscast and realized what she was walking in to. Sandra Charpentier gave her a crazy look, then they both exited the car.

From her window in the main office, the department secretary spotted the arrival of the silver sedan. The description and plate were familiar to her because she took it from the SPCA driver and had been passing it around to other police agencies. She had even faxed warrants over to the Manchester Police Department in connection with the vehicle owner's address. But how Pamela Paquin of Hayward Street, Manchester, New Hampshire, fit into this little mess still wasn't clear.

Paquin's short-cropped hair was a deep shade of auburn. With a flash of blonde and a similarly large body frame, the secretary thought for a second that the passenger coming into the station with Paquin was Sheila LaBarre. The secretary hurried over to the group of investigators and let them know the silver car and its passengers were there.

I sat idly in one of the lobby's three or four chairs, flipping through the pages of my notebook, waiting for something to happen. The walls in the Epping Police Department were shamefully thin. I knew, at that moment, that investigators were desperately searching for a silver sedan. And one had just pulled in.

With nothing more than a sound bite from gentleman-farmer Dan Harvey to show for a day's work, this appeared to be the big break we'd been waiting for (and by "we," I mean the media, not the police). But a TV reporter without a videographer was like Wyatt Earp without his six-shooter. Before I could get out of my seat, two mature women came into the tiny lobby.

They looked around for a moment, looked at me in recognition, then scanned the rest of the room for someone to talk to. Before I could say anything to them, the side door opened and a female detective stuck her head out.

"Pam. Why don't you come on in?"

The two women obeyed. They didn't question why the woman seemed unsurprised to see them.

The detective was NH State Police Trooper Jill Rockey. Wearing plainclothes, she was of medium height, with short straight dark hair and dark eyes. As an investigator, Rockey was solid. Lieutenant Russ Conte and Sergeant Robert Estabrook knew that having a female on the team was a plus in this case, especially when interrogating women. Rockey closed the secure door behind the pair, giving them the impression they were now cut off from the observations of the reporter quietly sitting in the lobby.

Assistant Attorney General Peter Odom, the lead prosecutor on the case, joined Rockey. Paquin noticed his fine dark olive suit. With it, the gray-haired Odom wore a light blue shirt with a button-down collar and a red necktie. The women felt a little inadequately dressed. Pam had on a violet colored top; Sandra wore a pink ribbed sweater. They both had on denim jeans.

"What's this about?" Paquin started in on Rockey and Odom. "How'd you know my name? Why were you waiting for me?"

Rockey explained how she had been spotted inquiring about Sheila's horses. Her tone was non-confrontational, as the police knew these women were the only good leads to finding LaBarre.

"Those horses are mine!" Paquin yelled, grimacing. "Sheila sold them to me! I have a bill of sale right here!"

"Where is Sheila?" Odom asked, the volume of his voice staying even.

"She's not with us anymore. We dropped her off."

"Where?"

"We're not telling you that." Paquin adjusted her eyeglasses and stared at the trooper and the prosecutor.

Odom put his hands in pockets and flashed a smile at the women. Rockey could tell he was up to something.

"Does Sheila think we're going to arrest her?"

"Well, aren't you?"

"We haven't seen her in two days. We haven't heard from her. We're already dealing with one missing person. We're afraid that we're dealing with two missing people."

Paquin and Charpentier exchanged glances. Were they wrong about what the real concern of the police had been? "No, Sheila's fine. She's been with us all day."

"She spent the night at my house last night. She sold me her horses."

"So you're friends?"

"I guess so. I just met her yesterday."

Odom reached for Paquin's bill of sale. He examined it and noted it had been notarized in the town of Raymond earlier in the day. The lawyer handed the paper back.

"Looks legit to me," he said. "Those horses belong to you now, I suppose. But we are going to have to hold on to them for a little while."

"That's okay," Paquin said. "I got no place to stick them."

"Yeah," Charpentier echoed. "She lives in the city. She hasn't any place to put the horses anyway." She laughed.

"Why would you buy the horses then? Seems like an awfully nice gesture for someone you hardly know."

Paquin sighed deep. "I don't know. Whenever Sheila talked about the horses, she'd start to cry. She really loves them. I just thought . . . I don't know."

"Pam's got a big heart," Charpentier came to her defense.

"Yeah. That's why I let her sleep in my son's bedroom."

The police officers motioned them to a nearby room. The four sat down. Odom knew if he didn't take notes, he'd never be able to follow where these two women were leading him. Paquin described for the investigators how Sheila approached her daughter at the pet store and how she gave Paquin's children a ride home. They detailed how Sheila discussed "Adam" after seeing the evening news and how they spent the day going to the bank, talking to lawyers and chasing the horses. The investigators asked what Sheila said about her boyfriend. They asked if the pair believed Sheila could hurt the boy.

"She didn't do it," Paquin said folding her arms.

"What makes you think that?" Rockey asked.

"She doesn't seem the type," she answered with confidence. "She's such a nice person. So caring. It makes me sad to think of what she's going through. And she's just so upset about what people think about her."

Paquin clicked her long, painted nails on the table, lost in sullen thoughts. Charpentier agreed with her friend's assessment of Sheila LaBarre. As a prosecutor, Odom had sat across from some malevolent people. Killers, sexual deviants. He was no longer surprised by the evils a person could exhibit. He wondered why others were so ready to dismiss the possibility those around them were capable of such acts. How could people vouch for a person's soul when they hadn't even known them twenty-four hours?

"Where is Sheila now?"

The couple fixed uneasy looks at one another. "I don't think we should say."

"Could you take a message to her?"

There was agreement. "We could do that."

"Would you ask her to come to the police station and talk to us? She's not under arrest. We're just trying to find out what happened to Kenneth Countie. She can help."

The women thought about it and agreed. "We'll see if we can bring her back ourselves," Paquin offered. "Give us a little time."

"And she's not under arrest?" Charpentier double-checked.

"She's not," Odom said. "We just want to know that she's all right, too. We haven't spoken to her since Saturday."

Rockey and Odom watched the two middle-aged women leave the police station on a new mission. "Nice job," Rockey commented. "They came in here ready for a fight and now you've got them working for us."

Odom seemed deep within himself. "How does she do it?"

"What?"

"Sheila. How does she do it? How is she able to manipulate people into doing anything she wants? Control them? Convince them of her innocence?"

It was more than mere Southern charm. It was like how Bram Stoker's villain could control the mist, the flies and the animals to do his bidding. How he preyed on the weak-minded and made them his servants. There was something unholy about it.

Like an assassin, I waited in the lobby for the two women to emerge. My plan was to jump them on their way back to their car and pester them with a string of questions. "Where is Sheila? What do you know about the disappearance of this man?" I wasn't sure if I'd get a substantive answer, but the theater of it all would please those I needed to please.

At the last minute, I heard Odom speaking to the women, telling them to bring their message to Sheila. I paused. *Could I fuck up this investigation with a stupid stunt like sticking a microphone in a witness's face?* I decided instead to let them go, to walk by me.

Pam Paquin and Sandra Charpentier pulled into a small cemetery not far from the police station. They found Sheila right where they left her: hidden behind some tombstones. She was dressed in the black outfit she purchased hours ago at the Manchester Wal-Mart.

"Did you get my horses? My animals?" she asked.

"Sheila, they don't think you did it."

"What do you mean?"

"You should go to the police station and talk to them. They think you're missing, too. Just like Adam."

"What?" All this talk was confusing her. She started

breathing heavy, hyperventilating. It was the beginning of a panic attack.

"Sheila, trust us. It'll be okay."

The wanted woman looked into the eyes of her two companions. She couldn't trust them anymore. She gathered herself. "Pam," Sheila said. "Give me the keys to your car."

Paquin complied. Sheila got behind the wheel, while Pam and Sandra piled in. The road out of the cemetery was rocky, but Sheila punched the accelerator.

"Whoa! You're driving like a maniac!" The car banged up and down on its wobbly shocks. Paquin and Charpentier both cried out for Sheila to slow down. They spun out of the graveyard and back onto the main road.

"The police station is the other way," Paquin yelled.

"We're not going that way. It's a trick."

What are we going to do? Paquin thought. *If she doesn't go back to talk to the cops, are we in trouble, too? Why won't she go help them clear up what happened to that kid?*

Sheila drove the car out of town, into Raymond on Route 27. No one was sure where they were going. Without warning, the car swerved to the side of the road near a townhouse development. Sheila began to have trouble breathing. Pam was sure it was a panic attack. The women began coaching her, telling her to calm down, when another car pulled up in front of them and boxed them in.

"Fuck!" was all her hyperventilating lungs mustered.

Two police officers got out of the sedan and approached them. Lieutenant Michael Wallace and another officer had been driving an undercover car, going the opposite direction on Route 27, looking for Sheila. The officers had not expected the car to pull over, nor were they ready to make a stop. The undercover car had no siren, no lights or any other emergency equipment in it. They actually passed the silver sedan, assessed the situation, then went back to make contact.

"Sheila, you have to step out of the car and come with me," Wallace said.

"Am I under arrest?" she asked.

"No, but the state police have a warrant to search your body."

Sheila told Wallace she had obtained counsel and wasn't going to talk to him. The lieutenant said that was fine and there wasn't going to be any conversation anyways.

"I'm worried," she told the cop, "about the $37,000 I have in the trunk of the car." Wallace assured her the money would be secured and she would be able to claim it.

Wallace radioed the Safety Complex and told them he had LaBarre detained in the town of Raymond. Three state police troopers, including Rockey, responded to that location and took Sheila back to Troop A barracks.

Ten minutes later, after the cruisers had left with their new friend, Pam and Sandra sat in silence on the side of the road, unsure of their next move. Should they just go back to Manchester and forget the whole day had happened?

"What do you want to do?" Sandra asked.

"Let's go back."

The two women sat for several hours in the lobby of the Epping Police Department, waiting for their new friend to be released. They had no idea, and nobody bothered to tell them while Sheila was being carted away, that she was actually being questioned at the state police barracks a mile and a half away. The sun set, and with the hot dogs from the market a distant memory, they were hungry. The women decided to leave and return home to Queen City. Charpentier told Paquin that Sheila would contact them if she needed them.

Long after Pam and Sandy had left, investigators Chief Dodge and NHSP Sergeant Estabrook quizzed Sheila. Seven hours passed, but to no avail. It was late in the evening, and for the second time in three days they had to release her. There is no "suspicion" charge in New Hampshire, and no one could prove yet that the pile of dust and bits of bone the officers had found on the farm was Kenneth Countie.

Sheila asked the state police for a ride to Manchester, perhaps to rejoin Pam Paquin. A trooper was ordered to follow her and keep constant tabs on her. Now they'd be able to observe her every move, making it easier to serve that arrest warrant when it surely would be drawn up.

The second practical matter had to do with identifying the bone and dust. DNA was a long shot, but they were about to get some samples from Countie's parents. Carolynn Lodge and Kenneth Countie Sr. were on their way to Epping. For Odom, this was going to be the most difficult part. He'd have to keep up the façade of the police's much-publicized missing persons investigation with the family. The entire time, watching these innocent people cling to waning hope, while being aware of the significance of what they'd found: that their son's body probably had been ripped to shreds by a woman with whom he never should have fallen in love.

CHAPTER 15

DISTORTED ANGEL

It was Tuesday morning, March 28, and Steven Martello caught sight of the woman as she came down the on-ramp to Interstate 293 in Manchester. The signs say he was going south, but a compass on his station wagon dashboard proved he was going east. The morning sun was glaring in his eyes, but he still managed to see her. She wasn't thumbing like a hitchhiker would. She was waving one hand at traffic trying to flag someone down.

What the hell, he thought. He'd been there before. Martello had spent years on the road as a truck driver. *There's nothing worse than being broken down and needing help.*

He pulled over quick, so as not to coast too far beyond the woman. The wheels vibrated loudly along the rumble strip cut into the side of the highway, and he watched the woman in his rearview mirror. Showing neither panic nor relief, she approached with calmness as if she'd been expecting his arrival the whole time.

"Hey," he greeted the attractive woman through the rolled-down window. Martello tried to get a read on whether she was a lowlife or not, examining clothes and misdemeanor. She was wearing a pretty black two-piece sweater set, looked him in the eye while talking and flashed a friendly smile. She seemed okay to him, so he asked, "What are you doing on the highway?"

"I had a fight with my boyfriend. My car's broken down in Manchester," she said.

"Do you need me to call you a tow truck or something?"

"I have to get to Boston." She said this and left it hanging there. The rush of trucks speeding by them shook the station wagon Martello was driving.

"Right now I've got to get to Derry," he said.

He's going south and that's the right direction, she thought, *and he didn't say no.*

"I'll pay you to take me to Boston."

The lady's smile warmed Martello. He rubbed the bristled white sideburns on his cheeks, but his hands couldn't conceal the smile he returned. *I've got nothing to do today,* he thought. "Okay, hop in."

Sheila slid in and buckled up. She was exhausted from Monday night's questioning from state police. They presented her with a search warrant for her body. They took pictures of her. They even took four swabs from inside her cheeks. But true to their word, they had not arrested her. They dropped her off in Manchester, at her request, at a motel near the mall and the highway interchange. She thought it was too risky to contact Pam Paquin now that the cops knew she'd befriended her. But Pam could still be of some use to her.

As the station wagon motored to the merge with Interstate 93, they left Manchester behind. Sheila didn't know it, but a state police detective had been watching her motel. Taking to the highway on foot, somehow she managed to slip the tail she didn't even know she had. It would be some time before investigators realized Sheila was gone.

"I have to make one stop first. I have to pick up my ex-wife and drive her to work." Martello then added sadly, "My soon to be ex-wife."

"That's okay. There's a fast-food place right off the highway. Drop me off there for breakfast. I'm starving."

Martello looked at his watch. It was quarter after seven. "What's your name?"

"Cayce," she said. She sat still with two hands on her purse.

He introduced himself as Steve. She smiled again and flirted with her eyes.

"Are you a biker?"

"What?"

"Are you a biker?" she asked.

He certainly looked the part. He was a big guy. His hair was long and on his shoulders. He wore a dark T-shirt. He had two looped earrings. His Fu Manchu mustache had grown into his muttonchops. Only his chin was clean-shaven; it looked like something had taken a bite out of his beard.

"Yeah. I'm a biker."

"I like bikers," she said.

It only took about ten minutes to get to Derry. The station wagon left the interstate at exit 4 and Martello pulled up to the door of the eatery.

"Now, I promise I'll be back. I just have to drop her off at work and I'll come straight back."

"I know you will, angel," she said, then gave him a kiss on the cheek and entered the restaurant.

Martello pulled away, watching Sheila/Cayce in his rearview mirror. He touched his scruffy cheek where the kiss had landed. His good deed had made him feel alive. Things had been so shitty for so long. Martello had been putting on weight, until he topped out at 400 pounds. He developed high blood pressure. His doctor diagnosed him with diabetes. Everything in his life was starting to fall apart. His health was prohibiting him from truck driving. He'd tried to keep it together at home, but his wife began to question some of her life choices as well.

Martello tried not to dwell on his family situation. He had dropped much of the weight he had added on, but he still couldn't drive a truck. He was estranged from his wife, but was taxiing both her and their children all over the state. She was asking for a divorce, and Martello was honor-bound to give it to her. But it wasn't until this hitchhiker showed him some kindness that he started to feel some happiness again. The whole day was full of possibilities.

Martello took his estranged wife to work and said nothing about "Cayce." He returned to the fast-food restaurant half wondering if the woman would even be there. But he found her sitting in a booth drinking coffee. She was busy writing something among the empty food wrappers, but she beamed when she caught sight of him. The big man took Sheila's tray to the waste barrel, then sat next to her in the plastic booth.

"I need to mail this letter," she said. "Do you know where the post office is in Derry?" Martello said he thought so and they left the restaurant together. She had more spring in her step now that she'd eaten.

The station wagon bounded into the gas station nearby. The gauge was low and a trip to Boston would require a full tank. Martello put the shift into park. Sheila reached into her pocket and pulled out a tight wad of bills.

She peeled off one hundred dollars and stuck it in his hand. "Take this for gas." It was much too much, and made Martello uncomfortable. *She gave me that too easily. She's acting like a rich person, but I don't think she is one.* He tried to protest and give the cash back, but she insisted.

They drove around the town for a little while searching for the post office. It wasn't on Broadway. It wasn't near the firehouse at the traffic circle. It wasn't among the businesses and cheap restaurants on Crystal Avenue, which leads back to the interstate. She pointed to a strip mall and asked if they could stop there so she could finish writing the letter.

They sat in the plaza with the engine idling. Martello was quiet as Sheila continued scribbling away on the lined paper. Not far from the car was a newspaper dispenser with an above-the-fold story on Kenneth Countie. None of the papers or TV stations had photos of Sheila LaBarre yet.

The mysterious hitchhiker looked up from the letter and smiled at Martello. "I'm sorry I can't find the post office," he said. "You wanna keep looking?"

"We better go before the cops come," she said. "They might question why you're here and give you a hard time." She dug into her handbag and eventually found two thirty-seven-cent stamps. She instructed him to take her to any mailbox so she could drop her letter.

That's funny, Marteilo thought. *Why does she carry that big roll of money in her pocket and not in her handbag?*

They found a blue metal postbox on the sidewalk. Martello pulled over, and the woman promised to be right back. But Martello got a good look at the envelope. It was from a bank. It was covered with coffee stains and what looked like scribbles. There was more writing on the back, like she still had more to say. He read the name and address on the front of the envelope before it disappeared into the box.

Martello and Sheila drove on Route 102 to get back to the interstate. The mood was light, comfortable. "Where you heading in Boston?"

"I have some tax trouble," she said, "involving the estate of my late husband." She told her new chauffeur that she was the wealthy widow of a doctor and she was on her way to Boston to contact the famous attorney F. Lee Bailey.

"The O. J. Simpson guy?"

"Yes. He has a satellite office in Boston. I've used him before."

"Hey look at that," the driver said. "Two police cars in a row."

The woman looked down the road. On the left-hand side, two Derry police cruisers were parked side by side. But not the "patrolman's 69," in which they sit driver's side to driver's side so they can chat through the windows. Both cars were pointing out at the road, seemingly on lookout.

"Oh!" Sheila reached around the back and leaned over the seat. There was a red plastic gas can back there. "I think your gas can tipped over. It's spilling on your jacket."

Martello thought she was being nice. "It's empty. Don't worry about it." She spent another moment reaching back there, her head sufficiently hidden from view, before turning around and settling in the front again.

She sighed. "I haven't slept in a couple of days. Can I sleep in the back?"

He assumed she meant not the backseat, but the rear cargo section of the station wagon. "No. You need your belt on."

She looked at him harshly for a second. There was no seat belt law in New Hampshire, but she remembered there was one in Massachusetts. "Right," she said. "You wouldn't want to get stopped."

Trees zipped by, and the pace of the conversation began to lag. Martello's passenger reclined in her seat and started to doze off with the purse still clutched in both her hands. She was comfortable enough to kick off her shoes. He watched as she did so. She was wearing blue socks, he recalled. But there was something on the heel. Something on the heel of the shoe and on the bottom of the socks. He was sure they were bloodstains.

"I spent the whole weekend hiking with the family I've been staying with," she said. "Do you mind if we stop along the way and I get some tennis shoes?"

"Naw. It's okay." *Hiking all weekend?* Martello thought. *Not dressed like that, and certainly not in those shoes.* Who exactly had he picked up?

The woman was curled up in the passenger's seat, not fully asleep. There was still too much running around in her mind that she needed to square away, but her body was telling her to let go and drift off.

"I forgot your name," Martello said. "What did you say it was?"

"Sheila," she said. Her body stiffened. She opened her eyes and regained her composure. With copious amounts of Southern charm she added, "But you can call me Cayce, 'cause that's my middle name."

Steven Martello drove on southward, still unsure of what to make of this hitchhiker.

Sheila/Cayce napped off and on as the station wagon continued into Massachusetts. Martello was thinking he needed five minutes alone so he could make a phone call. But he'd need to do it when she wasn't in the car.

"If you want," she offered, "we can stop and buy your son some clothes."

"You don't have to do that, Cayce."

She smiled richly as he used her name. "That's all right, angel. I'd love to."

They pulled off the highway and found some stores in Dorchester, Massachusetts. Sheila pointed to a drug store. "Can we stop there first? There are some things I want to get." Martello parked the car so he'd have a view of her exiting the store. As soon as she went in he pulled out his cell phone. *Is this an emergency?* he thought. No. So he called information and asked for the business line for the Manchester, New Hampshire, police department.

Martello noticed the time on the car's clock. *10:20.* He began explaining to the dispatcher that he picked up a woman, nicely dressed, with lots of money, who said she was rich. "But I'm kind of skeptical."

"Yeah?" the dispatcher asked, unsure where the caller was going with this tale.

He had been thinking about the direction of travel she was taking when he got her. Two towns in the opposite direction was the women's prison. "Has anyone escaped from the prison today?"

"Hold on. I'll check." The lines switched over to music, a horn blowing light jazz. Martello kept an eye on the front door. He thought he could see her heading to the checkout line. In his ear, more jazz. Then the music clicked.

"Hello?" he shouted quickly. But there was no one there. The click had been a splice in the music as the jazz riff looped from the beginning again. He watched a delivery truck pull up close to the front door, slightly blocking his view. What if she came out and caught him on the phone? What would he say? *Think of an excuse.* He'd say it was his son. *But my son's in school now. Think!*

Sheila stepped out of the store with a large white plastic bag. The deliveryman was passing her on the way in and they both stopped. Martello could not hear what they were saying, but they seemed to be chatting like friends. *Come on, cops. Pick up! Pick up!*

She continued walking, running a finger through the blonde hair over her ear. She hadn't looked in the station wagon yet.

"Hello, sir?"

It was the dispatcher.

"No, we got nothing."

Martello closed the phone and stuck it his pocket. *She's not a convict. Maybe she's on the level.*

"Can you believe that guy?" she yelled, getting in the car.

"What? The delivery guy?"

"He tried to grab my boob!" Martello hadn't seen anything like that. But he wasn't really paying attention either.

"Wanna see what I got?" she teased.

The plastic bag crackled as she dug in. Martello could see some feminine douche products and something that could have been a box of hair dye. She pulled out something else. A forty-dollar box of lambskin condoms. She shook them at him wickedly, then placed them back in the bag.

"There's a shoe store right there," she said changing the subject quickly. They went in and Sheila looked at tennis shoes. But she saw a pair of boots she really liked and decided to buy. Martello was amazed at the ease she displayed in carrying on a conversation with the clerk. It was as if they were long-lost friends. *She has a knack for it,* he thought. *Maybe I'm just not used to somebody being so friendly.*

"Let's go there," she said pointing to a motel. She made him go in alone with instructions to get a king-sized bed. She must have decided it was taking too long, because she came into the lobby anyway.

"They don't have king beds," he told her.

Sheila turned her charms on the desk clerk. "I know how things are. I've worked in hotels before. Do you have anything on reserve that we could have?" The clerk said there weren't any king-sized beds at this location. But he thought they had kings at the other chain motel down the road.

The pair went off without a word. Martello worried that saying the wrong thing would burst this bubble and the absurd, abrupt reality of this fling would be made apparent. So, he just drove to the next hotel and followed his lady friend into the lobby.

They entered the motel together, but Sheila did all the talking. Again, she won over the clerk and chatted like they were friends. "Where did you get that pin?" she gushed, and the woman behind the desk touched it demurely.

"I just need an ID," the clerk told Sheila, passing her papers to sign.

Sheila began to fumble with her purse. There were cards in there, he was sure of it. But his soon-to-be lover turned and said, "I don't seem to have my ID. Will you show her yours, angel?" Martello did. The room came to $102 and she peeled the money off her roll of bills, again instructing Martello to keep the change.

She likes to be in charge, Martello thought.

When they entered room 427, Sheila/Cayce began to make coffee in the small brewer. There was a small table and chairs, but Martello sat on the bed. It wasn't a coy suggestion; it was where the large man felt comfortable. He looked around the small room and wondered if she was going to stay here.

What am I doing here? he thought. *Is this going to happen? Her and me?*

Once the coffee was brewed, she poured some in the plain ceramic cup and joined Martello on the bed. They talked some more, like they did in the car. Martello had a hard time concentrating. He was aware of the time and of the odd luck of the situation. But the woman kept chatting, not even flirting, just keeping the conversation going.

Martello started to think it wasn't going to happen. *Maybe I should make a move.* It had been so long since he had been with a woman. It would be nice.

Sheila got up from the bed and took the drugstore bag into the bathroom with her. There, she removed one of the two douches and cleaned herself. An eternity went by. Then, Martello heard the bolt of the door click off the strike plate and she came out.

The woman was wearing her shirt and a towel wrapped around her hips. She walked towards Martello on the bed. He started to move back, against the pillows. She was still wearing the new boots she had bought.

"I'm very fussy," she said. He wasn't sure what to make of this statement.

"Okay."

"I want the blankets on me. Don't take my bra off. I want my bra on." These statements weren't presented as either requests or demands. They were presented as statements of fact, that her new paramour would be doing such things.

"Alright," Martello said. She gave him one of the lamb-skin condoms from the box. He lay back, and once he had rolled it on Sheila got on top of him.

The drapes were drawn and the room was dark, but Martello could see her face. She was gritting her teeth and pumping hard with her hips. "Fuck me," she commanded. He obeyed and thrust harder. He ran his hands over her powerful thighs and calves. That's when he first noticed some bruising.

Sheila began to moan and pant in equal measure. Now Steve Martello was getting into it. "Fuck my pussy," she said. He wanted to fuck her harder, bring her all the way on to him as deep as he could go. He reached up to her shoulders, then slid his hands down her arms. He grabbed hold and tried to pull her deeper.

I was right. She does like to be in charge.

"Argh!" She yelled and flailed her arm as if it hurt. Martello let go. The rocking rhythm of their sex was thrown off, but Sheila recommenced like a conductor in front of the symphony. She offered no explanation for the shout, only more passion.

"I have a tight little pussy," she declared. "How does it feel to have sex with a tight little pussy that's an angel?"

Martello grunted approval. But inside his mind was

swirling. *What the fuck is up with this chick? What's this angel shit? She's fucking wild.*

They went at it harder and harder. Both of them were running out of breath as salty perspiration dripped down their fleshy bodies. Sheila ran her fingers through his and they grabbed fists tightly. He couldn't look her in the eyes anymore. There was something scary about her passion. When he gazed in them, he didn't know who was there. As she looked down on him, he felt outmaneuvered, like she had more than two arms and legs. Like he wasn't a match for her intensity and that she would devour him. Just like a giant squid.

So he turned to avoid her gaze and noticed her hand in his. Across her knuckles were cuts, vertical cuts across the fingers and ridges of the knuckles. Then the fingers turned white as she squeezed his hands with incredible force. She let out a sigh that was neither sensual nor pornographic. More like having flesh torn away from the bone. Sheila collapsed on him, her bra sticking to his damp chest.

Then she made him change the condom and do it again.

Afterwards, when they were both too spent to feast on each other, they lay quietly on their sides. As soon as they were done, Sheila had gone back into the bathroom and douched again. His eyes now adjusted to the dark, Martello could make out some bruising on her arm. The marks were black and blue and looked like someone had grabbed her. It was the same arm that caused her to wince when he had reached for her, but the bruises were too established to be fresh.

Martello started examining her body. She had marks everywhere.

Sheila ran a finger on his shoulder, then nudged him to get up. "Go in the bathroom and flush those condoms down the toilet."

He didn't think he was supposed to, but Martello got up and did it.

When he got back she said, "If you don't flush the condoms, the maids will find them and impregnate themselves with them."

What? Of all the odd behavior Martello had seen, that stretched all credulity. *This woman is very strange.*

Sheila sat up with her purse, clutched again with two hands. "Oh, I worked in hotels. I *know* how people are. Evil. They can be evil."

The man didn't know where this line of thought was going, but he knew to stay out of the way.

"I had a boyfriend," she said, "who had child pornography. Can you believe that? The filthy, filthy thing. I took the picture from him and brought it to the police. But the police disposed of it.

"You know, police are pedophiles," she said without any emotion. "My boyfriend, he was a pedophile too."

"Really?" It wasn't so much a question as it was a log on the fire, fuel to keep the madness going.

"One time, I had died and they brought me back to life. And when I was dead I talked with God and the apostles. They spoke to me in Hebrew. And they said, 'Vengeance is mine, says the Lord.' And that's when I was sent back. As an angel. You had sex with an angel, Steve."

I want to get out of here, Martello thought. *I have to get the hell out of this hotel room.*

Sheila regarded Martello again. "Steve, what if someone touched your son?"

"What? What are you talking about?"

"What if someone touched your son? Would you kill him?"

"I don't know," he said, unsure what answer would be the right one.

"Seriously, if someone touched your son, would you kill him?"

Martello thought about it for a second. "Probably I would."

Sheila leaned closer. "God said that pedophiles have to die. God told me that *all* pedophiles have to die."

"You know, I've got to get back and pick up my son from school. I've got a long drive."

Sheila/Cayce nodded and looked at the time. "Absolutely, sugar. You don't want to be late."

Martello began to dress. Sheila pulled at a long strand of blonde hair from the top of her head.

Before he could leave, Sheila/Cayce asked Martello for his phone number. He gave her the digits to his cell, and she began writing them down backwards.

"Why are you writing them that way?" he asked.

"It's code. My boyfriend is very influential." Again, he had no idea what she meant by any of this. He was just focused on the door. "If you tell anyone you were with me today, he'll come back and hurt your son."

Martello lost a step. *A threat? Is she serious?* He was ready to go. He gave her a kiss on the cheek and made for the door.

"Is there any way," she called out, "you can get me some pot?"

His hand rested on the door handle. "No." When there seemed to be no further objection, he pulled down on the handle and left.

That night, Martello sat down to watch the six o'clock news. For the lead story, the reporter was standing in front of the Epping Police Department. He promised the first picture of Sheila LaBarre. It was a DMV photo of the face and blonde hair now familiar to Martello. The reporter described how several years before, Sheila LaBarre had been arrested for stabbing her boyfriend in the head with a pair of scissors.

"Holy fucking shit! I'm going to be charged as an accessory for taking her out of state."

Within an hour, Martello was at the police station talking with police. He showed them his cell phone to prove he'd made the call to Manchester police inquiring about his hitchhiker. He told them he thought this had been his lucky day.

Though embarrassed about having to reveal personal details, Martello told them everything about the day. He has an incredible memory for minutiae. He remembered the address the letter was sent to, the room number at the hotel, even the brand of feminine douche product Sheila bought at the drug store.

"You're lucky to be alive," someone in the room said.

Martello explained how Sheila insinuated someone would go after his son if he told his story to anyone. "I'm afraid she has connections. Someone who could come after me."

Someone else said, "Don't worry about it."

Martello said he could take them to her. She had told him she was going to stay in the room overnight, because it was paid for. He was sure she was still there. But these cops weren't all that interested. That's because Martello had contacted authorities in his hometown, instead of New Hampshire State Police or the Epping Police Department. There was no arrest warrant out for Sheila LaBarre and she had not been accused of a crime. The cops took the report and fed it into the system. By the time the info got to Odom's team, Sheila was long gone.

When Martello was done, the authorities said he was free to go. He paused a minute. Someone asked him why he had come in and he explained that he had seen the news report about Sheila once stabbing a boyfriend in the head.

He said, "I'm just happy she liked me."

CHAPTER 16

POST: MORTEM

By Wednesday, March 29, the news story of Kenneth Countie's disappearance seemed to have played itself out. I was baffled as to why the Attorney General's office still held the position this was a missing persons case, when the only searching that had been done was in the front yard of Sheila LaBarre's farm. Although New Hampshire State Police Sergeant Robert Estabrook quickly kicked the TV crew out on Monday morning, they still captured enough iconic shots that viewers could read between the lines. The burned mattress. The rusty brown fire barrel. Crime technicians pointing digital cameras at the blackened particulate matter piled on the ground. By Tuesday, news helicopters were flying overhead, peering down into the courtyard. Investigators in white jumpsuits walked back and forth from the home to the forest green state police crime van. Blue plastic tarps were laid on the ground, and stacks of white plastic buckets stood ready to collect the cruel fruits of the fires.

Despite the intrigue, the fourth day of coverage brought nothing new. Producers planned each morning for a big 6:00 P.M. story on LaBarre's arrest, but each afternoon were disappointed when it never happened. Some TV viewers began to question reporters: what's the big deal about this Epping story? There's a lot of innuendo, but couldn't Countie have run off? On the air and on the page, reporters' enthusiasm for the story was outpacing the actual developments.

What did the average person outside of Epping know about the case? Bits and pieces of a puzzle. Since Sunday, they knew state and local police and the Attorney General's homicide unit had been searching for Kenneth Countie. They knew his last confirmed sighting was at a business in Epping, but had no reason to believe he had been injured or was of a diminished mental capacity.

Of Sheila LaBarre, the public was aware she owned the property where Countie last lived and where police had been searching. They heard from neighbors who politely described her as "difficult" and that her relations with them were "strained."

There had been only one photograph of her published. It showed a woman with long blonde hair, pretty cheekbones and sculpted eyebrows. She stood in front of a light blue background, in what was presumably a DMV photo.

While the cops had been secretly trying to track her down, the reporters had followed her paper trail. They supplemented their property search reports with sidebars on Sheila's legal history. The news had revealed there was an unresolved probate dispute between Sheila and the children of Doctor Wilfred LaBarre over the 115-acre plot of land. It took a day of digging to confirm that Sheila had never been married to the doctor, but claimed common-law spouse status.

It was reported that Sheila had claimed she was the victim of domestic violence. The report was taken in March of 1996 in Hampton, New Hampshire. The defendant accused of simple assault was Wayne Ennis, born in Manchester, Jamaica. The pre-sentence report drawn up by the NH Department of Corrections listed his wife as Sheila. The couple's address was the same as Dr. LaBarre's clinic. Sheila was quoted in the report as saying her husband, a resident alien, was jealous and insecure and a period of separation would be beneficial. She asked that Ennis, as part of his plea, pay for her medical expenses.

A different set of affidavits tantalized reporters. They were from September 1998. In this case, Sheila LaBarre was the defendant, charged with second-degree assault. The victim was a twenty-seven-year-old man named James Brackett, who described Sheila as his girlfriend. The assault again occurred in the building that served as Bill LaBarre's office. The police officer's report said Sheila stabbed Brackett in the head with a pair of scissors during a lover's quarrel:

> [Brackett] stated he had an argument with Sheila La-Barre early this morning around 4:30 A.M. . . . He then pulled out a folding pocket knife, which he showed me and I logged into evidence. He stated he just had the knife to scare her away from him because she was "out of control." She then picked up a pair of scissors and attacked him, stabbing him in the head.

When he saw the television report of this incident, it was of particular interest to Steve Martello, who immediately contacted authorities about his disturbing afternoon with the woman.

The journalists missed two clues hidden within the police report. The officer said that Brackett "would sign a statement but had trouble writing." Also, no one questioned why there was no paperwork explaining whatever happened to the second-degree assault charge against Sheila.

Dusk fell right around news time. The mercury had climbed to the middle sixties, and it was comfortable enough to stand outside the Epping Police Station for the first time that week. The incessant coverage by the New Hampshire media caught the attention of the Boston TV stations and newspapers, which assumed they were missing something by not doing the Epping story. Engineers began wrapping cable, videographers stored their expensive cameras. Another day had passed with no major developments. Surely the team coverage would be scaled back now, until authorities announced some sort of breakthrough.

I, for one, assumed as much. Then I got a call that turned

the whole story on its head. Two women had just walked into the TV station with a letter from Sheila LaBarre.

Back on Manchester's Hayward Street, in a sea foam green ranch house, Pam Paquin spent the day wondering what had become of her new friend, Sheila. The newspapers did not announce her arrest and hinted that Sheila was unaccounted for. Sheila had left behind the pre-paid phone she purchased Monday with Charlie at Wal-Mart. Pam kept it in hopes Sheila would call the number, but the phone never twitched. The only call Pam got was on her home phone. It came from a female police officer who said one of Sheila's rabbits from the farm was sick. Even Pam saw through the ruse designed to get Sheila to contact police again.

Pam believed Sheila must be in hiding, but would be back for her rabbits. Pam's children were playing with the three bunnies in their hutch in the other room.

On the morning of Wednesday, March 29, the arrival of the mail was announced with the usual squeak and slam of the metal lid of the box. Mixed in with the junk mail and bills was an envelope from a bank. The preprinted address in the corner reminded Pam of the envelope Sheila got from Lucky, the bank teller.

The envelope had some coffee stains on it and two "Madonna and Child" Christmas stamps, which was double the necessary postage. She flipped the mail over and saw a series of loops and squiggles, which could have been either letters or designs. Above the enclosure, along the top line of the envelope, there seemed to be a postscript to the note inside:

Love to [your family] Snooky, Sapphire, Satin. They won't let you or me have my Beloved Horses, Dalmatian+other Beloved rabbits.

Love Always

The back was unsigned, but it was unmistakable who the letter was from. Pam got on the phone to Sandra Charpentier.

"Sandy, get over here," she said. "Sheila just sent me a letter!"

The two women stared at the letter over and over again, alternating heavy hands on their foreheads or thoughtful fingers scratching hairlines. It was clear that Sheila wanted them to bring it to the television station, but left the choice up to them. While they debated the merits of action, there was a firm knock on the door.

There were two Manchester police officers standing in the doorway. Charlie recognized them as two of the crew that drew guns on him in the kitchen Monday and who stood by while a tow truck hitched up Sheila's green car and dragged it off to the police station.

"Where's the letter?" they asked.

Pam's mouth dropped. *How do they know about the letter? It just arrived.* She had no way to know Steve Martello captured a look at the name and address before Sheila mailed it the day before in Derry. To her, there seemed only one plausible answer. *They've tapped my phone! I'm under surveillance!*

"We know Sheila sent you a letter. Where is it?"

"It's MY letter!" Pam roared. "I know my rights. I know the law."

"We're going to get that letter one way or another."

The women followed the officers back to the Manchester Police Department. There were many loud interjections from the room in which they met. Pam was adamant that she was walking out of there with her letter. The officers proposed a compromise. They would photocopy the letter. Pam and Sandy could leave with the copy; the original would stay with authorities. Pam stewed, believing she was well within her right to claim the original as her own. After conferring with her friend, the ladies agreed to take the photocopy and head straight to the local television station, as per Sheila's wishes.

Assistant Attorney General Peter Odom groaned when Manchester Police told him what had become of the letter.

Investigators were already referring to Pam and Sandy as the *Laverne & Shirley* characters "Lenny and Squiggy," and the continued errands they ran at LaBarre's behest were sure to complicate things. When the letter reached him, Odom blanched. It contained accusations that Sheila hoped would both improve her image in the media and denigrate the victim and his family.

Pam and Sandy waited in a bright white conference room at the TV station. In another room, news managers were huddled around the letter, picking it apart for the benefit of their lawyers on speakerphone. It always amused me when the men in the group would remove their ties and open their collars, signaling the great weight of their impending decisions. Ultimately, the decision was made to interview the pair and use selected quotes from the letter.

A video camera, a light kit and a pair of clip-on microphones were dispatched to the conference room that Pam and Sandy waited in. The idea of *being* on television hadn't occurred to them. Although they had spent most of their day trying to get there, the pair never talked about what might happen once they delivered the letter.

It took some cajoling, but Pam agreed to answer questions. Her name would not be used and her face would not be shown. Instead, the videographer pointed his lens at Pam's hands, her long red-painted fingernails and the white paper pinched between her fingers. As she had done for Odom two days earlier, the woman gave an impassioned defense of Sheila LaBarre.

Peter Odom did not see any mention of the letter on Wednesday's 11:00 news, but discreet phone calls to him and other colleagues led him to believe a full report was coming on Thursday, March 30. He called Carolynn Lodge and told her what to expect in the letter. She was horrified at its contents and felt helpless about what further pain she would feel. Again, Odom assured her they were working hard to locate Kenny and bring him home.

The station planned on doing two full reports on the

letter. I spent the next day, Thursday, working as hard as I could to verify the letter's authenticity. I tracked down the Manchester lawyer that Sheila first solicited (he refused to comment). I drove to the Raymond bank branch where Sheila had her rental agreement notarized. We compared signatures on the letter with those on other documents. We burned a lot of daylight doing due diligence; but we all wanted the story to be solid.

The scripts were submitted in mid-afternoon for approval from the station's lawyers. But approval came so late in the day that I couldn't get to Epping in time for the five o'clock news, so I broadcast the report from the studio before driving out to the Safety Complex for the six o'clock broadcast.

The stories revealed there were no confessions, no major clues that investigators were not privy to. The criminal allegations against Kenny were not reported. Instead, colorful highlights from Sheila's own hand punctuated the telecast. The personal comments from Sheila only tantalized the viewers, as the public's bizarre attraction to the case was beginning to catch up with the media's:

March 28, 2006

Pamela,
    You are a true friend and an angel. I am innocent and God knows that I am. Thank you eternally! Hold my "children" close each day and night, kiss them and tell them each+every day+night how much I love them.

The "children" Sheila LaBarre referred to supposedly are her three rabbits, Sapphire, Little Satin and Snooky.

The Epping police were called by me <u>around</u> 3/21/06 and I talked to Sgt. Sean Gallagher and played a legally tape-recorded statement that Kenneth M. Countie, aka <u>Adam</u>, swore to me in my official capacity as a Justice of the Peace and Notary.

At this point in the letter Sheila listed names, including relatives whom "Adam" allegedly molested. As she put it, Kenny swore he molested every child in the family. She neglected to say that during his sworn testimony Kenny vomited and passed out under duress. This passage from the letter was not reported:

> . . . The State Police and Epping Police stole that tape from my home and now are suppressing the evidence. Kenneth M. Countie wanted to change his name to Adam Olympia LaBarre. He asked me to marry him. I asked him to leave due to him molesting children. He said he had videotaped his rapes on kids and that they were hidden in [his roommate's] house at XX Grove Ave, Wilmington, MA. in his top left dresser drawer.

Sheila's insistence that Adam had changed his name made the news. The allegation of the videotape was not reported, although journalists did attempt to retrieve or verify the existence of the tape with his former roommate. They were not successful.

> . . . The State and Epping Police badgered me, lied to me, intimidated me, illegally had the SPCA take my beloved horses, rabbits and precious Dalmatian even though a notarized Bill of Sale was presented to them by you on 3/27/06 at the Epping Police Station at the same time the SPCA had my Beloved pets and you and I were following them.

What remains compelling is the emphasis LaBarre places on her animals throughout the letter. Of all the indignities authorities put her through she thought to underline the seizure of her horses, perhaps indicating this one was most egregious.

> Thank you for everything you have done for me and for the welfare of [my] pets. You are an angel.

I am in the N.H. area and will get another lawyer
since the other one wanted a $60,000 retainer. But I
won't Be Back at your house until this is settled.

Please release this to TV News only if <u>you decide</u>
and please do not give it to the police ever. You know
they can't be trusted.

Will Keep in touch.

> All My Love Forever
> Sheila

After the newscast, Carolynn Lodge asked Peter Odom
to contact the TV station and thank the staff for not reporting the molestation allegations. It would be one of the only
times she would communicate with the press.

Sheila had crafted the perfect letter. Through it she further
ingratiated herself with Pam Paquin, injured Carolynn Lodge,
the woman who had meddled into her affairs, and seeded
doubt among its readers about Kenneth Countie's purity. But
the broadcast reports of the letter's content had been encapsu-
lated to include only her rants about police treatment and her
love of animals.

Pam and Sandy continued to believe in Sheila. They felt
after submitting to the TV interview that the public would
have a different picture of their friend. They agreed to stay
in touch with the reporters.

"But our phone is tapped by the police. That's how they
knew we had the letter." Pam devised a code for the journalists. If they wanted to talk to her again, "Call and say we're
going for coffee. That we're going to *that place*."

Several days later, when a different reporter and cameraman visited the address on the photocopied envelope, Pam
Paquin shooed them away with squeals of panic.

"You didn't use the code!" she yelled at them, slamming
her door. "You didn't use the secret code."

Sheila left one postscript in the letter for Pam, but also
for the consumption of the others who would read it. Judg-

ing by the thick pen strokes and double underline, it was her most passionate assertion: "It's not over. I am <u>INNOCENT</u>."

It was a striking statement coming from a woman who had not yet been accused of a crime.

CHAPTER 17

WE INTERRUPT OUR PROGRAMMING . . .

Odom first met Kenny's parents on the evening of Monday, March 27. While Sergeant Rich Mitchell and Trooper Jill Rockey of the NH State Police were grilling Sheila LaBarre, the prosecutor was watching the couples arrive separately at the Epping Safety Complex. A dashing red sedan was the first to appear. It had a simple "GB" Euro oval sticker on the back proclaiming its driver's British heritage. Gerald Lodge got out and opened the passenger door for his wife. He was a burly man, neatly dressed, with a troubled look on his face. He scanned the parking lot and the small group of reporters who had gathered for their evening news live shots. No one bothered the couple as they entered the police station.

Kenneth Countie Sr. pulled into the complex driving a blue pickup truck with Massachusetts license plates. His wife, Suzanne, was by his side. Some reporters had knocked on the door of his home earlier in the day. He lived in a nice neighborhood in a well-maintained house only blemished by the temporary chalk artwork and hopscotch squares of the couple's preschool-aged daughter. The Counties had not been home to answer questions. Neighbors knew only that Mr. Countie was a youth hockey coach, his wife was a corporate party planner and they had two children. None of them was aware there was a Kenny Jr.

Behind closed doors, Odom's affection for Kenny's family

grew exponentially. "I won't lie to you," Odom told the parents. "But there may be things I cannot tell you." They seemed to appreciate his honesty and trusted that this man would work as hard as possible to bring their son home.

A victim/witness advocate from the Attorney General's office joined Odom for their meeting. When it was over, she agreed to walk with the parents and the prosecutor back to the parking lot. Darkness had fallen and the Safety Complex was likely to be empty. When the small group made its way through the secure door and into the lobby, they passed a small army of television and print reporters waiting to hear from Odom. They consisted mostly of news organizations from Boston, who were now further enthralled with the New Hampshire story because the missing man was from Massachusetts. Those reporters new to the scene had yet to meet with Odom, and deadlines for evening newscasts and morning papers were ticking closer. As the parents went through the front door and into the parking lot they heard someone behind them say, "That's them."

The gloomy lot exploded in white halogen light. There was a mad dash of TV cameramen to catch the parents, to get in front of them so the photographers could swing around and shoot their faces. Someone thrust a microphone into Carolynn Lodge's face as she tried to get into her car.

"Any comment?"

"Who are you?"

"Do you know where your son is?"

Odom had tried to sate the mob by standing in the lobby and offering himself for questioning, but the increasingly desperate news writers and picture-takers bolted from the building in search of better prey. Odom followed the crowd and watched the scene from the front door.

"You're not actually doing this?" he growled to no one in particular. The horde then scrambled away from the Lodge's sedan to the Countie's blue pickup. The media created pandemonium. "I can't believe you're actually doing this. I've never seen anything like this in New Hampshire."

The collective behavior of the gathered reporters so

disgusted Odom he toyed with not giving them any comments. Once the cars drove away, the group instinctively gathered around the prosecutor and fired away in the same manner.

"We take it very seriously. We're concerned at this point," Odom told them. "It's premature at this point, given the stage of the investigation we're at now, to talk about foul play."

When someone asked about Countie's parents, Odom pictured the tearful mother he just met. "I mean," he started with a heavy sigh, revealing emotion not usually displayed in these situations, "they're doing about as well as they can be expected to be doing under these very difficult circumstances."

Each day following that scene became more stressful for the Attorney General's office. Evidence at the farm was mounting but there were few results. There wasn't enough for scientists to say the remains they found were Kenneth Countie's or to tell the story of how he died. Meantime, LaBarre was not in custody, and on Tuesday she got away from the detectives trailing her.

I can't believe this week, of all weeks, this is happening, Odom mused.

Sheila's getaway was a sore subject back at the AG's homicide unit in Concord. The head of the unit, Senior Assistant Attorney General Jeffrey Strelzin, asked for a private conference call with Odom and Assistant Attorney General Kirsten Wilson, who had been assigned to Odom's case. Strelzin was an easy-going man, but methodically by-the-book when it came to the law.

Odom and Wilson found an empty room in the police department to hold the call. There were many details to discuss, but Strelzin remained incredulous that the state police let Sheila get away. The speakerphone sputtered some choice words.

When the teleconference was over, Odom discovered a long line of disgruntled New Hampshire State Police officers outside the room where the call took place. That was when investigators discovered what reporters already knew: the walls in the Epping Police Department were paper-thin.

On the morning of Wednesday, March 29, the Lodges and Counties returned to the Epping Police Department for an update on the search. Carolynn Lodge stepped outside for some fresh air. A television reporter kindly asked her if she was up for an interview and she politely declined.

"It must be tough waiting," he said to the mother.

"It's bloody awful," she replied with a British accent. The reporter later went on air and said Countie's mother called the wait "bloody awful." The phrase might have seemed slightly gruesome to New Englanders unfamiliar with the old English colloquialism.

Investigative protocol gave sole authority to comment to the press on a homicide case to the Assistant Attorney General. As more reporters turned up in Epping, each looking for a quote, requests for Odom's time were never-ending. There was an unspoken understanding each day that the prosecutor would talk but would most likely not have anything new to say. Surprisingly, the better-than-nothing philosophy was eagerly embraced by the press corps, who only seemed interested in getting fresh quotes.

At mid-afternoon, Odom emerged from the police department and held a press conference for the gathered reporters. He was sometimes awkward on camera. He'd inadvertently ruin someone's B-roll of him walking in or out of the building by looking at the camera and saying something to the videographer. He liked to point out that by Wednesday the reporters had seen each of the only suits he owned. Someone started the verbal jabbing by asking why this "missing persons case" was confined to the breadth of one property.

"We are working hard. We're still searching the property, talking to people. Kenneth Countie has not been located. Understandably, the family still is very concerned for his well-being."

As time passes, don't your chances of a good outcome diminish?

"With each minute, with each hour, with each day that Mr. Countie does not contact his family, they become more concerned. And we become more concerned," he stated.

How much longer will investigators be at the farm?

"I can tell you we've been there for several days. And the Major Crime Unit will be there until the job is done. I can't give you any predictions about how long that will take."

Why is it taking investigators so long?

"It's looking behind things and under things and testing things. In this case, as you know from reports that are already out there, there are several buildings that are involved. There's a farm. There're hutches. It's quite extensive."

The property owner hasn't been seen for a couple of days either. Is she also considered a missing person?

Trick question. "I'm not going to comment on that."

How are Countie's parents?

Odom breathed deeply before answering. "It's unimaginable what they must be going through. The waiting with each passing day. Becoming more worried about what might have happened to their child." He mulled it over some more. "They're doing about as well as can be expected in this very difficult circumstance."

On Thursday, March 30, investigators asked the State Fire Marshal's Office to help in their search on Red Oak Hill Lane. Deputy Fire Marshal John Raymond brought his accelerant-detecting dog to the LaBarre farm.

"What can you tell us about diesel fuel?" State Police Sergeant Robert Estabrook asked Raymond.

"Diesel burns longer than gasoline does. And it has a higher flash point."

"What does that mean?"

"The flash point is the minimum temperature at which the fuel will ignite. It's higher than gasoline, which makes it inherently safer to handle."

"So a higher flash point means you can pour it on an open flame like in a burn barrel," Conte asked, "and it won't flash up on you?"

"It won't flash up on you. Exactly," Raymond replied. The arson investigator got his dog, Clancy, from the back of his car. Clancy was a chocolate Labrador retriever that had been rescued from a pound in New York before receiving his special training. Raymond, a pleasant fire service veteran, was just as friendly as his canine partner. With his thinning salt-and-pepper hair and trimmed mustache, Raymond drew a striking resemblance to the late Dr. Wilfred LaBarre. The deputy tugged on Clancy's red cloth leash and sent him to work.

The front yard did not look as it did when Sergeant Sean Gallagher and Detective Richard Cote saw it a week earlier. After hours of meticulous photographing, cataloging and sifting, much of the ash and particulate matter from the fires had been moved around and stored for later study. The brown, rusty burn barrel lay on its side, its contents fastidiously removed. The blackened skeleton of the mattress remained on the ground.

Clancy put his nose to the dirt and led Raymond to an empty spot just outside the crime team's work area. The dog "alerted" upon that spot.

"There were accelerants used right here," Raymond told the police investigators. The dog was standing where the burn barrel had been.

As Clancy sniffed around some more, pawing his way over to the remains of the burned-out mattress. Again, the dog indicated that an accelerant had been used in this location.

Raymond stopped to examine the remains of the box spring. Estabrook, Conte and the other police investigators said nothing to him, so as not to bias his findings. He noticed that the twisted springs were not all even.

"Those springs, at the time they burned, they were compressed," Raymond said. "It's as if something heavy was resting on the mattress while it burned."

Estabrook stepped closer to ask the deputy fire marshal for his opinion. "What do you make of *that*?"

Raymond studied the fatty substance stuck to the springs. "That would be consistent with some type of flesh or tissue burning."

The cops watched Clancy trot off into the pasture. Between the horses and the wild rabbits, the investigators had gotten used to animals roaming the property. Raymond knew his canine partner wasn't looking for the use of a handy tree. The deputy turned to the police, pointed into the vast acreage of Silver Leopard Farm and said, "He's got something else."

Odom met with Strelzin and with NHSP Major David Kelley. Kelley was commander of Troop A, which not only had geographical jurisdiction over Epping, but whose barracks were located in the town as well. He briefed them on everything Conte and Estabrook had come up with. They finally had enough confidence in the physical evidence to proceed. Odom needed to find a judge and have a heart-to-heart discussion with Countie's family.

On Friday, March 31, Assistant Attorney General Peter Odom decided he now had to tell the parents of Kenneth Countie that he was dead and to explain the manner in which he died. Odom grimaced at the pain he knew he was about to cause.

Odom had been instinctively protective of the Counties before he even met them. He had read Sergeant Gallagher's missing persons reports filed by Carolynn Lodge, knew that Kenny was a special needs adult and sensed that Kenny's loss would be powerfully difficult for his family to bear.

There was a part of the prosecutor that felt wrong about not having been able to level earlier with the Lodges and the Counties about the nature of Kenny's disappearance. He had made sure not to mislead the families about what the police were finding. He was not in the habit of providing false hope to people and wished there was some truth to his public ignorance about the young man's fate.

Odom listened as the victim advocate broke the news to the Counties and the Lodges that police finally had enough for an arrest warrant, and that the warrant was for murder. The peace of the room was fractured with wails and sobs of grief. Homicide prosecutors usually were not present to deliver such news; notification of a death was usually quite quick and done by police officers. This display of emotion was the kind of thing a methodical, calculating attorney tried to avoid.

"Tell me, Peter," Carolynn Lodge howled, "did he suffer? Did he suffer?"

"I told you before: there are some things I can't tell you."

"But tell me!" she continued. "I'm a grieving mother. Tell me."

Odom was speechless. He would have liked nothing better than to say to this woman, "He never felt a thing." But he couldn't, knowing that Kenneth Countie had suffered for days, was beaten, butchered and then burned. It was the most horrible death he could have imagined. No matter what, he would *never* tell her that.

At the end of the day, Odom did what he customarily did. He got in his car, put on a ball cap and sneaked a cigarette. Then he made the thirty-minute trip to his home and carved out some much-needed personal time. He resumed packing his personal belongings. That weekend he was moving out of his house, separating from his wife and two teenaged children, and taking an apartment in Concord close to the State Department of Justice building. The biggest case of Odom's legal career had exploded during one of his most challenging personal journeys.

Just after 6:00 on Friday, March 31, television reporter Jennifer Millette signed off from Epping. An acclaimed journalist with several years' experience, Millette was changing careers to allow more family time with her new husband. The week-long hype surrounding the missing persons story had finally waned and that night Millette was the only reporter from any television station standing guard outside the Epping Safety Complex. Now, she would pull out her IFB earpiece for the last time and drive to a Manchester bar where colleagues were gathering for a farewell party.

"Jennifer, wait!" A tall, thin man in a gray suit sprinted from inside the police department. It was Senior Assistant AG Jeff Strelzin. As head of the homicide unit, Strelzin was often the public face of the investigation. He had just announced arrests in a pair of separate homicides in the consecutive weekends leading up to the LaBarre case. But Strelzin had been conspicuously absent from this crime, allowing Odom and Wilson to dig into it.

Strelzin pulled Millette aside before she could climb into the SUV and leave. "We have something for you. Stick around if you can."

Millette laughed in his face. "Don't you know it's my last day?"

Strelzin was keenly aware, because he was on his way to Millette's going-away party too. "In about thirty minutes or so, we're going to have an arrest warrant. So I'm giving you a choice."

"What choice?" she asked.

"You're the only one here. The chief, Major Kelley from state police and I can come out in a little while and announce it to you. Or, we can wait until another reporter can drive here from Manchester to replace you." Strelzin was letting her choose between punching out and greeting all her friends or getting one last exclusive.

"Well," she said, "so much for retirement."

At 7:00 P.M. Jennifer Millette, late for her own farewell party, reported live from Epping in a special news bulletin following the evening's national news. The heads of the Attorney General's homicide unit, the Epping Police Department and the Troop A barracks of the New Hampshire State Police announced an arrest warrant for Sheila K. LaBarre. She was accused of killing Kenneth M. Countie and incinerating his body. Authorities would not comment on the cause or mechanism of death, but said the manner of death was homicide. The crime LaBarre was charged with was first-degree murder, implying that the suspect had premeditation.

The investigators said that Sheila LaBarre was not in custody and her whereabouts were unknown. A nationwide manhunt for their suspect had begun.

CHAPTER 18

CAT EYES

She doesn't belong there, the man thought while sipping his soda. The parking lot at the Northgate Plaza in Revere, Massachusetts, was huge, so much bigger than it needed to be for a strip mall. Even when the stores were busy, the lot made the place seem empty. Kids skateboarded around there, a cavernous asphalt area that not even Christmas shoppers could completely fill. But this woman just hanging out wasn't right.

Steven Moscato sat in his car, eating a taco. A thirty-year veteran of the Revere Police Department, he played it really cool. From afar, he watched the woman talking on her cell phone. Now, she was starting to get nervous and began to pace. *She's about to bolt. I've got to get a unit here*, he thought. *Now.*

The sky appeared large, swirling with blue and white, the unobstructed view one expects to find near the ocean. The sounds in the air were those of engines pumping and tires stopping quickly off the rotary. It was a warm day following a mild winter, and spring was on the minds of those doing their weekend chores. The police had been here earlier in the day, less than an hour ago. But a good sweep of the plaza turned up nothing. Just another dead end.

The Mexican fast-food restaurant stood alone in the parking lot close to the road. With the department store and pharmacy floating so far behind it, the restaurant looked like an island unto itself. It certainly wasn't a convenient walk from the retail stores up the parking lot to lunch. So why would someone be hanging out in front of the restaurant who wasn't a customer?

Moscato had taken the call himself maybe an hour earlier. A uniformed officer, he spent most of his time inside the dispatch center of Revere's downtown police department. The radio room was always dark, boxed-in glass and shaded from outside light. Moscato knew enough to know when to leave the heavy lifting of street patrol to the Young Turks, but his experience was invaluable when judging what resources to send to a call, understanding what was happening in the field.

"You know that woman they want in New Hampshire?" the caller started.

"Yeah."

"I think she's in Revere."

So where is this going? Moscato thought. "Yeah? How's that?"

"I was with her. Last night. In Boston. She says she's going to Revere."

Moscato remembered something about a New Hampshire case from a day or two ago. A BOLO, *be on the lookout*. He spun around in the chair and asked the other guys boxed into the dispatch center with him, "Any of you guys hear anything about a woman wanted out of New Hampshire?"

Yeah, yeah, they said. Saw it in the paper. Today's paper, there's something about her.

"So," Moscato turned his attention back to the caller. "What's the deal? Where do you think she is?"

The caller said the woman was waiting for him at a restaurant at the Northgate Plaza. That was an ocean of asphalt, where unattended shopping carts could roll for hours without so much as ever denting a fender. The footprint of the restaurant fills roughly one-quarter of the parking lot, with a drive-through traffic pattern seemingly conceived by a demolition derby enthusiast.

Moscato took down the rest of the caller's information and looked up the description of the suspect. *I'm going to send two units to check it out. No, three.*

Moscato waited patiently for a report. "GOA," said one of the cops. "Gone on arrival."

Moscato folded his arms and drew into himself. The caller seemed to have good information. Maybe the cruisers scared her off. It's just a hunch, but maybe . . .

"I'm going to lunch," he announced, grabbing his jacket. Moscato went to his own car, with the windbreaker zipped up over his uniform shirt. *I'm hungry*, he told himself. But something else was tugging at his gut.

Earlier that week, Kenneth Washington found himself with nothing to do. It was Wednesday, March 29, and he decided to drive around some of Boston's urban neighborhoods. Washington was sitting in his parked car near a strip mall on Morrissey Boulevard when he spotted an attractive woman walking alone across the parking lot. It was the woman's red hair that made her stand out. It was a deep auburn color with violet streaks running through it.

Washington pulled the car around to the woman and rolled down the window. He was smooth. It wasn't long before she got in the car and took off with him.

The woman said her name was "Cayce" and she was in Boston from Nashville on a real estate deal but the airline had lost all of her luggage. She was carrying around some clothes in a shopping bag. Together, they cruised some more Boston neighborhoods: Dorchester, Roxbury, Mattapan. They grabbed some food and she paid. They got weed and she paid. They pulled into the Marriott hotel on Morrissey Boulevard. Washington signed for the room but "Cayce" gave him the money.

Washington spent the night with the woman, smoking pot and having sex. When they awoke in the hotel, she invited him out for breakfast. Washington didn't have a job and was pretty much broke, so he didn't have to think long about hanging with someone who was throwing around cash like she was doing.

At "Cayce's" insistence, they checked out of the hotel and cruised around some more. She picked up an apartment guide for the area. Anything Washington needed, "Cayce" paid for.

On Thursday night, March 30, 2006, the couple checked into a motel not far from where Washington had met "Cayce." It was the same drill: he signed for the room while she took care of the bill. When they awoke, they again went their separate ways. They spent two nights in that hotel.

On Friday, "Cayce" returned to a beauty salon in Dorchester. She came in for a wash and blow-dry. The salon owner remembered the walk-in customer very well.

It had just been on Wednesday, the day after her tryst with biker Steve Martello, that Sheila LaBarre found the little hair salon in the predominately Hispanic area of South Boston. Though she spoke no Spanish, she was able to communicate with the owner. Sheila ran her fingers through her long frayed hair. The shop owner regarded the blonde locks and gray streaking. The black roots were exposed.

"My boyfriend wants a change," Sheila said. That much the owner understood.

The owner sat Sheila down and showed her a color board. Together they settled on tone 873, a deep auburn in the middle of the chart. Sheila had already decided that she would have red highlights, so she selected red-copper.

The owner passed the woman off to one of her stylists. She tamed the long hair with a set of shears then applied the new coat of color. The process took longer than usual, because Sheila's hair was so damn long. Since she was a child, she liked to wear her hair long.

When the stylist was done, Sheila had a long bob. The cut was off her shoulders and her head felt lighter than it had in years. The color was not quite the same as on the shade chart. The new look was very common for the Latina regulars in the neighborhood.

On this Friday when the walk-in returned, the owner had no problem remembering her. Not just for the unusual cut-

and-dye job. The bill that day had come to $125. Sheila passed two large bills, tipping seventy-five bucks.

Kenneth Washington had been enjoying the company of his new lady friend. He wasn't really interested in getting to know much about her. He hadn't even asked "Cayce" what her last name was. Washington *was* getting used to the Southern lady throwing her money around. Whether it be food, drink or pot, "Cayce" had it covered.

On Saturday, April 1, "Cayce" had insisted they move out of their current hotel room, saying the conditions at the hotel were sub-par. Washington agreed, and he took the woman to yet another hotel in the Boston area. This time, however, Washington had plans that didn't include chillin' with "Cayce." He dumped her in the new hotel room, then left for his cousin's place.

Saturday night, Washington played videogames and watched the Final Four of March Madness on CBS. The late game was a poorly-played match between UCLA and LSU. Washington stuck around to see the Bruins win and then caught the beginning of the local news.

WBZ-TV featured a story about the manhunt in New Hampshire for a woman accused of killing a man and incinerating the body. There was a photo of the suspect.

"Ah, shit." It had all been too good to be true.

Kenneth Washington did not want to go to the authorities. He had passed some bad checks in his time. He had used some fake names. He didn't want to get involved with the police. But he really didn't want to be involved with a murderer.

On Sunday, March 2, Washington didn't go meet "Cayce" in the morning as he usually had been doing. He gave some lame excuse and said he'd get with her later. She was in Revere and told Washington to meet her at a fast-food restaurant. She was hungry and wanted lunch.

Washington called everyone he could think of. The Boston police. The Massachusetts State Police. The Revere Police

Department. No one seemed particularly interested that he had a lunch date with a wanted homicide suspect.

"She's wanted out of New Hampshire?" one of the dispatchers asked him. "You should call New Hampshire to see if the warrants on her are still good."

Like I'm *going to do that,* Washington thought. *I'm going to be the cop. Fuck this.*

Washington decided to wash his hands of the whole thing. No matter how many times she called his cell phone, he decided he wasn't going to answer.

It's just about two and a half miles from the Revere Police Department to the plaza, about ten minutes by car. Statistically, the most dangerous part of this errand was fighting the traffic going through the rotary. And technically, Steve Moscato was not on a call. He was just getting something to eat.

She was there sitting outside the restaurant, talking on the cell phone, trying to get hold of someone. Moscato could guess who. He grabbed lunch and watched her from his car. She was getting frustrated. The guy wasn't returning her phone call, and she was realizing that he wasn't coming to get her. So she started to walk.

She's not blonde, like the BOLO said, but the rest of her fits the description, Moscato thought. He pulled out his cell phone and called dispatch. "I got her," he said.

"Got who?"

"The woman from New Hampshire. I got her."

Pause. "I thought you were at lunch."

"I was. But I found the subject in the BOLO."

Back in the dispatch center, the officer covered the receiver and turned to the others in the darkened room. "You're never going to guess who just tracked down that suspect on his lunch break. Steve Moscato!" The young guys all had a laugh.

"I'm at the Northgate Plaza," Moscato said. "Get those units back here. She's taking off."

The woman kept walking up Squire Road, back towards the rotary. Moscato got out of the car and followed her. He kept his hands in his jacket and kept his distance. He felt a rush, like he did when he was a rookie cop.

He could see the unit approaching as the woman passed a burger fast-food restaurant. There was another coming. The cars pulled into the lot of a family restaurant and boxed her in. Moscato read the woman's body language as a uniformed officer stepped out and moved towards her. No fear, no panic. She betrayed nothing.

"Can I talk to you?" Lieutenant Sean Randall asked, but the sharpness in his voice lashed the woman who slowly turned to him. This was not a request. "Come here, please."

The woman approached with gentle steps. She was forty-ish. Her face was made up tastefully. Her hair was combed neatly and hung to the end of her shoulders. The sun made her dark auburn hair shine and the color streaks gave her hairdo some depth. It wasn't until she got up close that Randall could tell the vertical streaks were purple. The coat was dark and fashionable, with some kind of fur collar. She wore a black twin sweater set top that was flattering to her buxom figure. She was carrying a brown paper bag.

She was clean, not someone who had been working the streets. But he felt she gave the impression of someone who was there because she had nowhere else to be. Someone on the run.

"What's your name?" the lieutenant asked.

The woman stared back regarding Moscato, as if just then realizing the guy in the windbreaker was a policeman. She revealed no emotion. "Cayce Washington," she said with a slight Southern drawl. Not the sharp accent of a New Englander who drives a "cah," cheers for the "Sawx" and addresses him as "aw-fi-sah."

Washington? Moscato thought. *That's not the name, but this has got to be her.*

"Do you have any ID?"

She shook her head *no.*

"Can I have a look in your bag?" Again it felt more like an order to her, no matter how casually it was delivered. "Do you have anything on you I should know about?"

She handed the bag to him. Inside was a newspaper folded open to the real estate and apartment listings. She had been scanning them for a place to stay. There was also a packet made of aluminum foil. The cop took it out and began to unpeel where it had been folded on its edges. He could smell something pungent before opening it all the way, revealing faded green, mossy leaves.

"Is this marijuana?" he asked, already knowing the answer. The woman didn't respond. Her eyes flashed down to the packet and back to the officer's face, but she made no other reaction.

Nailed dead to rights and still calm and cool, Moscato thought. *And with what's hanging over her head? The violence required to do what she did? This cool? I don't think I've ever seen anything like this before!*

"What did you say your name was?" Moscato was watching over their shoulders. The woman spied him without turning her head and repeated in a Southern spice, "Cayce Washington."

The cop suggested Sheila LaBarre's name. "No," she replied.

"What's this?" There was more in the paper bag.

Randall started to pull out money. Lots of it. Big bills wrapped together as if they'd just come from the bank. He thumbed through them. The bills were new and in sequence. At first he thought five, then ten. But there was more. More than he could hold in his hands.

"Gotta be about thirty thousand dollars here." His flat Revere accent made "dollar" come out as "doll-ah."

If there was some anticipation of an explanation, the woman didn't feel it. Maybe the cops would take some and let her go on her way. They stood in silence. The lieutenant shoved what he could back into the bag and dug around some more. He pulled out a fat piece of paper. A cashier's check from a bank, drawn in Manchester, New Hampshire.

"This is made out for fifty thousand dollars," Randall said to Moscato. They threw out Sheila's name again. She just shook her head and said she was Cayce Washington. "What about this name on the check? What are you doing with this kind of money?" She gave no response.

A2! thought Moscato. *Page A2 of the* Herald. "Anyone got a paper?" he asked the other patrolmen there. One of the cops went back to his car and got his copy of the *Boston Sunday Herald.* Moscato pointed out the color photo on the front page. Above the masthead was a grainy picture of a woman. Blonde hair, much longer. Her skin appeared blotchy in the photo. The woman in the picture seemed heavier, but something was unmistakably identical. The eyes. The woman in the snapshot appeared to be giving a calm grin, but the expression was coming from the eyes. Ms. Washington's face was like a stone. But her eyes moved like a cat's: not in a panic, but methodically moving everywhere they needed to be to see what she needed to see.

The photo was in the top right-hand corner of the paper. It promised more about this New Hampshire woman on page A2.

"Look," the lieutenant asked, "is this you or not?"

"Yeah," she finally said looking back at her tabloid reflection. It was less about how she looked and more about what she had become. "That's me."

The photo was framed in bold letters with a quote from the woman's ex-husband: "SHE'S JUST CRAZY."

The house on Silver Leopard Farm in Epping, NH where Sheila LaBarre tortured and murdered Kenneth Countie, Michael Deloge, and possibly other men who were her lovers.

Courtesy of Kevin Flynn

After discovering burning human remains on the farm, Epping police attempted to kick their way into the farmhouse through a door on this side porch, just as Sheila returned home.

Courtesy of Kevin Flynn

Sheila LaBarre was born Sheila Bailey, the youngest of six children, growing up in Fort Payne, Alabama.

Courtesy of the Bailey Family

Sheila's high school yearbook photo. As a teen, Sheila had dreams of leaving town to become a singer or a model.

Courtesy of the Bailey Family

Sheila posing in a red dress on her front steps. Life in her parents' house was often filled with horrible memories for Sheila.

Courtesy of the Bailey Family

Sheila posing topless for the camera. Many said Sheila used her sexual prowess to control men and intimidate women.

Courtesy of the Bailey Family

Sheila and her mother, Ruby Bailey, at Sheila's birthday party in July 2000. *Courtesy of the Bailey Family*

Dr. Wilfred "Bill" LaBarre was a respected chiropractor and a kindly widower from Epping, NH. LaBarre was looking for companionship.

Courtesy of the Bailey Family

Sheila's DMV photo that appeared on the front page of the *Boston Sunday Herald* under the headline "Just Plain Crazy."

Courtesy of the New Hampshire Department of Safety

Sheila's first husband, single father John Baxter, whom she married on New Year's Eve 1981.

Courtesy of Wendy Baxter

Mike Deloge with his infant son. Deloge was one of Sheila's boyfriends who disappeared, but whose personal items were later found on Sheila's property.

Courtesy of the Deloge Family

Kenneth Countie joined the Army looking for some direction in his life. After he washed out, Kenny met Sheila LaBarre on a telephone chat-line, then moved to her Epping farm.

Courtesy of the Countie Family

Battered and beaten, Countie is pushed through the Epping Wal-Mart by Sheila. This is the last time anyone would see him alive. The diesel in the containers on his lap fed the fire that incinerated his dismembered body.   *Courtesy of the New Hampshire Department of Justice*

The long, wooded road leading down Red Oak Lane to the Silver Leopard Farm. The twisty, bumpy path lasts nearly a mile, surrounded by beautiful farm and pastureland, its location completely isolated from those living there.

Courtesy of Kevin Flynn

The 115-acre property at the end of Red Oak Lane was a point of contention between Sheila LaBarre and the children of Dr. La-Barre. In the years following the chiropractor's death, the farm was populated by free-range rabbits and a series of men who would do Sheila's bidding. *Courtesy of Kevin Flynn*

Prosecutor James Brofetti shows jurors a metal screen that Sheila LaBarre allegedly used to sift through ash in search of human bones.

Courtesy of Kevin Flynn

Jeffrey Denner, one of Boston's most venerable defense attorneys, makes the case for Sheila LaBarre.

Courtesy of Kevin Flynn

The prosecution listens to the closing argument of the defense. On the easel before them is an enlarged photograph of the burn barrel discovered on Sheila's farm.

Courtesy of Kevin Flynn

LaBarre greets her lawyers as she enters a Rockingham County courtroom accused of murder. During the trial, La-Barre often turned to the media or the families of her victims and glared at them.

Courtesy of Kevin Flynn

This shrine to Kenneth Countie was created by his mother, Carolynn Lodge, and other loved ones just a stone's throw away from the gate to the Silver Leopard Farm.

Courtesy of Kevin Flynn

This ceramic angel is among the many mementos left near the LaBarre farm in tribute to Kenneth Countie.

Courtesy of Kevin Flynn

PART 3

BECOMING SHEILA

"All things truly wicked start from innocence."
—Ernest Hemingway

CHAPTER 19

A QUIET CONFRONTATION

Despite the best efforts of reporters to get them to talk, neighbors wouldn't say anything until Sheila was in custody. However, the *Boston Herald* had luck interviewing on the telephone a man identified as Sheila's second husband, Ronnie Jennings.

"She's just crazy, to put it bluntly," Jennings was quoted in the Sunday paper as saying. "Sheila didn't care about anyone. She just wanted everything her way." The editors liked the quote so much, they placed it on the front page above the masthead with a photo of a blonde-haired Sheila.

The suspect had to appear in a Massachusetts courtroom for an extradition hearing before she could be charged in New Hampshire for the murder of Kenneth Countie. At roughly 8:30 A.M. on Monday, April 3, Sheila LaBarre entered Chelsea District Court. Aside from blurry photos, it was the first time the press or the public had a chance to see the woman who had so captivated the news.

Sheila was gently escorted through a side door to a prisoner holding area. She stood behind a bulletproof glass partition on the right-hand side of the courtroom. Less than twenty-four hours after her arrest, she had already obtained counsel. An attractive, well-dressed attorney whispered to her through a hole in the partition. Sheila remained demure. Her lips never moved and her face never changed. Her eyes took in the attorney; she nodded if she needed to, but she never said a word or, at first, betrayed an emotion. But, as the hearing continued, she looked back at the camera in the room and failed to suppress a smile.

Peter Odom sat in the benches with the Lodges and Counties. The New Hampshire Assistant Attorney General was only an observer in this courtroom. Police Chief Greg Dodge and several family friends were also there, watching with interest.

Counsel for the accused informed the judge that she would not fight extradition. She would be taken immediately back to New Hampshire where an arraignment could be scheduled. The hearing was over.

Odom turned to Carolynn Lodge and whispered in her ear. They stood to exit, but after a few steps Lodge stopped and sat down on another bench unable to go any farther. She began debriefing her family, who had gathered beside her, but couldn't take it anymore. The mother put her face in her hands and softly wept. Relatives, sensing the camera's gaze upon her, made a wall around Lodge to give her some privacy.

Stepping outside the Chelsea District Courthouse, Odom saw a scrum of reporters. There were about eight television stations, several radio stations and a healthy sprinkling of pad-and-pen journalists waiting for him. With Dodge by his side, the AAG steadied himself and walked into the center of the fray.

"I've never had so many microphones in front of me," he started without a hint of nervousness.

"Welcome to Massachusetts," was the wry response.

A reporter asked about the $80,000 in cash and checks Sheila had on her at the time of her arrest. "What conclusions you draw from the fact that she had a large amount of cash on her is for you to draw," Odom said. "Not for us."

Accustomed to a more liberal disclosure from prosecutors, the Boston media pressed for more about what was happening on the farm. "As the investigation is ongoing, that means there's still people to be spoken with. There's still forensic evidence to be examined. And we're not going to jeopardize the investigation by getting the particulars of it out there," Odom said firmly.

A reporter attempted to ask Chief Dodge a question about the mood in Epping. Odom cut him off. "I'll be doing the talking."

About five minutes after Odom completed his press availability, Sheila LaBarre's defense attorney took his turn in front of the microphones. Jeffrey Denner was a familiar face to many of those who covered the crime beat in Boston. The son of a Polish immigrant who fled the Nazis, Denner grew up with modest means in Hackensack, New Jersey. His family never would have been able to send him to Yale, then Harvard Law School, had it not been for the academic scholarships he won. Upon graduation, Denner took a $1100 loan and put up a shingle in Boston. He spent the late 1960s and early 1970s defending radicals in Cambridge and taking on civil rights cases. Thirty-five years later, Denner had become the most venerable criminal defense attorney in Massachusetts. The Denner Pellegrino Law Firm occupied prime real estate in a Boston skyscraper and had offices in Springfield, Providence and on New York's Fifth Avenue.

Denner's firm had a solid reputation for being aggressive—and successful. He had a good track record of acquittals for those accused of white-collar crimes. He once convinced a jury that a client was not guilty of his alleged rapes because he was sleepwalking. He also won the acquittal of a man accused of killing a woman aboard his yacht and dumping her body at sea. Denner's legal successes were recounted in the book *Counterpoint*, which was later republished under the name *A Scream on the Water*.

In perhaps the boldest move of his legal career, Denner took on the case of John McIntyre, a Quincy fisherman who disappeared in 1984. McIntyre had been a key player in a gun smuggling operation that involved the IRA and the Irish mafia in Boston. Allegedly, James "Whitey" Bulger and Stephen "The Rifleman" Flemmi tortured and murdered McIntyre when they learned the gunrunner had blown the whistle to authorities. In 2000, Denner represented McIntyre's family in suing the FBI and three mobsters from the "Winter Hill Gang." For thirty years, Bulger and some of his lieutenants were informants for the government, providing investigators with information on their rivals in the local Italian mafia. Denner alleged federal agents returned the favor, giving Bulger the tip that McIntyre had turned rat. During the six years it took to get the case to court, Denner received a death threat every other week. "Just so I can be clear, are you with the mafia or are you with the FBI?" he asked his would-be assassins on the phone. A federal judge eventually sided with Denner's client, awarding his family three million dollars. The FBI paid up. "Whitey" Bulger is still at large and on the Bureau's Most Wanted List.

Sheila had contacted Denner's office following her arrest that Sunday evening. Denner was always in demand, turning away more cases than his team of forty lawyers could ever take on. But he was interested in the case as he understood it and Sheila had presented herself to the law firm as a woman of means.

Tall, with strong cheekbones and short wavy hair, he stood in a pressed white shirt, blue necktie and a fine wool top coat as he began Sheila's public defense.

"She's obviously very broken up. She's thinking she's found herself in a horrible nightmare," Denner said of his new client. His voice was soft, evenly paced and thoughtful. "Suffice it to say she proclaims her innocence loudly. My expectation is that someday we'll have a trial and both sides will be heard and the truth will come out."

Of the details of the homicide, Denner could share no knowledge. All he knew was what he had read in the newspaper. The state had yet to offer the defense any of the evidence it had collected. Writers pressed him on why Sheila was carrying so much money. Was she planning on making a getaway? "Of course, it's not against the law to carry cash. Or a cashier's check. Obviously her life was changed for a variety of reasons that I suggest are unrelated to a homicide."

About an hour later, Sheila rode back to New Hampshire in a car with Epping Police Chief Greg Dodge, NHSP Sergeant Robert Estabrook and NHSP Trooper Jill Rockey. The mood was, despite the circumstances, quite jovial. Sheila smiled when photographers rushed their car looking for another photo of her. It was as if she was enjoying the attention.

"Do you think they'll do a movie about me?" she asked. No one knew for sure. Perhaps, they said. Then it turned into a party game. "Chief, who do you think should play you?" Dodge shrugged it off, not sure who would want to pretend to be in his shoes. Sheila began to ask the officers who should play her, and dropped the names of actresses whom she fancied could pull it off.

"I don't know who would play you, Sheila," Rockey said, "but I want Sandra Bullock to play me." Everyone laughed.

Because some of New Hampshire's smaller district-level courts aren't staffed each day, locations for some arraignments seem to be chosen by a spinning wheel. Crimes in Epping were heard in the Exeter District Court (which was actually located in Brentwood). On Tuesday, April 4, Sheila LaBarre was arraigned in the Portsmouth District Court, the largest one in Rockingham County.

Carolynn Lodge sat in the front row on the aisle talking quietly with supporters around her. Her adult son was beside her, Gerald Lodge next to him, with Kenneth and Suzanne Countie at the far end next to the wall.

Sheila entered the courtroom at 9:08 A.M. wearing a rain jacket over her clothes, her hair untamed. Instead of the dapper sweater set, she was wearing the orange jumpsuit of the county house of corrections. As a uniformed state police trooper in a rain-speckled trench coat escorted her down the aisle, Sheila looked down at the blonde woman in the gray windowpane business suit. The woman held up a photograph. It was Kenneth Countie in green Army fatigues, a camouflage hat on his shorn head, in front of an American flag. His military portrait. The woman nodded her head slightly and held the photo out so Sheila would see it and get a good, long look at the life she stole.

The prisoner was escorted to a chair in the empty jury box. Other mundane arraignments for drunk driving and domestic assault continued, the opening act in a larger legal concert. Kenny's mother, Carolynn Lodge, was white-knuckled holding the photo. It began to shake in her grasp. After a moment, a trooper told Sheila her lawyers were in the building and she could leave the room to speak with them in private. Escorted back up the aisle, her hands cuffed behind her back, Sheila caught Lodge's gaze again and finally realized who she was. Sheila flipped her head to adjust her hair, a gesture that helped her eyes escape the looks of hate beaming her way.

Lodge sat in silence, her jaw clenched. She stared at the photo of her son, imagining Family Day when her son was in Basic Training. *He looked wonderful.* Her right thumb caressed Kenny's cheek in the picture. Another immaculately French manicured nail picked at the paper edge of the print.

"He was my best friend," she whimpered.

At 9:18, her other son put an arm around his mother, drawing her back from the trance she was in. The touch from her only living son did not embolden her. Lodge dabbed her nose with a tissue, then tried to stifle one large sob which burst forth from her heart. Her son's comforting hand around his mother's shoulders folded into a fist and he pulled her closer to him.

Those gathered for the first order of business in *State* v. *LaBarre* waited until 9:34 for the defendant and her lawyers to re-enter the courtroom. Sheila's hair was now combed and her face powdered. The click of digital cameras punched the silence. Her raincoat had been left in the conference room, so this time she walked in wearing nothing but the pumpkin suit and the iron bracelets.

Again, Carolynn Lodge turned in her seat and held up Kenny's Army picture as Sheila walked by. This time, Sheila did not look down at it. Lodge's body was locked in place, but her eyes followed LaBarre like a falcon. Then

Lodge slowly turned to face forward and watch the proceedings.

Defense attorney Denner and co-counsel Brad Bailey took their places up front. Denner spoke to Sheila in a low voice. She never spoke back, only nodded when appropriate. Her lips remained painted shut. At one point she squinted at Bailey, choosing this gesture instead of speaking to indicate she didn't understand what he had just said. At 9:36, Judge Sawako Tachibana Gardner began the case.

"I'm going to read the complaint to you," Gardner told LaBarre and began reading the form typed up and signed that morning by Sergeant Robert Estabrook. "The state alleges that on or about the twenty-first of March 2006, you committed the offense of first degree murder, in that you 'purposely caused the death of Kenneth Countie, date of birth 7/18/81, and did incinerate the body.'"

At the word "incinerate," Carolynn Lodge shuddered, then shook her head in disbelief. Both Gerald and her son reached for her, sensing her limit was near. The woman dropped her face in her hands, first holding back tears, then letting them go. Her son rubbed her neck while she cried. In one of her manicured hands she clutched a tissue to her temple. In the other, she clung to the photo. The only other sound besides her muffled weeping was the staccato rapid fire of camera shutters now zooming in on a broken Carolynn Lodge. *It's a hell of a picture*, the photographers thought.

Because her crime was a felony, no plea could be heard by the district court. Such a plea would be taken up by the superior court at a later time. The judge ordered Sheila held without bail and scheduled a Probable Cause hearing in three weeks time. At 9:42, Sheila was escorted out of the courtroom.

Afterwards, Denner stood before eight television cameras and said he still hadn't been provided with any documentation from the State and had no first-hand knowledge of what evidence there might be in the case.

Of Sheila LaBarre's ultra-cool persona in court, a reporter asked, "Could you describe your client's demeanor?"

"Her demeanor?" Denner replied. "I'm not quite sure what you mean. She's sad. She's depressed. She's in shock. Her demeanor is appropriate for what she's facing."

Peter Odom looked refreshed that morning, like he had finally gotten some sleep. But his answers to the media were the same, offering little in the way of new information. "We'll let the evidence take us where it will. We are still investigating."

The follow-up question seemed like an underhanded pitch served up for a slugger to smash. Each reporter had heard crazy rumors about the parade of young studs on the horse farm. Each had a hard time tracking any of them down. "Are you looking into the possibility there are other bodies on the farm?" one reporter pressed.

Odom shook his head. The only sane answer would be "No." Anything else would equal a "Yes." Even a hesitation could be inferred as a yes. And a "yes" answer would be horrible, evil, unspeakable. This one crime was so depraved. How could any community not cringe at the thought this had happened before? Multiple murders? A serial killer? A black widow? Surely now we can awake from this nightmare and enjoy the sleep of the Just.

Odom did not hesitate. He was quick with an answer, too quick, almost like he had anticipated such a question and had prepared a response.

"Nothing would surprise me," he said. "But right now, the complaint on file is for Kenneth Countie."

Later, Carolynn Lodge and her family drove to Epping to visit the farm. State police detectives were still on the property and no one could get close to it. So Lodge walked the roads, peered through the trees and fought the images of her son's last moments that were running through her mind.

CHAPTER 20

FIRECRACKER

About a month after Sheila LaBarre was arrested, I got on a plane to Alabama. The station had sent me with a videographer on a four-day excursion to Fort Payne to see if I could dig up any dirt on the woman who had grown up as "Sheila Bailey." Cooperation from the local authorities had been hard to come by. On the telephone, local police refused to answer any questions or make available any documents. But I had the feeling that if I could just get down there and start nosing around, I could get at the truth.

After checking into a hotel, I went to the Orange Street house that Sheila's mother, Ruby Bailey, called home. It was a one-floor ranch, surrounded by yellow grass, old cars and a highway interchange. To an outsider, it might appear fabricated to typify a rural neighborhood in the Deep South, complete with sticky heat and soothing shade from fruit trees. Mrs. Bailey sat quietly in her wood-paneled living room, surrounded by dozens of family portraits and snapshots and souvenirs from a lifetime of living. There was an afternoon show on her television set where people with real problems went to a fake judge, but the program was interrupted by a firm knock at the door.

The frail old woman moved slowly to the entrance. When she opened the heavy door, she noticed a bee buzzing around on the inside of the screen. On the outside of the screen I stood in a clean shirt.

"Watch out for that bee, Mrs. Bailey," I said. She cracked the screen and gave the stinging insect its freedom, but I was still there. "I hate to bother you, Mrs. Bailey. I come from New Hampshire."

She quivered slightly, as if a monster were on her front step. "Oh, no. I don't know a thing to tell you. Honest to goodness, I don't."

I nodded. "I believe ya. I believe ya."

"She's got a temper, like we've all got a temper, far as that goes," Ruby Bailey continued. "But that dope business, that's just the wrong thing for anybody to touch."

"The dope?" I said casually. I made a mental note, not wanting to reach for my notebook and obstruct the free flow of the woman's tongue. "Yeah, that can ruin people's lives. Can't it?"

"I hadn't talked to her in a while." Mrs. Bailey squinted her eyes, thinking back to some recent past. "You know her father's dead and two of her brothers have died since she's gone up there. But her daddy said, 'Sheila, you'll regret it one day.' And she said, 'Momma, Daddy was right. I do regret coming up here.'"

We stood casually in the doorway, letting the conversation find its own path. Another man sat in a rental car, the engine running. I peeked around the homeowner and took stock of the 1970s-era photographs on the wall. There was Sheila, perhaps twenty years old, thin and comely. Red dress, red lipstick. Long brown hair.

"They'll probably cut her hair, won't they?"

"I'm sorry, ma'am?"

"They'll probably cut her hair off. She's got real long hair." Until now, most people had only seen Sheila LaBarre with the red and purple hairdo or in her bleached-blonde license photo. Few knew her as her family did: a woman with long, flowing hair.

"It had been cut one time in her life when she was six, seven years old," her mother said. "She got it cut off. That's when she started school and I was working. It cost well at that time, and I thought she could handle it better with short hair. That's the only time it has ever been cut."

I shifted my weight from one foot to the other, leaned in and lowered my voice. I spoke directly and intensely. "So, like I said ma'am, I did come all this way. And I'd like to ask you if I could borrow you for just ten minutes to sit you down in front of the camera and ask you just a couple of quick questions."

The man in the car got out and retrieved something from the trunk. It was a TV camera.

The force mounting to get a comment from this gentle old lady was greater than our chatting in this Alabama yard. We had been sent 900 miles with instructions to get this woman on camera. I would dread it if I had to make the phone call back to the newsroom to tell superiors that, despite the money and effort to get to her doorstep, the mother of Sheila LaBarre was simply not going to talk.

By mid-afternoon, I found the DeKalb County Courthouse resting at the top of a hill. As this was a paper chase and camera equipment would not be necessary, I went in alone and told the videographer to relax in our rented car. From the front steps of the courthouse, I could see a Confederate soldiers' monument to my right and Lookout Mountain in Chattanooga in the distance. I kindly asked to be directed to the clerk's office and was sent to the second floor.

The Circuit Court Clerk's office had architecture common in 1950s public buildings. There were large, heavy doors. Expansive ceilings. Crisp echoes of footfalls in the hallways. Jim Crow was born and nurtured in these walls and eventually left to wither and die.

The office was staffed by half a dozen women. One rose from a desk and greeted me at the counter.

"I'd like to do a criminal records search on a former resident."

"What is the name?"

"Sheila Bailey."

The name was like a whip crack in the air. All work ceased. One woman snapped her neck up from her paperwork and stared at me, her mouth wide open. Another woman casually got up from her seat and slipped out a side door, as if leaving a saloon before a gunfight.

"I have a date of birth and a Social Security number, if that will expedite things."

The woman waiting on me made a brief note, then asked if I would have a seat. Outside. In the hallway.

I sat up straight and tried to exude pride. *This is a stonewall and this* Nawthroner *is going to be kicked out of a public building he has every right to be in.* My next three days in Alabama were going to be pretty uneventful if I couldn't get any information.

I heard someone come out from a passageway and walk up behind me. I assumed it was the person who was going to throw me out. It was a woman in a professional suit sporting a brave smile. Her face was oddly familiar. She offered her hand without reservation and I recognized the name even before she explained who she was.

"I'm Lynn Noojin," she said, looking at me without a hint of shame or aggression. "I'm Sheila's sister."

Lynn Noojin's office at the Circuit Court Clerk's was well-kept if not well-appointed. She ushered me in and offered me a seat. On her desk was the photograph of a young woman I had seen about one hour earlier.

"Ah, that's your child," I said.

Noojin was taken back. "Yes, that's my daughter." Then she tried to sound unconcerned when she asked, "How did you recognize her?"

I smiled casually. "Your mother showed me her picture, along with all the grandchildren."

Noojin made some effort at more small talk before excusing herself to another office. I thought perhaps before she was going to talk to me she needed to call her mother and tell her what a damn fool she was for letting a reporter into her home.

* * *

Lynn Noojin remembers the day her parents brought her baby sister, Sheila, home from the hospital. That's because they let four-year-old Lynn help carry the newborn wrapped in a blue and green blanket into the house.

Sheila Kay Bailey was born on July 4, 1958, destined for larger things than her small hometown could contain. She added an "e" to her middle name because she thought it fancier. The Baileys grew up in Fort Payne, Alabama, a tiny mill community in the Tennessee River Valley tucked along the famed Trail of Tears. During the forced eviction of the Cherokee in the 1830s, a stockade was erected there by Major John Payne to house the Indians until they could be removed to Oklahoma. Some historians have likened the Army's Fort Payne to a concentration camp.

Sheila Bailey was the youngest in a family of six children. Manuel and Ruby Bailey had spaced it nicely, with three boys and three girls. Their oldest, Jimmy, had been born premature at a time when such infants did not often survive. The couple would have two other sons, Richard and Kenneth. The girls were Judy, Lynn and Sheila.

Because she was born on the Fourth of July, Ruby Bailey gave her the nickname "Firecracker." But the moniker also seemed to fit the child's explosive personality. From young Lynn's perspective, the baby was always crying. Though a large family, both Lynn and Sheila were late in coming around, as their parents were already very old and their siblings nearly grown. The two often felt essentially alone in the world.

The children grew up along the front lines of the insurgent Civil Rights Movement. While Huntsville and Northern Alabama were looking skyward, building the Jupiter rockets of the Space Race, the Deep South quarters of Montgomery and Birmingham were looking within, pondering their choices about segregation and discrimination. The Freedom Rides were underway, and integrated riders were assaulted by angry mobs. Governor George Wallace stood in the doorway at the University of Alabama to block

African-American students from registering for classes but stepped aside when President Kennedy federalized the state's National Guard and ordered them to the campus. Race riots and bombings were the images that many had of Alabama during that era.

The youngest Bailey sisters shared a room in the cinder block home. One night, Lynn awoke to hear Sheila screaming. She turned to see what had frightened the four-year-old. There was a man's face in the window peering in at the sleeping children. The girls ran to their parents and told them of the stranger peeping in at them. Father and mother weren't interested, accused them of having a bad dream and sent them back to bed. The next morning, Lynn discovered a cement block turned on its side beneath their bedroom window. Despite this evidence, her father still didn't believe her.

Manuel Bailey had perhaps the most influence on his daughters' young lives. Both Lynn and Sheila remember the man as sometimes being loving—however there was an unspoken, everlasting fear throughout the house about him. He was, as Lynn Noojin put it, "pretty bad in to drink on the weekends."

One time, Manuel came home with a load on and a chip on his shoulder. It wasn't uncommon for him to be violent when he stumbled home, but something had launched him into a wild tantrum.

Manuel Bailey started tearing up the house. He toppled the iron stove the family used to heat their home in the winter months. He grabbed on to the refrigerator, but the huge icebox would not go over. Instead, he opened its door and began tossing its contents across the kitchen.

Ruby Bailey came out in her dressing gown and watched the spectacle with chagrin. Lynn, about ten years old, and Sheila, around six, got out of their beds only to see a nightmare before them. Their father began throwing eggs and other food from the fridge at them. Ruby ushered her children to quickly get their shoes and escape out the back.

Lynn grabbed the keys to the family's car and handed them to her mother. Ruby had scooped up Sheila in her arms. The girl was small for her age; she was always small. The three of them crawled onto the front seat bench. Ruby engaged the clutch and turned over the engine.

The rev of the motor brought Manuel out to the carport. He appeared in the headlights of the car, stumbling out of the house. The little girls screamed when they saw their drunken father's face. Ruby tried to balance the gas and clutch as the car rolled in reverse, but she took her foot off too soon and the engine bucked and died.

Manuel Bailey came around to the driver's side and reared back to smash the window with his hand. He was too hopped up to notice the window was already rolled down, so the momentum of the shot carried his body into the front seat. The mother and daughters scrambled to get out on the passenger's side while Manuel fumbled to free himself from the window.

The father went back to the carport and grabbed the first thing he saw. It was a metal can of antifreeze. He swung the container at the three fleeing females.

Ruby had been pulling Sheila's hand. Sheila put up her other hand to cover her face. The can flew on a smooth trajectory right at them and struck the child in the head. The can hit with such force that its bottom edge left an indentation on Sheila's four fingers.

The father ran right to that spot and reached down to pick up the metal can again. Sheila was screaming in pain and fear. Ruby had to go back for Sheila who, upon being struck, had let go of her mother's hand. Another blow from the can at that close range could have been fatal.

As Manuel bent over to grab the antifreeze can, Lynn jumped on his back and grabbed hold of his neck. He was stronger, but not so coordinated in his drunken state that he could throw her off his back. They wrestled a little bit. Lynn knew she had no chance of pinning her father, but thought the unexpected counterattack would buy Mother and Sheila enough time to get around the front of the house and across the lawn.

When he finally separated himself from his daughter,

Manuel watched Lynn sprint around the house and into the darkness. She ran to the edge of their property, which was lined by a cornfield. The weather was warm and the stalks were high. Lynn dove headfirst into the field, rolled to one side, and then froze in terror.

She held her breath as her father made his way to the edge of the cornfield. She could hear his heavy breathing. Lynn prayed that the night was dark enough and her father's eyes were poor enough that she would not be discovered. Manuel rustled some of the seven-foot stalks, cursed for his daughter to come out. It was hopeless. She might have only been a few feet from him, obscured by a few corn plants, but it was as if she had dived into the ocean.

Lynn closed her eyes and held her breath for an eternity. She knew her father had given up looking for her, because she could hear him on the other side of the property, kicking the house and cussing. The night *was* dark and she realized she was alone under a blanket of leaves and growing produce.

"Mother?" she whispered. "Where are you?" She felt around with her hands as if she were blind. "Momma?"

Suddenly, a hand grabbed Lynn's wrist and pulled it. The child gasped. It was Ruby, carrying Sheila on her hip.

"Come on. We're going to your brother's." They continued on through the cornfield and across Alabama farmland to get to his house, forgoing the sleeping homes of friends and neighbors during the five-mile walk. Ruby never pressed charges for the assault against her and her daughters.

The girls knew two things about their parents: that they were never safe around their father and that their mother was powerless to stop him.

Interest in the story of Sheila LaBarre's life and times came to a crest after April 25, 2006, when many of the inside details that were common knowledge among the police and press were finally made public. These facts were released during the defendant's Probable Cause hearing, a perfunctory proceeding the defense often waives. Because the defense had no knowledge of the actual accusations and had not seen any of the evidence collected by the state, attorney Jeffrey Denner insisted on holding a PC hearing. It would force the State to finally publicly declare what the Epping woman allegedly did.

The preliminary proceeding was held in Goffstown District Court, just outside of Manchester and more than one hour away from Portsmouth, where Sheila's arraignment was held. Goffstown was just another stop on the spinning wheel of how courtroom space was allocated among New Hampshire's towns.

There was so much interest in this preliminary hearing that one TV news program even streamed it live on the Internet. The one-hour proceeding occurred on April 25, 2006. There was only one witness called by either the state or the defense: New Hampshire State Police Sergeant Robert Estabrook. Assistant Attorney General Peter Odom walked Estabrook, the lead investigator, through a fifteen-page affidavit the prosecution made public for the hearing. Although sections were redacted, it was filled with stunning details from the murder probe.

Estabrook's glasses and phlegmatic speaking style matched his professorial intelligence. His utter coolness and lack of emotion, which in some cases dulls the edge of recounting horrific details, only underscored the absolute ruthlessness of the offenses and the bone-chilling result of LaBarre's work. For the first time in public, investigators explained Countie's mental deficiencies, LaBarre's seduction of him, their trip to Wal-Mart for diesel fuel containers and LaBarre's tape-recorded interrogation of Countie that resulted in his vomiting and passing out. There was also the implication that other people might have been killed on the farm.

Much of the press, already in the know about the mechanism of Countie's death, almost buried these facts underneath the bizarre details of the LaBarre/Countie courtship. Now the rest of the world knew that Sheila allegedly killed him on the farm, dismembered his body and then burned it in some fire piles on her front lawn. The stoic Carolynn Lodge broke down and sobbed uncontrollably when Estabrook described the remains that Epping police officers discovered on the property. Estabrook said that the bone sticking out of the hay pile was covered with a "meaty mass." The gruesome image shocked the courtroom and unhinged the victim's mother.

Over the next few days, the violent details were not easier for Noojin to digest, even all those miles away in Alabama. Sheila's sister and brother decided that Ruby Bailey wasn't to hear these horrific disclosures. They told the old woman her daughter was in jail on a drug arrest. Noojin ordered her mother to hang up the phone if reporters called. The newspapers had already badgered Sheila's siblings, her ex-husband, her ex-mother-in-law and anyone else they could find connected to the woman. Police in Fort Payne were uncooperative with journalists looking for information. This was a courtesy to Noojin, who was well-liked within the town and county. The Southerners threw up as much of a defensive wall as they could, but Noojin knew it would only be a matter of time before they came to her.

Lynn Noojin looked overwhelmed when she returned to her office. I was still sitting in front of her desk, looking at the photos of her three children. She confessed that she had called her mother and given her Holy hell for granting me the interview.

Ruby Bailey had given an impassioned defense of her daughter. She also offered us looks at family photos, complete with the names of relatives that I discreetly copied into my notebook. When she escorted me to the screen door, she told me she always prayed with Sheila just before they were to hang up the phone with each other.

"She's my baby," she said, the only time her voice cracked with emotion. And then she cryptically said, "But sometimes, people can fool you."

Despite her reservations about my visit with her mother, Noojin did not hurry to kick me out of her office. There was no TV camera and I only softly asked once if she felt like going on TV to defend her sister. We spent an hour talking about what was happening. We both asked questions of each other.

I requested some court paperwork on Sheila. Some of it Noojin had copied weeks ago in anticipation of such a request. There were other documents located in the courthouse basement. Noojin asked if I could return the next day for them.

The following day I returned to the second floor of the DeKalb County Courthouse and was greeted by the same staff. This time, the women were completely at ease and hospitable.

Noojin brought me back to her office and gave me the documents I requested as well as some photographs of a smiling Sheila. I spent another hour in her office, with no discussion of whether she'd submit to a TV interview. The woman held nothing back.

Noojin flipped a large wall calendar back two months to March 2006. She pondered the dates, trying to remember what night her sister had called.

It was Tuesday, March 14, only a few days before Sheila and Kenny had been seen for the last time in Wal-Mart. The call came in late at night, so Lynn wasn't sure who it was.

"Lynn, Lynn, Lynn," a voice barely louder than a whisper pleaded.

"Sheila, is this you?"

"Lynn . . ."

"What's the matter?"

"He's looking at me," she said, "with demonic eyes."

"Who is?"

"He is."

"Where are you?" Noojin wanted to know.

"On the floor. Under the table."

"Who's there with you?"

"Kenny."

"Let me speak to him," Noojin demanded. She waited for Sheila's boyfriend to get on the line. They had spoken once before. "What's the matter with her?"

"She won't let me . . ."

Sheila interrupted Kenny's explanation. She screamed, "Tell her! Tell her that your mother's been fucking you! You've been having sex with kids!"

Kenny took the phone back. "My mother . . ."

"Look," a tired and weary Noojin stopped him. "I don't want to hear this shit. Leave. Get out. I got enough on me without this."

Sheila took the phone back. "Mommy scalded me."

"What?"

In a baby voice, Sheila said, "Mommy scalded me."

"My God, Sheila, she did not!" There had been plenty of drama in their childhood, but she was certain that that had never occurred. Noojin expected Sheila to respond with some kind of deep insistence. Instead she turned her attention to someone on her own end of the phone.

"STOP LOOKING AT ME WITH THOSE DEMONIC EYES!"

Noojin was unsure what was left to do. "Tell him to leave."

"I can't."

"Sheila, let me call the police."

"No, they hate me."

"Let me call an ambulance."

"No. They gave me too much radiation."

"Let him go."

Sheila then spoke in the tiniest voice possible. "He doesn't have a car. It's cold."

The older sister tried to soothe the younger. "Get off the floor. Eat some soup. Put some pajamas on . . ."

"I don't sleep in pajamas," Sheila inserted.

"Put some on, it's cold. Then go to bed."

"Okay." With that, Sheila hung up the phone. Two days later a perky Sheila called to say she was feeling better.

Lynn Noojin turned in bed to her husband and said, "I don't think she's going to last another six months up there."

I learned that much of Sheila's family in the South either thought the case was a railroad job or were dismissive of the entire thing. No one wanted to bring up the topic of Sheila.

"You have no one here to talk to about this, do you?" I asked. Noojin shook her head, so we talked some more.

I left the office without an interview, but with something unexpected: a confidante.

Lynn Noojin had no direct knowledge about the death of Kenneth Countie, but she did have other information that she still wasn't willing to part with. She didn't know whether her sister was innocent or guilty, but she instead offered this observation of the horrific crime:

"There isn't anything I've heard," Noojin told me, "that I don't think my sister is capable of doing."

CHAPTER 21

THE LARGEST SEARCH IN HISTORY

The hearings for Sheila LaBarre did not slow down the pace of the Countie murder investigation. In fact, in the wake of LaBarre's arrest for Kenny's death, suspicions about her relations with other men continued to mount. Investigators were left with the daunting task of searching the 115 acres of pastureland and the adjacent properties to which Sheila had had access. Hour after hour while the legal wrangling went on, crime scene technicians continued to spread out, combing each section of the land and buildings at 70 Red Oak Hill Lane.

Police had sent digital photos of the bone evidence they had found on the farm to the State Deputy Chief Medical Examiner, Dr. Jennie Duval. A published researcher in the area of anatomy and pathology, Duval had spent several years at the Institute of Forensic Sciences in Dallas. The morgues of New Hampshire were rarely as busy as those in Texas; there was more run-of-the-mill medical refereeing than the challenging and sensational cases in the Lone Star State. But Duval enjoyed the work. Her starting salary in 2001 made her the second-highest paid state employee in New Hampshire, behind only that of the chief medical examiner and well ahead of then-Governor Jeanne Shaheen, who appointed her.

Duval consulted with a professor from Maine who had

been helping New Hampshire law enforcement on such cases since the early 1980s. Dr. Marcella Sorg is a world-renowned forensic anthropologist who specializes in the study of bones and tissue remains. She is one of only sixty-five certified forensic anthropologists in the nation. Taphonomy, the study of decaying human remains over time, is of particular interest to Sorg. With a Ph.D. and more than twenty-five years of experience, she has written more than a half-dozen books on the subject. Sorg was in demand not only for criminal procedures, but also for input on archeological digs in the Northeast. She studied findings from pre-colonial Maine settlers and Indian tribes, as well as prehistoric remains. Sorg's examination of bone fragments led her to draw conclusions and to publish treatises on such seemingly obscure topics as the infant mortality rate of the Upper St. John Valley French population and the prevalence of diabetes among inhabitants of Vinalhaven Island.

Duval told investigators that the digital photos sent from Epping were suspicious and probably human bone. She e-mailed the pictures to Sorg for further study, for she was unquestionably the expert in this area of pathology.

Samples from the LaBarre farm were sent to Sorg at the university where she taught as an adjunct faculty member. Upon inspection, Sorg was able to identify the tiny fragments as coming from a human hand. Based on the size and density of the bones, Sorg determined they belonged to an adult male under the age of thirty-five, but most likely in his twenties. Kenneth Countie was twenty-four when he disappeared.

Duval, meanwhile, was working in New Hampshire with the rest of the body parts collected from the farm. Her laboratory was located at Concord Hospital, just over one mile away from the Attorney General's office. Duval meticulously went through the many buckets of ash that the State Police Major Crimes Unit had filled. It was a needle in a haystack–type of undertaking that required a talented scientist's eye and a saint's patience.

Duval discovered many white chips and spokes of bone

and began laying them out. Some of them came from the Wal-Mart bag that Sheila had pointed to when officers talked to her at the farm, saying Kenny was "in the bag." There were fragments of skull that Duval set aside. She separated a rib and several knotty bones she believed to have come from the spine from a mix of small carpal, metacarpal and tarsal bones that came from the feet and hands. Duval also identified longer, thicker sections from the radius and ulna, the forearm bones.

The best find among the remains were three teeth. The heat from the fires destroyed the nuclear DNA present in the bones, melting it away. But teeth are a good source to mine for a different kind of DNA. Mitochondria DNA (mtDNA) is present in hundreds to thousands of copies per cell, unlike the two copies per cell of nuclear DNA. Despite the degraded state of the samples, Duval was hopeful some mtDNA could be extracted from the teeth. Also, mtDNA is inherited only from the mother, so a match from Carolynn Lodge would be proof of the victim's identity.

The samples of human bone and teeth numbered more than one hundred. Sorg continued the work of piecing the body back together in hopes of discovering a trauma or another clue as to the cause of Countie's death. The process would take months. Within those buckets of ash were also dozens of red herrings. Not every bone fragment recovered from the burn pit was human. In fact, Sorg identified more than ten different animal species in the materials taken to her. Perhaps in that burn barrel there really had been a rabbit or two.

A small army of investigators gathered on Gordon Winslow's farm. State police were using the area in front of his barn as a staging area for a massive search. It was fittingly reported as the largest search related to a murder case in state history.

Close to two hundred police officers, most from the small town departments that surround Epping, gathered in an effort to comb the hundreds of acres in and around the Silver

Leopard Farm. Many of the cops wore combat boots and camouflage pants or black jumpsuits, forgoing their dressier polyester uniforms for the sake of comfort for the long hours that were ahead. Some of the officers were members of SWAT teams and other special units. New Hampshire Fish and Game officers, who normally led the way in dangerous mountain rescues or wilderness searches, also knapsacked their way to Epping.

Throughout the day, shoulder-to-shoulder lines of officers walked the pasture fields around Sheila's farmhouse. They blazed trails in the wooded sections and followed knee-high stone walls. The search area was no longer limited to the 115 acres of LaBarre property. Teams trekked through neighbors' properties and unclaimed parcels, any bits of land to which Sheila would have had access. More than 180 police officers covered better than two thousand acres over a two-day period.

At first, Daniel Webster Harvey and his wife watched the proceedings from afar. But all the neighbors eventually walked a portion of Red Oak Hill Lane, offering small talk and encouragement to the police who went by.

Since Sergeant Estabrook had kicked out the TV crew on Monday, March 27, the perimeter of the crime scene had been several hundred feet from Sheila's wooden gate. Now, it stretched all the way back down Red Oak Hill Lane to Gordon Winslow's driveway, three-quarters of a mile from the burn pits. Winslow was agreeable enough to let police stage on his property. He almost had no choice, as the commotion on his nearly-abandoned dirt road had reached a crescendo. Winslow enjoyed peace and quiet, enjoyed farming his land and mostly enjoyed the prospect of no longer having Sheila LaBarre for a neighbor. Letting these officers camp out for a few hours seemed a small price to pay to secure his personal paradise.

Having already covered the morning court appearances, television news crews made their way to the property by early afternoon to shoot some more video. From the sides of roads, from neighbors' backyards and even from the cow pen on Winslow's farm, macro-zoom lenses on cameras locked down on steady tripods followed small groups of officers stepping through the early spring grass. News helicopters hovered and panned the great fields, shadowing the searchers from above.

Winslow shouted at a cop and TV crew standing by his fence. "Those helicopters are flying too low! They gotta be five hundred feet!" he said. "They're scaring my cows!"

The reporters Winslow was yelling at were not from the same station as the choppers, who quickly got enough footage anyway and flew back to Boston. The shots of the many police vans and communications vehicles parked all around Winslow's property made the six o'clock news. For weeks later, when newscasters referred to the farm where the nefarious murder took place, video editors mistakenly used the aerial footage of a neighbor's property. It so annoyed the neighbor that he called the local station to complain.

Residents of Red Oak Hill Lane watched as officers in groups of nine or more walked across their lawns and through their yards. At one point, the line stopped to examine something on the ground. No one could see what they were looking at. An officer motioned to a neighbor to ask about something.

"Oh, no," the neighbor said to the searchers. "That's just ashes from our stove."

The line continued policing the ground. They examined a decorative stone wall. Two officers used shovels and rakes to remove a dark object and placed it in a white bucket. Another made a notation of the item and the location where it was found. When the resident approached, the officers showed her where they were digging, but would not say what they took.

The internal search of the LaBarre farmhouse also took several days. Peter Odom declared that the real heroes of the investigation were the men and women who spent hours and hours inside the squalid home collecting microscopic evidence. The Assistant Attorney General often felt guilty that while those technicians were sweating in paper suits, he was sitting in the climate-controlled comfort of the Epping Safety Complex, eating dinner that Chief Dodge provided for him from one of the town's restaurants. The Major Crime Unit collected hundreds of blood samples from inside the home, most of them mere flecks or drops. The largest blood sample was from the chair that crime lab technician Tim Jackson had found at the foot of the stairwell.

Jackson and technician Kim Rumrill worked in the upstairs bathroom, spraying LCV on the sink and bathtub fixtures. To their surprise, nearly everything glowed bright purple when hit with the spray. There were dilute bloodstains over the entire surfaces of both fixtures. The amount of blood represented was much more than an average household cut or bloody nose.

The technicians spent more time examining the plumbing in the upstairs bathroom, going through pipes and traps, looking for additional evidence. Rumrill discovered something odd about the bloodstains. Some of them were fresh, from the previous week or so. But other bloodstains were older. They had layers of dust and dirt over them. They had been there for quite some time.

In the dining room, Mudgett discovered a sheathed knife in a hutch cupboard. With a gloved hand, he pulled the blade from the leather scabbard. The knife was covered in reddish brown stains.

He also found several notebooks. Mudgett showed one to Trooper Jill Rockey, who agreed the handwriting appeared to be Sheila LaBarre's.

"She kept a journal," he said.

Investigators discovered that Sheila had indeed been keeping a journal since her youth. It filled dozens of notebooks and legal pads. Most entries were poems and song lyrics that she wrote and tried to sell, but there were also the occasional letter or postcard meant for loved ones.

On one page of a journal, dated July 2005, there was a sketch of what appeared to be a horizontal body made of circles. Under the sketch were the following notes:

110 lbs 5'4"
incinerated-burned-ashes flushed scatter
water-
Bury c shovel
private pilot/helicopter/boat
    DEATH
    Torch

The word "DEATH" was circled. Aside from the fact the note pre-dated his appearance on the farm by more than seven months, Kenneth Countie was neither 110 pounds nor five-foot-four. On the next page of the notebook, Mudgett read:

Daniel 3
the fiery furnace
Hotel furnace?
crematoriums?
4000 F

What did this mean? The name "Daniel" did not appear in any other journal as a person whom Sheila may have known, so investigators thought the notation might be a different kind of reference. Estabrook looked up the third chapter of Daniel in the Old Testament. The passage was about the deliverance from "the Fiery Furnace." In it, King Nebuchadnezzar says all people must worship the gods of Babylon or be thrown into the fiery furnace. When three devout Hebrews refuse to renounce God, Nebuchadnezzar's soldiers dispatch them into the inferno. But the king turns to see the three men and the Son of God walk out of the blazing furnace:

"They saw that the fire had not harmed their bodies, nor was a hair of their heads singed; their robes were not scorched, and there was no smell of fire on them." (Daniel 3:27)

Had this meant something to Sheila, and if so, why had she referred to it in her journal? What kind of fiery furnace had Sheila LaBarre created as a test of faith?

At another location on the LaBarre property, investigators were seen working with shovels and a stationary backhoe. Deputy Fire Marshal John Raymond and his dog, Clancy, had led them there.

In addition to the burn sites in front of the farmhouse where investigators had been sifting, Raymond and Clancy discovered two additional burn piles and one ash dump site. Unlike the smoldering, diesel-fueled fires police stumbled upon the previous week, these burn piles were not fresh. Raymond estimated each of the piles had been there through the winter and most likely dated back to autumn 2005.

While searching through these older burn piles, investigators found the remnants of clothing. They also found the charred remains of a zipper.

While detectives were contemplating what this new find meant, Mudgett's team turned up something else inside the house: personal items that didn't belong to Sheila or Kenny or Dr. LaBarre. Another person had lived on the farm, stayed in the house and left without taking those belongings with them.

Was it possible they had finally found out what happened to the man named Michael, who was last seen stumbling away from Sheila's farm in a bloody haze?

CHAPTER 22

SOUTHERN COMFORT

Among the documents I obtained at the DeKalb County Courthouse was a divorce decree for Sheila Bailey and John Baxter. A quick Internet search came up with a residential listing for John Baxter. The cameraman and I rolled up to a modest ranch-style house with several cars parked in the driveway.

I walked up to the front door, but before I could knock, a woman in her mid-twenties greeted me. I asked for John Baxter.

"He passed away about four and a half years ago. This used to be his home." *So much for this lead,* I thought. But then the woman offered, "I'm his daughter."

"As you may know, your father was married for a brief time to a woman named Sheila Bailey . . ."

She shook her head, frowning. "I remember Sheila, plain as day. When my daddy was married to her, she used to lock me up in the bedroom with a pot from the kitchen and told me not to come out or she'd beat me."

So, I thought, *I really am getting a grip on Sheila's past.*

The young woman closed her eyes and rewound as far as she could. "The last thing I remember about Sheila," she said, "is Daddy pushing her out of the way to take me out of the house. Then the next thing you know: the car's gone, the credit cards are gone. Everything's gone. And she's gone with it."

* * *

By the time Sheila Bailey got to high school, she had blossomed into a gorgeous teenager. Her brown hair swept behind her as she moved down the halls. She had a lot of charisma and everyone thought she was a knockout. Many of the boys were interested in her, but she showed little interest in them. She dated a little, but never had a serious boyfriend.

Sheila came from modest means, but always seemed to wear nice outfits. She entertained dreams of being a fashion model or a photographer. Sheila and her sister Lynn practiced dressing up and striking glossy-magazine poses around the house or in the yard where the light was better. Both girls became shutterbugs as they grew up, but even Sheila admitted that Lynn had the better eye.

Writing was a talent that Sheila possessed. She dealt with adolescence by jotting down free-flowing poems. They were always written quickly, usually late at night while sitting in the Baileys' front parlor or while alone in her room.

"My writing is the only faithful companion I've ever had," she wrote in her journal. "It never leaves. It never hits. It never refuses to protect me . . . If I ever really get to know myself, it'll be on paper."

On the page, Sheila worked out the troubles in her head and sketched rough drafts of her life. In her mind, she dreamt of being swept away by a rich man, someone who would take her away from the life she had been living. But the verses were also filled with angst and longing. Love notes were marked by desperate pronouncements; poems of love lost burned like torch songs. To read between the lines, one might assume the woman believed herself to be fragile and misunderstood.

She always signed and dated the poems, adding them to the growing volumes of *objets d'art* that she was fabricating. When she entered the Junior Miss pageant, Sheila read an original poem for the talent competition. During high school, Sheila joined the Alabama State Poetry Society, the first step for her on what she hoped would be a publishing career. There were also the first clues to a damaged psyche:

> *It's unfair that other hands*
> *must judge our body*
> *before the right hands*
> *finally touch home.*
>
> *We grow from childhood*
> *to womanhood*
> *never knowing who will finally stake his claim*
> *on our trampled territories*
>
> *Other mouths must taste*
> *our sweetness and*
> *nibble at our pampered smoothness –*
> *never bothering to remember our name*
>
> *It's unfair that other men*
> *must enjoy what we*
> *truly want to save*
> *for one special lover [. . .]*

Those who knew her say that Sheila Bailey may not have been the smartest in her class, but she was the sharpest. Those who viewed her charms as being obtained merely by looks failed to appreciate the way her mind worked. Things seemed to go her way when she concentrated on accomplishing something. She had a way of reading people and convincing them to do what she said.

Sheila Bailey graduated from Fort Payne High School on May 21, 1976. She had a string of unremarkable jobs and less-than-notable relationships. As she described it, Sheila had her "share of bastard ass men." She had been in love and heartbroken at least twice by her twenties. She spent more and more anxious evenings losing sleep and pouring her heart out in verse.

In December of 1981, things got serious between her and a young man named John Willis Baxter III. Less than twenty years old, Baxter was already divorced and the father of a young daughter. Some of Sheila's friends thought Baxter was a little boring, but the dark-eyed woman saw something else in him. The young man had a good job as a utility lineman, and a sweet-looking black sports car. There was an attraction between them. He needed a mother for the little girl he had at home, but Baxter was often compulsive in matters of love.

"You have to be sure. I hate divorces," Baxter told her. He was still stinging from the pain of his breakup with his first wife just weeks earlier. "If we get married, it'll have to be forever. Okay?"

John Baxter married Sheila Bailey on New Year's Eve, December 31, 1981.

Wendy Baxter remembered a young woman with long hair who smiled sweetly at her father, but who had little patience for caring for a child who belonged to another woman. When Baxter went to work and left Wendy home with Sheila, his new bride showed a different face.

"She was nice and polite and took care of me," Wendy said of Sheila years later. "She played Daddy real well."

Wendy Baxter recalled that Sheila placed her in a small bedroom, not much bigger than a closet, if the child became too needy. Wendy, who was just old enough to use the toilet, was given a pot in which to urinate. Wendy claims her new stepmother locked the door and left her in there all day until her father came home.

"If I cried or asked to get out or I needed anything, she tore up my toys," said Wendy. "She beat me."

"If you ever tell your daddy, I will kill you and your daddy both!" she claims Sheila told her.

Sheila's poems reveal a different perspective of the marriage. She resented being brought into the household to become maid and nanny. She was still young and believed she was giving up her dreams of a career as a writer or performer. In a composition titled "Soon, So Soon" and dated

January 13, 1982, she lamented her decision to marry into the Baxter family:

> *Put away your dreams & wishes*
> *Cook the food & wash the dishes*
> *Domestication is the word*
> *Monotonous & absurd.*
>
> *He gave you warmth in*
>   *body not heart*
> *He planned & plotted*
>   *from the start*
> *To add you to the family tree*
> *As the "Mother Star" for all to see*
>
> *You loved him as a man*
> *You loved him as a boy*
> *Until he made you feel*
>   *like his extra toy*

One night, young Wendy crawled into John and Sheila's bed to snuggle with her father before he was called out into a storm. They watched Baxter get dressed, put on his yellow crew helmet, his thick eyeglasses and his heavy workman's gloves. When the man left, Sheila shoved the child out of bed and chased her from the room.

"You don't have the right to be in my bed!" she yelled.

Thinking Sheila really would kill her and her father, Wendy was afraid to tell Baxter about what was going on. Instead she told her mother, Nancy, who had met John Baxter on a blind date to a drag race. They both had a love of cars and racing. She was taken aback by how quickly John remarried, but Nancy had always suspected Baxter of being unfaithful in some way during their marriage.

Fort Payne was home to dozens of hosiery mills and considered itself "The Sock Capital of the World." It was a place where a woman like Nancy could travel from factory to factory and make a good wage, all in cash. She did not have custody of Wendy and was working double shifts at the city's various mills to save money for a new family lawyer. She had no love for her ex-husband and had no time for the crazy lady he married.

While dropping Wendy off at Baxter's home after a visitation, her mother sent the child inside with a bunch of bananas. Sheila Baxter blocked the child from entering, grabbed the bananas and threw them at Nancy's pickup truck. Otherwise, the two women had virtually no previous contact.

Wendy told her mom that Sheila forced her to drink a liquid she poured from a dark bottle. The child said it tasted horrible. Nancy Baxter suspected it might have been brandy, but knew for certain her daughter had not been prescribed any kind of medication. Wendy also squealed about being forced to stay in her bedroom all day.

Nancy confronted John about the incidents. She never considered him much of a husband, but believed he was an excellent father. The young man was shocked at the allegations, but didn't doubt them. He had wanted this new marriage to work, to place a caring female into his home for the sake of his daughter. Baxter was decisive on this matter upon hearing of the mistreatment. The man scooped up his little girl and made for the door, ordering Sheila out by the time he returned. After a brief stay with his parents, Baxter returned to his home to discover his new wife had cleared out, taking his beloved black sports car with her.

Instead of forever, the marriage lasted only six weeks. The divorce was filed at the DeKalb County Court on February 14, 1982 (twenty-four years later, the ex-Mrs. Sheila Baxter would spend the anniversary having dinner with Kenneth Countie). The paperwork cited the reason for the breakup as "incompatibility of temperament." One of the only conditions spelled out in the settlement was that Sheila was to return the sports car, something that she didn't do.

Turning to her notebook again for comfort, Sheila wrote a poem dated April 2, 1982, titled "Broken Pieces":

I wish sometimes the world would end
And all the stars would break and bend
Forming another place to live
Where everyone would want to give
The treasures deep within their souls
<instead of broken pieces>

Yet life goes on and time is based
On what you achieve, the amount you
waste
Searching for love, or money, or fame
Knowing who to thank — knowing who
to blame

Some men give treasures
Some men give pleasures
Some men give nothing at all

Some men like daughters
Some men like nieces
Some men prefer broken pieces.

Nancy figured with Sheila out of John's life, she would be out of hers. But Sheila seemed to blame no one other than Nancy for the dissolution of her union with John Baxter. In the late winter and early spring of 1982, Nancy went into virtual hiding in Fort Payne. She lived out of a trailer she parked on a campground and told no one, not even her parents, precisely where she was staying.

Sheila badgered Nancy's friends. She banged on their front doors at all hours of the night, demanding to know where "that home wrecker" was. Some people found roofing nails sprinkled all over their driveways or forced into their tires.

Nancy drove a large construction-grade pickup truck. While pumping five dollars of leaded fuel, she heard a screech and then a bang. Baxter's black sports car had shot across the filling station parking lot directly at Nancy. She had been standing on the other side of the iron brackets around the pumps, and the car came to a stop there, killing the power. Sheila Bailey jumped out of the sports car wielding a claw hammer. Nancy was sure there were roofer's nails inside that car too.

Nancy's father was a hunter and she owned a .22 rifle, but she'd been taught not to grab a firearm in anger or desperation. Instead, she reached into the cab of the truck and pulled out the only other instrument she had: a twenty-four-inch-long machete.

"Well, don't that beat all," the filling station attendant said, looking out the window to watch the former Mrs. Baxters circle one another in the parking lot. One waved a hammer; one waved a machete. The women danced around each other, a soundtrack of jungle fight music playing in their heads. Then, they could hear the sirens from the Fort Payne Police Department a half block away, so they both jumped into their vehicles and vanished.

The stress of being stalked was showing on Nancy's face. The only time she felt safe was while working at one of the sock mills, because productivity-obsessed foremen did not allow hammer-wielding visitors on the floor.

Nancy's favorite place to grab a bite to eat was a local burger joint. She could get a bag of food and eat it while driving to another mill to work another eight-hour shift off the books. The mother of one of her good friends would start putting together her favorite burger when she spotted the pickup pulling into the parking lot, and the order would be ready by the time the hard-working mother got to the counter.

"You always fix me up right," Nancy said one time, taking the bag.

Walking back to her truck, the smell of the hot burger and fries was heaven to a hungry mill girl. She was ravenous after another day of work and not looking forward to another shift. She opened the bag to see that her friend had thrown in extra French fries for her. That's when the bag went sailing from her hands.

Nancy looked up to see that Sheila Bailey had slapped the bag of food away, the burger and fries scattered all over the asphalt. No other words were said. The two locked mad-hatter eyes and reached for each other's throats.

Nancy had her hair pinned up, because she had just come off work. She was able to get her fingers wound up in Shei-la's extra long tresses. Grabbing hold of Sheila's hair, she pulled her attacker to a parked car and began smashing her head into the steel bumper. After several blows Sheila was out cold, and Nancy dragged her unconscious body to the middle of the parking lot.

The exhausted woman got into her pickup and turned the key. She lined up the front left tire with the mangled mess of hair left unmoving on the ground.

"I'm going to pop your head like a grape," she mumbled, then stepped on the accelerator. Deducing its trajectory, a man jumped on the hood of the pickup and implored her to stop.

"Leave," he said. "You've already done enough."

Sirens could be heard in the distance. Nancy turned the wheel the opposite way and went around the back of the restaurant. On her way by, her friend reached out the window and handed her another hamburger in a bag.

"You ladies have to stop fighting over John," the police lectured them. In Nancy's mind, the cops were missing the point. She'd let Sheila have John, for all she cared. Her momma never liked the boy, and now she knew why. She and her friends were being stalked.

One afternoon, Nancy gave her friend a ride to the Laun-dromat. She thought it was only fair, because the night before Sheila had been banging on her friend's door and raising Cain. When he woke up the next morning all four of his tires had been slashed, and now he had no way of bringing his clothes to the Laundromat.

She was waiting at a stop sign, thinking about how much four new tires were going to cost her (she insisted on paying; her friend was an innocent bystander to all this tomfoolery). Two-hundred dollars would cut deep into her lawyer's fund.

Before rolling through the intersection, something caught her attention in the rearview mirror. A familiar firebird decal on the hood of a black sports car bearing down on her. She could see Sheila Bailey sticking her head out of the driver's side window. In her left hand, she was waving a pistol and then leveling it at the truck's cab.

Nancy grabbed the stick of the three-on-the-tree column and jammed it up in reverse. The tires spun so fast they burned out on the street. Her friend could have sworn the giant pickup had more than one gear for reverse. The mighty pickup slammed backwards into the sports car and kept crawling up the engine block until it stopped at the windshield.

Both vehicles stalled out. The friend, who had some unfinished business with local law enforcement, ran from the cab and disappeared into Fort Payne's neighborhoods. Sheila got what was left of the engine to turn over and pulled away, sure to be making a beeline to the police station.

A man ran into the street and picked up the pistol that Sheila had dropped during the crash. "Get the hell outta here. I don't want to know you."

Nancy hastily conducted some minor repairs to get the heavy-duty pickup running. Despite Sheila's head start, she still beat Sheila to the police station and filed a report saying the sports car had rammed her from behind. The collision had wrecked the car's radiator and all of its fluids ran out, causing the muscle car to overheat. The pickup only had a few scratches on its steel bumper.

Sometime later, the District Attorney asked to speak with Nancy. She was certain they were going to arrest her for the crash and filing a false report. But the authorities said they believed her version of the events. Sheila had been quite indignant about the police's view of the confrontation.

"You should take this," the D.A. told Nancy. He handed her a blank gun permit. "That woman's elevator doesn't go all the way to the top."

Wendy Baxter agreed to a television interview on the back porch deck. Afterwards, we went inside. She gazed out the sliding glass doors, on to the deck, where her kids and the neighbor's kids were playing with the dogs. John Baxter's picture was still on the wall of the living room, a shot of him in a cherry picker tying a Christmas bow to a utility pole. Baxter passed away in 2002 of cancer, having been married four times. He left everything in his insurance and retirement package to his daughter, including the home. Her attractive face still bore the freckles of her youth; her heart still belonged to Daddy.

"I wish we had done something twenty years ago," she told me, "and saved that man's life in New Hampshire."

There was peace in the house, even with the squeals of children outside. Baxter looked at her pre-school-aged daughter through the back window and quivered at the thought of how anyone could do such things to a child.

"I wonder what I would do if I ran across her here in Fort Payne," the woman thought out loud. "What would I do now because I'm grown? I'm not four or five years old anymore."

CHAPTER 23

CHATTANOOGA

I found Ronnie Jennings sitting at a desk behind the counter of the fast food eatery where he worked. Unlike Wendy Baxter, he was not pleased to see me.

Few people from up North had been able to get Jennings to say much, not after the *Boston Herald* report. They got him to call Sheila crazy and then they ran with it.

A producer from my station called his workplace looking for Sheila's ex-husband. A woman answered the line.

"I'm looking for Ronnie Jennings," she said. "But I don't know if I have the right Ronnie Jennings."

The woman on the other end asked, "Where you calling from?"

"New Hampshire."

"You got the right one." Then she yelled at the top of her lungs, "RONNIE!"

On the phone, Jennings had refused to answer any questions. Now here I was in front of him, asking him to come on camera and talk about those tumultuous years. I had no idea that I was standing right where Sheila once tried to kill herself.

"You can ask all the questions you want," he reiterated, "but I'm not answering."

Following her divorce to John Baxter, Sheila Bailey got a job at the local burger drive-in on the main drag through

Fort Payne. The drive-in was always hopping with shift workers speeding in or teenagers hanging out.

The interior of the restaurant was cramped. During the day, it always seemed like the cooks and carhops were dodging each other as they grabbed orders and brought them to parked customers waiting outside. It was loud, with the carom of voices and grill grease sizzle bouncing off the walls. Things were quieter at night, when cool Alabama breezes sailed through the open windows and stirred the papers on the shift manager's desk.

One night, working the closing shift, Sheila found herself without a ride home. "Do you need a lift?" a young man asked. His name was Ronnie Jennings. His mother owned the restaurant.

"Yes. Do you think you could take me home?"

The pair shared a car ride, and a romance bloomed. Jennings was tall, dark and attractive. Physically, he fit the description of the often-dreamt-of stranger who would take Sheila away from her small town life. He was not a man of means, but he could capitulate and aid in her getaway.

Sheila's friends were cautious of Jennings. They saw him as being kind of fast, as being unsettled. Jennings ran with a wild crowd. The two of them smoked marijuana together. To the beauty queens and epicene boys who gave Sheila counsel, Jennings was a player who had been through several relationships. But as with Baxter, Sheila saw something else in Jennings that drew her to him. It may have been nothing greater than that she was the focus of his attention (which she sorely missed since the end of her first marriage) or it may have been as deep as being drawn by his sincere devotion. Either way, Sheila held on to Ronnie Jennings tightly.

However, the young woman was apprehensive about certain aspects of Jennings's character and behavior. In a six-page letter she composed, but never sent, in September of 1982, Sheila wrote to Ronnie:

I'm in my bedroom, listening to the traffic on the Interstate. I'm lonely. I miss you very much.

The actual thing that is bothering me is this "illegal" thing, you're doing to "make money for you." I feel it will hurt us, and create problems. It makes me nervous more and more . . .

I am considering stopping seeing you until you find a way to stop this "illegal" whatever. I simply <u>cannot</u> nor <u>will not</u> have anything create problems for me again.

The "illegal" activity Sheila refers to is not explicitly enumerated. Throughout the letter, she tries to lay down the law and convince Jennings to change his ways. Sheila dreamt of moving to southern California and getting a Ph.D. in psychology. She had been taking prescription painkillers and an antidepressant since her car crash with John Baxter's first wife. But she couldn't hide how much she truly needed to have Jennings in her life, and she talked herself right out of the ultimatum:

. . . Do you believe you would always be happy being mine? . . . I don't want to take away your freedom. I would only want to feel that my love was the best kind of freedom and warmth you could know.

Please, allow me the changes of my many moods. The seasons are changing and so am I . . . Yet it is the season I somehow must become. I do not know why. I only know it's permanent.

I love you, Baby.

I love you so very, very much.

Only months after signing off on her divorce from John Baxter, Sheila and Ronnie eloped. The couple found a judge in Georgia to perform the ceremony. It was a quick and private affair, one that Jennings thought his bride truly wanted. Marriage had been her idea, and he knew her well enough to realize she would eventually get whatever she wanted.

The couple left the ceremony hand in hand. They strolled blissfully back to their car. No sooner had Jennings slammed the driver's side door than Sheila broke down into tears.

"We shouldn't have done it! We shouldn't have gotten married!"

The change of heart wasn't as discouraging to Jennings as it was disturbing. He had not seen that reaction coming. On their quiet drive home, he started connecting some of the things he'd seen, the flashes of irrational behavior he'd witnessed and wondered if his new wife had deep problems he hadn't recognized before.

A year later, Ronnie and Sheila Jennings left northeastern Alabama and traveled up Interstate 59 to Chattanooga, Tennessee. Her brother and his wife had moved to the city, which sits on the Georgia/Tennessee border just fifty miles outside of Fort Payne.

Sheila had worked at a hotel in her hometown and was able to get a job at the same hotel chain on South Market Street. In 1989, the hotel moved down the street to the famous Chattanooga Choo Choo complex, where tourists could climb all over the retired train or spend the night in a sleeper car. Sheila's time working at this hotel was brief, as she later found a job at another of the city's historical businesses. Sheila worked the front desk at a local hotel. Within three months, she was promoted to office supervisor. Three months after that, she was the assistant front office manager.

Ronnie Jennings found work as a cook. His new wife accused him of running with a dangerous crowd. According to Sheila's journals, their relationship was strained. She wrote a draft of a letter to leave for her husband:

Dearest Ronnie,

I have brought some things to help keep you warm. And some kitchen items, also.

Unlike you, I find it very painful to be away from our home. But I can't live with you anymore until you stop hitting me and stop staying very mad for long amounts of time.

I do love you, Ronnie.

The margins of the draft are filled with her signature, "Sheila Jennings," practiced in numerous fashions, each reflective of a different note she tried to strike. Some defiant, some loving, some invulnerable.

Two weeks later, Sheila journaled about her mundane days and the uneasy times at home:

November 20, 1983
Monday

No words hardly in AM. No kisses. Ronnie made his own lunch. I honestly planned to go to a lawyer. During the day, I found myself looking at the Bible and thinking of our marriage vows. – They're sacred. I've been sick all night and day – bowels, headache. Gave the cat a bath. Fed her/him (?) one worm pill in whipped cream. No arguments. Went to wash. Had fun together. Prayed, talked of God.

For his part, Ronnie Jennings was becoming more and more nervous about the mental state of his wife. His perceptions of their days together were not the same. He found Sheila to be unreasonable and bossy. He remembered himself as the victim, not the perpetrator, when things got physical between them. Some of his emotional distance was due to his uncertainty about her sanity.

At one point, Jennings spent an entire night awake in bed with Sheila beside him. He feared she would attack him once he fell asleep. More specifically, he believed she would try to stab him in the head with a pair of scissors.

Sheila's isolation in Chattanooga grew as time went on. Although her older brother was also in town (and she occasionally lived at his house when she and Ronnie were on the outs), the woman felt cut off emotionally. If she had hoped Jennings would provide the comfort she desperately desired, she was crestfallen.

Sheila Jennings ran a strict operation at the front desk of

the hotel. The original building was first used for lodging in
1847. In 1861, upon resigning from the United States Senate,
Jefferson Davis gave a speech at the hotel on the issue of
Secession. This enraged the owners, who called Davis a
traitor and nearly came to blows with the future Confederate
president. Union troops turned the building into a military
hospital when they seized Chattanooga about a year later.
The house survived the Civil War only to burn to the ground
in 1867. The new owner built a new hotel in 1871, which
operated until 1926, when the modern day facility was con-
structed.

The hotel was an architectural gem, displaying much of
the Roaring Twenties swagger commonly found at the time
of its rebirth. The facility had a certain ostentatious manner
that fit both Chattanooga and Sheila. The large windows and
decorative moldings were typical of Georgian architecture.
The ceilings were high and arched. A large fountain sprang
forth in the lobby. The indoor pool boasted a trio of water-
falls.

Sheila's larger-than-life persona was at ease in the brick
walls of the hotel. She excelled at operations, finding new
ways to save the hotel money on the way it did guest registra-
tions and dinner reservations.

By 1985, management at the hotel began the process of
terminating Sheila Jennings. Co-workers were complaining
that Sheila was leaving the front desk uncovered for long
periods of time and that she was fraternizing with male
guests in inappropriate ways. One hotel worker discovered
her shooting pool with a man and flirting with him. On one
occasion, the staff was unable to locate her because she was
upstairs with a guest. While there was plenty of innuendo,
no one ever caught her in a truly compromising position.
Nonetheless, the hotel and Sheila Jennings soon parted
company.

After leaving the hotel, Sheila got a job working for a local company as a secretary. The workload was easy for her
to handle; she had been a surgical secretary in Fort Payne
when she got out of high school. Though the pay was steady,

her hands were not, as they trembled at the sight of one of her bosses.

Sam Billiams was one of the sons in "Billiams & Sons Construction." A family business, the company was very successful. Their projects reached into most surrounding states. Larry Billiams was more than the father of the clan; he was the undisputed boss.

Sam was a vice-president in the company and the likely successor of the business. The fortyish executive was good-looking and had a hearty laugh. His pockets were always flush with cash. His new secretary caught his eye. They shared a love of music, a curiosity about the finer things. They also shared strained marriages from which they desired to escape.

Their affair began innocently enough. Sam took Sheila with him on business calls and site inspections. He taught her how to operate a loader on an empty job site. They had dinner and drinks and fell easily into bed with each other, making foolish declarations of love and devotion.

The couple found their way to many hotels in the area, spending torrid afternoons and long, hedonistic evenings together. Their pillow talk was tender. Sam whispered *bon mots* and Sheila recited poetry. They soaked in warm tubs and slid across fine sheets, ignoring the clock, the phone and the rest of the world.

The man was torn between his wife and children and the rush that being with Sheila gave him. It took only a matter of weeks. In the weakness of ecstasy, Sam promised to leave his family and start anew with her. He feared the confrontation it would surely bring and begged his lover for time to arrange matters before doing so. Between the sheets, they schemed of a life together.

The secret lovers rang in the New Year of 1986 together. Sam made excuses and escaped his family to meet Sheila in clandestine locations. Sheila gave few excuses to Ronnie Jennings of her frequent absences. She often slipped out without an alibi.

Sheila seemed poised to have it all. A man of wealth to

provide for her, to care for her. One with his head screwed on straight and who pledged his love for her. One who accepted her for who she was. He was a bit older and that symbolized security and strength.

The two were naked in bed in one of Chattanooga's finest hotels. The lovemaking was done and the smell of sweat was in the air. Sheila Jennings fantasized about telling Ronnie that she was leaving him for a rich businessman and tried to imagine the look on the miserable son-of-a-bitch's face. The telephone on the dresser rang and shattered the idyllic mist the couple had created in the room. Neither breathed, nor moved toward the receiver.

"Who's calling us?"

"Who knows we're here?"

"No one."

Sam Billiams picked up the phone as if it were a serpent about to strike. "Hello?" The man listened quietly. Without saying another word, he hung up and began to get dressed.

"Wait here," he said as he left the room. Sheila was too shocked to say anything. *It's his wife,* she thought. *He's been caught and now has to face her. Now he'll tell her of his love for me. Our life together begins now.*

Sheila sat up in bed, waited naked beneath the sheets for her lover to return. She would envelop him when he came back. She tried not to look at the clock, fighting the urge to imagine the tears and slaps and angry kisses happening in the lobby.

Sam's key hit the lock of the hotel room door and the bolt clicked off the strike plate. He entered and stopped at the foot of the bed, his shoulders bent. Sheila slid toward him in a crumple of silk material, her face aglow with joy.

"That was my father," Sam said. "He knows of our affair. He says I must end it."

There was silence. Sheila believed Sam had the strength to stand up to his wife. Even in her lusty fool's paradise, she knew Sam would never stand up to Larry Billiams. His father was not a man to cross, and he held the financial well-being of each of his sons in his hand. Larry's word was final.

"He says," Sam continued, "that you're fired. You can pick up your things this weekend."

Sheila protested. "Don't leave me!" she yelled over and over, and grabbed on to Sam's overcoat as he tried to slink from the hotel room. Out the door went her grand lover and her dreams of escape to another home than this.

One warm night in Alabama, a Fort Payne police officer knocked on Lynn Noojin's door. He was a friend, and asked Noojin to come with him a couple of blocks down the way.

The cop took her to a car accident. It involved one vehicle that had gone off in a deep ditch. The metal frame all around was crumpled and firefighters were working to pull someone from the vehicle. The car looked like her brother-in-law's, but she could see the long, straight hair of the victim.

Sheila was unconscious, her thin body flopping around like dead weight. She was bleeding from the head. The ambulance driver was trying to put a neck collar on her and another rescuer yelled out, "She's got a pulse."

Lynn watched helplessly as her sister's unresponsive body was carried from the car and loaded into the wagon. They were taking her to Baptist Medical Center. Lynn knew she had to make one stop before going to the hospital. Sheila still lived in Chattanooga and Lynn could think of only one reason why she would be in Fort Payne this time of night.

Lynn screeched into the fast food drive-in, pushed the call button, and asked for Ronnie to come outside. He had been making the drive from Chattanooga to Fort Payne to work in his mother's restaurant. He seemed neither surprised nor concerned to see Lynn there.

"Did you and Sheila get into an argument?" she asked him. Ronnie shrugged. Every day was an argument with Sheila.

"Did she take anything?" she pressed.

Ronnie quietly nodded. He still hadn't asked Lynn why she was asking these questions.

Earlier in the day, there had been a fight back in Tennessee. There was yelling and stomping and all sorts of general dissatisfaction between the married couple. During the argument, one of the kittens curled itself around Ronnie's feet. The man's heavy shoe came down on the kitten, crushing its back.

Sheila was horrified. The little cat was screaming out in pain. Sheila became apoplectic watching the pet suffer. Ronnie took the kitten out to back of the house and ended its misery.

Later that night, Sheila burned into his workplace and found Ronnie flipping burgers and drinking. Sheila had no problem with making a scene.

"I can't believe you're cheating on me," she cried.

"I'll fuck whoever I want to," he yelled back. Ronnie went back to the burgers and said Sheila would never get a divorce from him, because he'd never give her one.

"You want to know how bad I want out of this marriage, Ronnie?" The rage in Sheila's voice turned to despair. "I'll show you how bad I want out of this marriage."

Sheila took a bottle of pills from her purse. She popped the top and swallowed all the little red pills in front of Ronnie. Her husband didn't react. Sheila stormed out of the place, jumped in Ronnie's car and drove off into the night.

Sheila continued on for about three or four miles. As the pills took effect, all the buildings she passed seemed to turn golden. She felt an overwhelming sense of calmness and peace right before she passed out and crashed.

Lynn Noojin drove at breakneck speed to the hospital. She ran into the emergency room to find her sister still unconscious and doctors unable to revive her. They had already summoned a helicopter to transport her to Birmingham.

"She swallowed some pills! She took a handful of pills!" she called out. The medical staff quickly changed gears and started pumping Sheila's stomach. Lynn watched as all of the contents, stained bright red from the pills, were ejected into a bucket.

Sheila Jennings was taken to the hospital at the University of Alabama at Birmingham. She was in a coma for eight days. When she awoke she was admitted to the Neuro ICU, the hospital's psych ward.

Sheila spent thirty days in the unit, with no visitors allowed. Everyone in the family wondered what Sheila would be like when she got out. Upon her release, Sheila told Lynn the time in the Neuro ICU was the worst time of her life. She called it a horrendous experience, surrounded by mental deficients and deviant staff. She said an orderly tried to rape her and she fought him off. She swore she'd never go back to such a place again.

Her resentment was directed largely at her husband. Ronnie had been the one who'd had her committed. What was left of their marriage soon evaporated. The couple filed for divorce in Hamilton County, Tennessee, on February 12, 1986.

Sheila reported something else happening to her while in the psych unit. She recalled being summoned down a hallway by men dressed in white. There was a bright light and she was at peace. But the men sent her back and they didn't say why. It was left to her to decide her purpose.

Another year tore off the calendar and Sheila Bailey Jennings resolved to get what she wanted out of life. Sometime around Valentine's Day 1987, she browsed the personal ads in the *Globe*. She kept records of her replies to about a half dozen ads, from California to Idaho. Ad # 8185-G was a widower doctor living in New Hampshire. The five-feet-five brunette snapped a topless photo of herself in her bedroom mirror for enclosure with the letter she mailed to Wilfred LaBarre. Sheila made no notes of which other letters she sent to men around the country also included photographs from that same session.

This time, Sheila was intent on finding the man who could give her everything she needed. A beautiful home. Financial security. Support for her artistic aspirations. A loving bed. And a safe haven from the demons she'd been fighting all the years of her life.

Before I left Fort Payne for good, I made one last stop at Ronnie's workplace. The videographer and I both went in this time, the camera on his shoulder ready to capture a photo or any reaction we might get from Ronnie Jennings.

We didn't get very far in the door before another manager jumped out, threatened us with trespassing and kicked us out. Ronnie was somewhere in the building, still working at the drive-in, just as he had when he first offered Sheila Bailey a ride home.

As we drove out of town, it occurred to me that our run-and-gun tactic wasn't dissimilar to the ambush of the Counties and Lodges by the Boston press in Epping. I thought I would never be a part of something like that. Perhaps it helped that I knew I was never coming back to this town again.

CHAPTER 24

LOST SOULS

Police Lieutenant Michael Wallace placed a long-distance phone call to Sheila LaBarre's sister, Lynn Noojin, in hopes of learning something more about the nature of Sheila's relationship with Kenneth Countie.

Noojin received the telephone call from the police officer with grace and humility, as was her nature. She believed everyone in New Hampshire must presume her guilty by association with her sister. She worried people from the North looked upon Southerners as backward and unintelligent with funny accents.

Noojin had heard enough bitching about the police department, even if it was from Sheila. She knew Sheila had a grudge against Chief Greg Dodge, so some of what she was told had to be scrutinized. Noojin couldn't imagine the law enforcement professionals of Fort Payne or DeKalb County telling a woman not to bother them with her concerns. Mostly, she was at a loss as to why they didn't do more to protect Kenneth Countie. Why hadn't they taken him into protective custody when they discovered him bruised and burned at Wal-Mart? What were the laws like in New Hampshire? She couldn't imagine the police officers she knew in Alabama putting that boy in Sheila's truck and watching them drive off into the night.

Wallace asked Noojin some basic questions about Sheila. There was little for her to offer, as she knew almost nothing about Countie. The relationship had been short before its deadly conclusion. But the family never got to see Kenny, although Sheila had taken other boyfriends to Alabama, sometimes in the company of Dr. LaBarre himself.

"There's nothing I can tell you about him. I'm sorry."

"Fine, Mrs. Noojin. Is there anything else you could tell us? About anyone else who might have lived on the farm?"

Noojin thought a moment. A name popped into her head. "Do you know anything about Michael Deloge?"

Wallace made a note of the name. "Where is he?" he asked.

"I don't know," Noojin replied. "You tell me."

Noojin remembered the young man who had been Sheila's last boyfriend. Deloge, she recalled, had moved to the farm sometime in 2004 and had been there for about two years. During one of her long-distance rants, Sheila had said the Epping police were giving her grief about her horse farm.

"'You had a homeless man living with you,'" Sheila had indignantly recalled an officer saying to her.

"Homeless!" Noojin had interrupted. She never heard before of a homeless man staying on the farm with Sheila. The older sister was afraid this might be the kind of ne'er-do-well who'd take advantage of a woman who lived alone in the woods. She pressed Sheila for details about the man they were talking about. Was it Michael? How did she meet a homeless man? Where was he now?

"Oh," Sheila said with as much casualness as she could muster, "he left."

"Left?" At the time, Noojin had not wanted to let this go. "When did he leave?"

"Months ago. I can't remember."

Sheila refused to talk about it anymore. But something about the exchange bothered Noojin deeply. Later she told the story to her niece. "Your Aunt Sheila doesn't let a man 'just leave' and not talk about it for so long."

* * *

Upon returning to New Hampshire from Alabama, I was greeted at the airport by people sticking their heads out of cabs and congratulating me on my reporting. I felt like I had begun an investigation I couldn't just put aside. I had to go on and find out the whole truth. I just hoped that people found the story as fascinating as I did.

After an early morning flight out of Huntsville with a change in North Carolina, we stumbled into the newsroom in the early afternoon. There were a lot of handshakes and back slaps from reporters and cameramen. We were like those big game hunters who went to the mysterious Skull Island and came back with Kong; we found the big story.

We had only been back for a half hour before a bulletin came across the wire. A family in Somersworth was telling the papers that their son had worked on Sheila LaBarre's farm . . . and he hadn't been seen for two years.

Michael Deloge grew up along Long Island Sound in West Haven, Connecticut. The city was blue collar, just one town over, yet a million miles away, from Yale University. Michael had a rough edge to him. He struggled with substance abuse and other demons and though it was common for the young man to lose touch with relatives, he had not been seen for more than two years.

Michael's parents met around 1967 in a bar in New Hampshire. Deloge had just gotten out of the Army. Donna Boston already had a world-weary expression when she was young, and she was impressed by the physical stature of Deloge. He took Boston, their new son and Boston's daughter from a previous relationship to his native southern Connecticut. Deloge bought a home and took a job on the New Haven Fire Department. The couple stuck it out for several years, but the family split in the early 1970s. The girls, Donna and her daughter, returned to New Hampshire. The boys, Mike and his father, stayed on Long Island Sound.

Mike Deloge was a tall man, kind of thin, with a long face. He was a clown who loved a good joke, but was also sensitive and protective of loved ones. Like his father, he kept his emotions bottled inside him. As a teen, Michael grew his hair long to emulate the rock stars he idolized. Deloge struggled to find himself as a young man. He dabbled in drugs. He was a heavy drinker.

Mike had a love of music and lyrics and fancied himself a songwriter. He didn't play an instrument or read sheet music, but he composed rhyming couplets. Deloge often went to a famous rock club in New Haven. It was a tiny venue located somewhere between Hartford and New York City, but premier musical acts like Billy Joel and the Rolling Stones often slipped in and played their songs. In the late 1980s and early 1990s, Deloge brought his notebooks of lyrics to the club for readings and open microphone nights. He tried to market his songs, but never found any takers.

In 1990 Mike's father met Joy Storer through a mutual friend. They married. Joy already had a young daughter, and the couple soon welcomed another son to their growing family.

In 1993, Mike's girlfriend, Loretta, became pregnant. Encouraged to do the right thing and settle down, Deloge proposed. The couple was married that summer in a public park, with Mike's stepsister, Tracey Storer, serving as flower girl.

Their son was born before Christmas, and Michael seemed like a doting father. Beneath the surface, his relationship with Loretta was slowly deteriorating. Deloge was often without work and had trouble retaining it when he found it. He was still abusing drugs and alcohol. Loretta couldn't stand the drama anymore, so she made a clean break. When she left him and took their son, she completely cut ties with Deloge and his family. The man was heartbroken over the separation from his child and found comfort in the repeated cycle of substance abuse he had turned to throughout his life.

Michael Deloge worked hard to finally obtain and maintain his sobriety. He spent five years on the wagon before deciding he needed a clean slate to start his life over. Though the miles separated them, Deloge had always kept in touch with his mother. In 2002, he decided to move north and try to make a go of it in the Granite State.

I tracked Donna Boston down to a subsidized housing complex in Somersworth. Attached to a strip mall, the Plaza Terrace apartments resembled a roadside motel. It was a Sunday and the only thing open in the mall was a Chinese restaurant that seemed to specialize in Indian food. It wasn't far from the apartments that Sheila owned and still collected the rent on.

A man was standing in the doorway of apartment number two. About sixty, he was wearing a T-shirt and flannel pajama bottoms. He was holding a can of beer.

I introduced myself and he said he was Donna Boston's boyfriend. She had gone to the store for groceries and would return in a half hour. The cameraman and I returned to our SUV.

Soon we spotted the woman being dropped off by a neighbor, groceries filling the trunk of the car. We gave her enough time to put away the goods before knocking.

Through the storm door, I could see Donna Boston sorting through pills and putting them in a weeklong dispenser. She had a dispirited look on her face.

"I don't feel good today," she told me when I asked for an interview. "I'm not up to it. I've got four types of hepatitis and cirrhosis of the liver. I need a day off."

Michael Deloge found himself at a homeless shelter in Portsmouth. How he made his way there is unclear. But the record shows that Sheila LaBarre met Michael Deloge at the facility and invited him to live on her farm in Epping.

Deloge was not the first man to live on the property since the passing of Dr. Wilfred LaBarre some four years prior. Gordon Winslow and others saw many young men being escorted down Red Oak Hill Lane to the Silver Leopard Farm. Some stayed for the day, to help Sheila with her horses. Others stayed for months. Some of these visits overlapped. It gave the neighbors fodder for jokes, that Sheila was operating a stud farm, not a horse farm.

One day, Deloge phoned home with news that he had met a nice woman named Sheila. He told his father he was in love and that Sheila had been taking excellent care of him. There was a noticeable difference in their ages, more than ten years, but no one objected. There were never any visits between the two households, but it was understood that things were going fine. His parents were relieved that Michael finally seemed happy and in a stable relationship.

However, as 2004 progressed, Michael's phone calls to his father were less enthusiastic. He no longer praised the love of his new woman. Instead, he grumbled that they were having their share of problems. One time, he told of a fight the couple had while they were driving in Sheila's truck. He said Sheila pulled over and threw him out in the middle of nowhere, and he walked for what seemed miles on deserted roads with no streetlights and no homes.

"I spent the night in the woods," he told his stepmom of another incident. "She threw me out of the house and I slept in an orchard."

Mike's parents did not closely follow the shifts in Michael's relationship. The couple was too busy managing their own struggling marriage. In the summer of 2004, Joy was living alone in the family home. Late one night, the telephone rang. Joy pawed at it, if only to stop its jarring clangor. Still half asleep, she answered the call.

"How could you do that to your son?!"

It was the shrill voice of a woman that Joy did not recognize. "What?" she mumbled.

"How could you molest your own son like that? You'll burn in hell!"

Joy thought she was having some sort of strange dream. The woman continued to rant and quote scripture. Joy had no idea to whom the woman was referring. There was also a man, either in the background or coming from another extension, who was mumbling incoherently. Neither ever identified themselves.

"How could you let him molest your children! You were supposed to protect them. Tell them how you molested your brother and sister!"

Joy was getting annoyed at the circular logic swirling around her, so she hung up the phone.

A moment later, the telephone rang again. This time, she chose to let the answering machine get it.

The next weekend Mike's father joined Joy and the children for dinner when the subject of the mysterious phone call came up.

"You have to listen to this crazy message I got," Joy said. She played the tape of the man mumbling and the woman yelling that "he" was a child molester and that, "he is going to burn in hell for his sins."

"That's Michael," Mr. Deloge said.

"What?" No one had recognized the man's voice.

"That's Michael. And he's either drunk, on drugs or drugged. But that's him. And he's making no sense."

None of it made sense to the family. As far as any of them knew, Michael was not a child molester. But there were some disturbing facts that confused them.

As a child, Michael Deloge claimed to have been a victim of molestation. The culprit was supposedly a friend of his older half-sister. After his and Loretta's marriage fell apart, the drifting Deloge flopped at homes of relatives. While staying with one family, his cousin's husband accused Deloge of being inappropriate with the children and threw him out. He told this story to his mother, Donna Boston, who later recalled it for reporters. The New Hampshire media declared that Deloge was a confessed child molester (though no records of arrest or formal accusations could be found). After the incident, however, Deloge went to his father and said his cousin's husband had had enough of him living in the basement and was looking for an expedient excuse to get rid of a freeloader.

"I swear to God, Dad," he said, "I never molested those children."

The lack of clear evidence was not protection for Michael

Deloge. *What if he told Sheila about that incident?* Michael's stepmom thought. *Would she have had a bad reaction to it? Would she have freaked out?* She could not have anticipated the words LaBarre later said to her afternoon lover, Steven Martello: *God said that pedophiles have to die. God told me that* all *pedophiles have to die.*

The phone message remained enigmatic. "I got a phone call from Sheila last month," Michael's father confided in them. "She said Michael needed money. But he was asleep and couldn't come to the phone to ask for it."

"How much did she ask for?"

"One hundred dollars."

The family did not hear from Michael after that late night phone message.

There was little concern at first. Deloge traveled a lot, especially in his younger days of drunken skullduggery. Then weeks passed by. Mr. Deloge resolved to ask Michael what that phone business had been all about when his son called to wish him a happy birthday. Mr. Deloge's birthday came and went, and no phone calls from Michael. Michael's father stopped talking about him after that. At first, Joy thought he was hurt by Michael's thoughtlessness, but she knew that Michael always called his father on Mr. Deloge's birthday no matter what. Mr. Deloge could not bring himself to call Donna and ask, could not bring himself to call Sheila and ask. He just knew. Something had happened to his son.

The West Haven home of the Deloge family is spitting distance from Long Island Sound. Saltwater mist blows across the neighborhood and into the family's lawn and walls. The day I visited them, photographs of their missing son lay on the coffee table. The family seemed like they were in a state of shock.

"All that stuff about him molesting me and my brother," Tracey told me. "It's plain not true. It never happened. Michael never touched either of us."

The claim was puzzling. *If it wasn't true, why did Sheila*

say it? Why was she so motivated by it? If it wasn't true about Deloge, was it true about Countie?

The interview was done with only Mike's stepmother and stepsister. Michael's father was still too upset to talk about his son. The only thing he ever said to Joy when the news of gruesome discoveries on the LaBarre farm came out was, "That would explain why Michael never called me on my birthday."

"I know Sheila killed him. I know it," Joy said. "Will they charge her for it?"

It was a difficult question to answer. I knew the forensic evidence on Kenneth Countie had been troublesome for investigators. There was nothing left but dust and slivers of bones. How they'd be able to prove Countie had been stabbed or shot or poisoned or strangled . . . it seemed unachievable to do with legal certainty. How they could prove to a jury Michael Deloge had been murdered—when there was even less physical evidence—seemed impossible.

"Where is he? You tell me where he is," Lynn Noojin said on the phone to Epping Police Lieutenant Michael Wallace. *Somewhere on that farm?* he thought, but didn't say.

Noojin was about to hang up on the officer, when she remembered something. "I can tell you this. Sheila put the telephone bill in his name."

Wallace was puzzled. "What do you mean?"

"It was just something Sheila did. She didn't want the phone in her name. She was afraid of crank phone calls. She put the phone in Michael's name."

Wallace thanked the Alabama resident for her cooperation. He was about to confer with state police investigators when he decided to check something on a whim. He reached into his desk and pulled out the Epping telephone book. He looked up "Sheila LaBarre."

Nothing. Not listed.

Then he thought about it some more. He thumbed backwards to the D's and looked up "Michael Deloge."

"Son of a bitch."

Michael Deloge. . . . 70 Red Oak Hill Lane, Epping . . . 679-XXXX.

Could it really be? Had this man been missing for two years and the entire time an address for him was listed in the telephone book?

CHAPTER 25

ISLAND LOVER

Life in Epping, New Hampshire, was just what Sheila Bailey wanted. When she came to town in 1987 and moved into that wonderful farmhouse at the end of Red Oak Hill Lane, she went by the name "Sheila Bailey Jennings." It wasn't long before she began referring to herself as "Sheila LaBarre."

Each night, when the old doctor came home, she showered him with affection, praised his bedroom prowess. Each day for several weeks, Sheila purchased a greeting card and left it for LaBarre before he went to work. The cards varied from the romantic to the silly to the suggestive. She had all sorts of sexy nicknames for the old man, which he seemed to get a kick out of. Each card contained a note expressing her deepest love for Bill.

LaBarre was supportive of Sheila's dreams. She told him she wanted to be a singer and a songwriter. However, New Hampshire was not the best place to break into the recording industry. But LaBarre encouraged her to try. He took her to Nashville on a working vacation to network with as many country music stars as possible.

"Sheila Jennings" did not sound like a suitable stage name, so she adopted a new moniker. She took the name Cayce. The name came from both a young niece who had mangled Sheila's name until it came out like "KC" and in honor of author and mystical psychic Edgar Cayce, whose writings about visions of angels fascinated the young woman. Since Sheila had appropriated her lover's last name, she introduced herself to Tennessee musicians as "Cayce LaBarre." (Ten years later, she used the alias "Cayce Washington" when hiding from police during a murder dragnet.)

Sheila continued to dabble in all forms of writing. She tried unsuccessfully to get poems published, messages embossed on greeting cards and jokes printed in magazines. She continued to write songs and sought out local musicians to score the tunes with chords to match the melody.

"Honey," LaBarre told her, "never get discouraged that you don't have it all. Your past failures were not failures. They were simply the necessary steps on the ladder of life to get you here."

As comforting as the sentiment was, it did not satisfy Sheila's desire for self-fulfillment. Dr. LaBarre and his girl-friend discussed ways she could help out with his real estate holdings. LaBarre owned some rental property on the seacoast. It required maintenance of both the buildings and the tenants. Sheila took over the duties as landlord, collecting rents and evicting deadbeat occupants.

Sheila made a more direct impact on the doctor's economic situation at the clinic. The LaBarre Straight Chiropractic clinic had been doing a steady business with Bill LaBarre and his cousin Ed Charron. There was a small staff who handled the appointment book and the other paperwork. Among those who worked there part-time was LaBarre's daughter, Kelly.

Older than Sheila by only a couple of years, Kelly did not have a good feeling about her father's new companion. Kelly remained close to her mother, Leone, who had moved out of Epping after the divorce. Many of the neighbors, including the Harveys, also kept counsel with Leone LaBarre. Kelly knew her father had deeply loved Edwina, his second wife who died of cancer several years earlier, and he was lonely in her absence. Kelly cared immensely for her father and was willing to accept she couldn't choose his lovers for him. But she felt Sheila Jennings Bailey regarded her as some sort of enemy, a rival for Bill LaBarre's affections. There was much tension between them from the beginning.

"Dad," Kelly told him many times, "you don't want her in your life. She's bad news." The old man always consented, agreeing to send Sheila packing, but tears from the long-haired beauty always changed LaBarre's mind.

"The first thing she ever said to me when we were alone," Sheila LaBarre later said of Kelly, "is, 'When my father dies, I get the farm.'" Others wondered if this was a creation of Sheila's mind, part of her battle plan to win her probate case.

The first project Sheila assigned herself was going through the books of the LaBarre Straight Chiropractic Clinic. Much of the paperwork was rudimentary, with just patient names and fees recorded in a ledger. She discovered much red ink, to the tune of six figures.

"What have you and Eddie been doing all these years?" she quizzed the doctor. "You've got patients who aren't paying and insurance companies that are gypping you."

Much to the dismay of the regular patients, Sheila became the office enforcer. She was heavy-handed with them, sometimes insisting on payment with a pronounced tongue-lashing in the middle of the small office. No longer could patients make a promise to pay at another time or compensate the doctors with fresh produce or horse tack. Sheila's overbearing stance and Southern accent rubbed the locals the wrong way.

The addition of Sheila to the business was troubling for Dr. Ed Charron. LaBarre's cousin and life-long partner, Eddie was like Bill's right hand. Charron lived in the furnished apartment on the second floor of the clinic building in Hampton. Even as he grew older, Charron carried himself like the athlete he was in his youth. Both LaBarre and Charron had their list of regulars who confided in them during the intimacy of a procedure.

"That woman at the desk is horrible," Charron heard from his patients. "On the way out the last time I saw you, she threatened to drop me if I didn't pay my balance." Charron heard this often and mostly from those who could least afford the needed treatments he provided. The doctor would take a twenty-dollar bill out of his wallet, slip it to the patient and instruct the person to give it to the lady at the desk.

Although Sheila sensed the resentment from patients, she turned a blind eye to Charron's attempts to circumvent her efforts. Her work managing the office helped clear the clinic's debt and made it lucrative for the doctors. She discovered some money missing from the business and investigated by tracking down patients on the books who were listed as not having paid. Sheila discovered many of them claimed to have paid in cash, having given the money to one of the other office workers. This led Sheila to crank out letters to each of the patients, asking him or her for a notarized statement to be used against the employee.

Sheila then turned her attention to the one tenant of the Hampton building: Ed Charron. LaBarre's life-long partner had lived in the apartment above the clinic with his Doberman Pinscher for next to nothing. Sheila demanded Charron pay seven hundred dollars in monthly rent.

The demand took the old buck by surprise. LaBarre just threw up his hands, indicating Sheila, even as an employee, was beyond his control.

Charron told Sheila he would not pay that much rent to live in the clinic he helped Bill build. Sheila insisted; Charron resisted.

"If you don't pay me that seven hundred dollars," Sheila told him, "I'll kill your fucking dog."

The Doberman was probably the only living creature in Hampton not afraid of Sheila's shadow. Charron threw her out, refused to talk about it any more with her.

Three days later, Ed Charron's Doberman mysteriously dropped dead.

Sheila and Kelly continued to bicker. The daughter felt Sheila was not merely a gold digger, but that she was also ruining the friendly practice her father and uncle had spent their lives building. Kelly confronted Dr. LaBarre about these feelings. What they said to each other is unknown, but Kelly spent less and less time at the clinic or at the farm while Sheila was there.

By the early 1990s, people began to notice a change in Dr. LaBarre's personality. He seemed sad, drawn out. Even the most casual of acquaintances could see that his stress and unhappiness came from Sheila.

The stress from dealing with Sheila was beginning to affect Bill LaBarre's health. He was having chest pains, lying down between patients. He developed hypertension. His own physician said it was stress. For long stretches of time, LaBarre lived in an apartment above the clinic and left Sheila alone on the farm. He did it to get a break from her.

"Why don't you leave her?" some asked in the privacy of the treatment room. "Just send her packing? Get her out of your life?"

He believed Sheila was too smart and could outfox anyone. No one else understood it was impossible for Bill LaBarre to extract Sheila from his life. Maybe she just plain intimidated him. Twice he got restraining orders; twice she convinced him to drop them. She was like a briar on trousers after a walk on the farm.

"Oh," the doctor sighed heavily, gave the patient a wry smile and said cryptically, "she's got too much on me."

Sheila enjoyed being the center of attention when she made her way around Epping. People often spotted her silver luxury car coming at them a little too fast. She was still young, still trim and still sexy. She loved wearing tight pants and tossing her luxurious long hair over her shoulder so it could float behind her when she walked. Sheila revealed in mixed company that she was a practicing dominatrix and that she got pleasure from inflicting pain on her lovers. No one presumed she was referring to Bill LaBarre, and they were appalled she'd be so indiscreet at the expense of the doctor. She had the ability to shock, and she seemed to love it.

Sheila flirted with everyone, but turned the heat up for any good-looking man she came across. The flirting sometimes led to dating, which sometimes led to wild sex. She treated her boyfriends the same way she first treated Bill LaBarre. She was complimentary and attentive. She fed their egos. Then she tried to control them.

Sheila was less than subtle around the office about her taste for new men. She eyed the hot guys who came in for chiropractic treatment or made deliveries to the clinic. Kelly couldn't stomach the behavior in her father's own office.

Sheila did nothing to keep her dalliances a secret from Dr. LaBarre. She showed him photographs of her lovers, told him about her dates. All the while, she sent the doctor cards of love, gave the doctor kisses of tenderness and wore the doctor's last name like a designer dress.

Like Sheila, Wayne Ennis came to New England looking for a better life. The twenty-nine-year-old man had been born in Manchester, Jamaica, and bounced between odd jobs like driving a taxi and harvesting local crops. In New Hampshire, Jamaican migrants could still move from farm to farm, picking fruit, like apples and blueberries, doing the work that an uninterested generation left for their fathers to outsource. Men of color were rare in New Hampshire, and Ennis's island accent made him seem even more exotic to the people who met him.

He had been in a serious car accident in 1994. He was left with aches and pains that made it hard to do manual labor. Ennis sought treatment at the LaBarre Straight Chiropractic Clinic and immediately caught the eye of Sheila LaBarre.

As a young woman, Sheila had dreamed of finding a dark-skinned lover from Jamaica, writing about it often in her journals. She vacationed on the island in 1989 (with Dr. LaBarre's money and without the doctor). Sheila and Wayne became a couple and told the doctor they were to be married in September of 1995.

If there was a glimpse of freedom from Sheila, LaBarre did not realize it. Inexplicably, even after Sheila married Wayne, the woman did not leave LaBarre's life. The woman he wooed a decade earlier to come to New Hampshire continued to work in his practice. Her new husband became a handyman on the doctor's property. The couple later lived on the farm with the doctor. Sometimes, they lived in an apartment above the Hampton clinic, next to Ed Charron. The doctor's tolerance for the curious relationship confounded neighbors and acquaintances.

Sheila used her old typewriter to compose a pre-nuptial agreement. Ennis had little in the way of personal wealth, and Sheila was eager to set her affairs straight in case her third marriage went the way of her previous two. The document included the standard divisions of stocks, automobiles and jewelry. But, some points seem to have been shaped well to Sheila's advantage:

COMES now Sheila Kaye LaBarre and Wayne Alkins Ennis to make and declare this to be their Prenuptial Agreement . . .

Any proceeds from Sheila's singing, songwriting or acting remain hers alone.

One can infer that Sheila still believed she would become a star and her future wealth needed to be protected. The agreement was reasonably balanced to both sides regarding assets acquired before and during the marriage. However, at the end, the language spelled out which assets were not to be divided:

It is further agreed that Wayne will never make any claim to any real estate currently placed in trust for Sheila . . . It is agreed by both that neither will make any claim against the other for anything the other inherits from anyone and any time . . . Any monies from life insurance will be the exclusive property of the beneficiary and neither party will make a claim against the other regarding same.

It's unclear whether Ennis was aware at the time that Sheila held the trust to Wilfred LaBarre's properties and that she was to be the beneficiary of the doctor's life insurance. Regardless, Sheila's intentions were to keep those assets to herself.

Wayne Ennis loved the view on the farm. He enjoyed walks through the pastures. To a poor island boy, it was like he was a millionaire himself. It was the best time of his life.

However, he was puzzled by his wife's sudden mood changes. She cursed him, threw things at him, struck him. Ennis kept from hitting her, mindful that Dr. LaBarre was also in the house.

One dreary autumn evening, the arguing reached such a fevered pitch that Sheila chased her husband out of the house with a .380 handgun. In a clap that echoed over the empty fields, she fired a shot over his head.

"I'll send you back to Jamaica in a box! I swear to God!"

With nowhere to go, Ennis made the long trip through the drizzle back down Red Oak Hill Lane. He did not stop to ask for help at the Winslows' having been warned by Sheila that they were crazy. Instead, he made it on to the main road and stumbled through the night into Dan Harvey's orchard. Ennis climbed into the bow of one of the six-foot trees and tried to go to sleep there.

"Darn fool," Harvey whispered to his wife. The old farmer summoned the refugee out of the tree and into the house, where he offered Ennis a hot drink and a couch to sleep on.

Having spent all his life in Jamaica, Ennis had never seen a blizzard. One night, he watched the heavy flakes stream diagonally under the floodlights. That was before a fight sent Sheila into a rage. She directed her ire at both her husband and her lover, throwing them both out of the house and into the accumulating snow and barring the door. The men looked at each other, the snowflakes sticking to their bare heads, then headed for the horse barn.

LaBarre had a small camper he kept on the far side of the barn. He offered to share it with Ennis, but the young man refused, shameful of what his wife had done to him and the old man. Ennis took a blanket and went into the barn. The horse named St. Serious whinnied when he came in from the storm. Ennis looked around for some clean hay to rest in. The barn provided shelter from the snow, but its high roof and wooden interior trapped the cold air in and offered little warmth. His island blood was too thin. He shivered and got little sleep.

Until now I didn't know a place on earth so cold, he thought. *I am going to freeze to death before morning.*

Both men lived to see the sun come up and were granted re-entry into the house at 70 Red Oak Hill Lane.

But the peace between Sheila and Wayne was temporary. More fights ensued. Even with his marriage to an American citizen, Ennis was still only of resident alien status, a point Sheila wielded like a sword. Ennis tried to convince Sheila that her violent outbursts were going to get her in trouble with the Epping police.

"Who are they going to believe?" she mocked him. "A black man or a white American woman?"

Sheila called Ennis' mother in Jamaica and threatened her, too. The Jamaican man became despondent. *I don't want anyone back home to know I am living this way,* he thought.

Ennis came home to the farm one night, only to be dragged by Sheila out to her truck. She was clearly agitated about something, but he suspected it wasn't him so he went along with her.

The two drove off in the darkness, down the bumpy, root-laden path from the farm to the main road. Sheila was driving too fast, and everything inside the cab and the bed bounced. Ennis started to wonder if getting into the vehicle had been a mistake. At first Sheila said nothing. She pulled the truck on to the asphalt and spun the tires, darting off along the back roads in the tiny New Hampshire town.

"Do you know what I wish?" Sheila posed. Ennis said nothing. He feared his wife when she was angry and a wrong answer could very well rollover the speeding truck.

"This is what I wish," she continued. "I wish that a horse would kick that old man in the head."

Ennis was shocked. "Dr. LaBarre?!"

"One of those horses could kick him right in the head and kill him."

It was true that a blow from a shoed horse would possibly be fatal to the old man. St. Serious was jumpier than the other horses, needing gentle coaxing to calm him in the stable.

"I've thought of it myself," Sheila went on. "I've thought of strangling him myself. Killing him right there in the house."

"Sheila," he gasped, "why would you say such a thing?"

"If Bill dies," she said, "we inherit the farm." It's unclear if Ennis knew the farm was only in Sheila's name and his pre-nuptial agreement nullified any claim he could make to the property. At that moment, Ennis was only concerned about the ravings of his wife.

She said, "You should kill him."

"What?" Before Ennis could protest, Sheila cut the wheel and made a sharp turn onto another street that sent cassette tapes and other debris skating across the truck's cab.

"I want you to kill him. Then we can be rich."

Ennis was afraid to say anything. He was afraid to tell his wife no. *If I refuse her, she'll turn on me. I don't trust her when she's like this.* Suddenly, Sheila spun the steering wheel the other way and the force slammed Ennis into the passenger-side window. He was scared, remembering all too well his other car accident.

Sheila pressed him several times for a commitment, a commitment to kill Dr. Bill LaBarre. Ennis resisted. In what seemed like a deadly version of an amusement park ride, the truck continued speeding on side roads as stray branches smacked the windshield and fenders. All the while Sheila made her fatal sales pitch.

I cannot kill Dr. LaBarre. He is like a father to me, Ennis thought. But the words would not come out of his mouth. Finally in frustration, Sheila slammed on the brakes.

"Get out," she ordered him. Ennis quickly complied, though he had no way home. His wife peeled the truck out on the loose sand and zipped off, leaving Ennis to make his way home through the woods.

The couple spent some time away from Dr. LaBarre, living above the Hampton clinic. One evening, Ennis was sitting on the couch watching television. The program took place at the beach, and the sand and warm sunshine reminded him of Jamaica. Catching a glimpse of the show, Sheila saw that all the women were wearing bikinis. She chastised Ennis, calling him perverted.

Sheila's eyes were wild, just as they were during their truck drive, and he knew there would be no reasoning with her. Ennis fled the apartment, but without an overcoat he quickly grew cold. The man stuffed his hands in his pockets and walked to a nearby bar to warm up.

In Hampton, there weren't any dive bars a forlorn husband could slink into. The town sat on the ocean and Hampton Beach was one of the state's biggest tourist attractions. The businesses ranged from family seafood restaurants to Colonial-style taverns. Ennis calculated how long he'd have to wait until Sheila cooled down, had a few drinks and then braced himself for the cold walk home.

When he returned, he hoped to find Sheila asleep. However, instead of cooling off, she had been simmering. Her ranting continued just as it had before he left.

"You've been cheating on me!" she spat.

Ennis denied being unfaithful to his wife, though the prospect of a less dramatic relationship had crossed his mind. Sheila crossed the room and pounded on his chest. "How dare you! How dare you!" Her husband remained motionless, bewildered by the new line of verbal attack.

"Come on! Come on! Do it!" Sheila was now goading him. He feared striking her. *Why would she want me to hit her? So she can call the police? It's a trap.*

"Stop it, Sheila. You are my wife. I will not hit you."

Sheila froze too. For a moment the two stared at each other; the only thing moving was the fire flickering in Sheila's eyes. She let out an anguished scream. Ennis flinched, fearing it was the battle cry of an assault. Instead, Sheila reached up to the collar of her shirt and pulled as hard as she could. The material ripped a scream of its own. She dug her fingers into the side of her neck and raked them across her own flesh. She slapped her face over and over, working her way closer to her mouth. When a blow finally landed that split her lip, she paused. But the insane rage did not leave her eyes. She bit down on her own finger and worked it between her teeth like a mongrel. The sight horrified Ennis, unsure if intervention would only fuel the masochism.

When she stopped the tirade, Sheila admired her mangled digit. Her gaze then turned to her husband and she smiled. With blood smeared around her lips, Ennis thought it was an evil smile, as if the devil himself were looking right at him. Sheila then walked around the apartment, calm as day. *Have the demons been exorcised?* Sheila strolled to the telephone, punched seven numbers and smiled once more at her husband.

"Is this the Hampton police?" she asked smoothly. "I need an officer to come to my house. My husband just assaulted me."

As part of the pre-sentence investigation into the simple assault charge against Ennis, a worker for the state Department of Corrections Division of Field Services interviewed the couple about how to proceed. A restraining order was placed on Ennis for the time being. Sheila told the investigator that her husband was terribly jealous, blamed his abusive personality on having grown up "in a more violent culture" and said he had "a problem with women in general." The investigator wrote that Ennis described "the marriage as being 'shaky,' but he would like to try to resolve the problems 'one more time.'"

As employer and friend to both parties, the investigator questioned Dr. LaBarre about the marriage. He said both confided in him and they both had tempers.

While his written report referred to the victim solely by her husband's name, she continued to call herself "Sheila

LaBarre" throughout the marriage. The investigator made this note:

> Dr. LaBarre employs Mrs. Ennis, but they are not re-
> lated, and have not been married. Apparently, she de-
> cided to change her name after a bad marriage, and
> she had known him for some time.

Bill LaBarre had every reason to resent Ennis. But he knew that the Jamaican laborer wasn't the reason his once-happy relationship with Sheila had devolved into this soap opera. It was all her doing, as was this dangerous business between him and Ennis.

Dr. LaBarre helped Ennis pack some things in the doctor's car and drove him to the bus station in Manchester.

"You have to get away from her. You have to go some-place and start over. It's the only way."

Ennis listened to LaBarre's words. He had always admired him, and he knew the doctor spoke the truth.

"You must go. If you stay, there's no telling what trouble she'll get you into."

At this, Sheila's husband thought of the wild ride through the darkened back roads in which Sheila solicited his help to kill LaBarre. Now LaBarre was rescuing him from the real threat to his own safety. *How could I have kept quiet that night? Why didn't I speak out and defend this man?*

When they got to the station, LaBarre gave Ennis some money, got his bags from the car and wished him well. The man promised he would not return.

It was a promise Ennis found hard to keep. For the sixteen months of their marriage, he continued to return to the woman he thought he loved.

The marriage finally ended in December 1996. The Jamai-can returned to 70 Red Oak Hill Lane to see Sheila. Her car with the "CAYCE" license plates was parked in the yard. Dr. LaBarre's car was gone, so Ennis assumed he was still at the clinic.

Ennis opened the front door of the home and came in out of the cold, his boots wet from the snow. At first, there was silence in the house, then he heard Sheila's commands coming from the bedroom. They were the familiar orders she gave in bed to her new lovers.

Wayne burst in to find Sheila on top, her bra on, her long hair waving over her shoulders. Her face betrayed surprise when she saw her husband standing there. For a moment, it felt like the only time in their relationship when Ennis had the upper hand.

"You . . . son of a *bitch*!" she bellowed.

In a battle of who could be the angriest, Sheila LaBarre was not about to lose. She leapt from the bed and began screaming at him. How dare he come here! How dare he spy on her! Her lover, Ennis noted, was a young white man who just watched the act unfold. He thought the man seemed slow. Sheila reached for the cordless phone and threw it at Ennis, striking him in the head.

The next day, Sheila began divorce proceedings in Rockingham County Court.

After the divorce was finalized, Sheila petitioned the court in May 1997 to seal her file. She said she enjoyed her privacy, and the family court judge agreed to the request. Sheila, who was never too long without companionship, had already replaced Ennis with a new lover, maintaining the triumvirate on the farm.

Wayne Ennis dropped out of sight and was never seen in Epping again. Sheila told people he had gone back to Jamaica. His absence was never really questioned until investigators tried to list the different people who had once shared Sheila's bed.

The investigation into Sheila LaBarre had been underway for nearly a year before the public learned what really happened to the farmhand.

CHAPTER 26

THE DEATH OF DR. WILFRED LABARRE

No sooner had Wayne Ennis disappeared from Sheila's love life than another young man turned up. James Brackett had also been a patient of Dr. LaBarre's. Sheila was attracted to him and soon they were living together back and forth between the Epping farmhouse and the apartment above the Hampton clinic, the same arrangement she had with her ex-husband.

Brackett was a young guy in his mid-twenties, but he had a thick bush of salt-and-pepper hair. He had worked odd jobs and was employed at a garage in neighboring Raymond, New Hampshire. Jimmy was mostly quiet, seemingly shy. There was a subservience to his nature, which attracted Sheila to him.

Jimmy Brackett was slow. Unlike school children still struggling to learn, there isn't much use for diagnoses in adults. It was sufficient for those who met him to know that Brackett was slow. It was obvious to anyone who had spent time with him. His speech was drawn. His penmanship was infantile. But they also came to like Brackett, because of his sweet nature and his good soul.

The three of them, LaBarre, Brackett and Sheila, spent Christmas 1997 together on the Epping farmhouse. Sheila's greeting card to Bill praised him as being the greatest man she'd ever loved. Brackett's card to Sheila was signed to "my wife." The dynamic of this relationship was hard for people to understand.

Just after sunrise on September 26, 1998, Brackett walked into the emergency room at Exeter Hospital. The next day was his twenty-seventh birthday, which he planned to spend with Sheila in their Hampton apartment. He was standing before a triage nurse bleeding from the forehead. He said he'd been stabbed with a pair of scissors.

At 7:30 A.M., Doctor Travis Neely walked into exam room two to evaluate Brackett. In addition to the laceration to his forehead, the patient had a cut on his right earlobe. He had a clean medical history, just a bee allergy and some past chest pains. He was alert and oriented. The cut on Brackett's head was about two inches long, running vertically near the scalp.

"Are you in any pain?" the doctor asked.

"No."

"How'd you get this?"

"I got into a fight with my girlfriend," Brackett told him. The young man said they argued often, sometimes tossing each other around the apartment.

Brackett said the fight begun around 4:30 in the morning. It ramped up to tussling immediately, with both people tossing each other around the apartment. Sheila told Brackett he was going to get his ass kicked, not by her, but by her new boyfriend. Brackett didn't know who that boyfriend might be, but he assumed it was someone who could make good on her threat.

Now Brackett was scared. While Sheila was yelling at him, he pulled out a folding knife and pointed the blade at her. He didn't want to hurt her. He wanted her to be scared, too. Brackett thought Sheila was out of control. The sight of the blade did not slow her down. Brackett cut the palm of her hand with the blade. Sheila screamed. She reached for the first thing she could find: a pair of cuticle scissors. She let out a death cry that frightened Brackett more than the weapon did. Then she lunged at him, driving the point of the scissors into this head.

With the blood pouring down Jimmy's face, Sheila and Jimmy rolled around the living room, locked arm in arm. Brackett knew he had to stay on his feet. If he went to the ground, she would stab him again. Somewhere. His eye. His chest.

The pair crashed around the apartment. Sheila let out a high-pitched screech, sucking air in between her teeth. She had been cut on her finger, either by the folding knife or the scissors. They broke the hold. Brackett got away, left the apartment. There was no major medical facility in Hampton. Three hours later he turned up at Exeter Hospital, less than four miles away.

Before Dr. Neely stitched the wound, he called the Hampton Police Department. They waited until 8:00 for an officer to arrive at the Emergency Department. Officer William Bourque asked Brackett to write out a statement, but the man said he had trouble reading and writing. Instead, he dictated the incident to the cop, who wrote the statement for him. Brackett had the folding knife with him, so he turned it over to the officer. Bourque took some photographs of Brackett's head and ear, then left for Sheila's apartment above the chiropractic office.

"Come by the police station when you're done here," Bourque told him. Once the officer left, Neely put four stitches in Brackett's head, treated the ear wound and gave him a tetanus shot.

Bourque and Officer James Patton went to the apartment on Winnicunnet Road. Sheila reluctantly agreed to speak with the cops. In her recollection of events from that night, Brackett attacked her with the knife and she defended herself with the scissors. Bourque placed her under arrest, put her in the back of cruiser #308 and brought her to the police station.

While being booked on second-degree assault, Sheila asked Officer Bourque why Brackett hadn't been arrested yet. "He's still at the hospital," Bourque told her, but they would be arraigned together at the courthouse later that day.

Sheila told the patrolman that she had crashed her car the

week before and that she had suffered internal bleeding. Then she started to list her injuries inflicted by Brackett during the fight. She told Bourque she had injuries on her hand, on her neck and to her private parts. Sheila began to lift her shirt to expose herself to the cop. "That's not necessary," he said, putting a stop to it.

Bourque asked a female secretary if she would photograph Sheila's injuries. When she learned the tall, uniformed police officer would not be behind the camera, Sheila told them she was no longer interested in having her body photographed.

During the booking process, Sheila began to complain she was bleeding from the vagina. Someone offered her a sanitary napkin, but she refused. "No, I'll use toilet tissue instead."

When Sheila was taken to Hampton District for arraignment, the court staff was stunned. The LaBarre Chiropractic Clinic was right down the street from the ancient public building, and Sheila had appeared *pro se* on behalf of the business for dozens of small-claims cases. Though Sheila had a reputation in Epping as being tempestuous and promiscuous, she had always been the gold standard at the Hampton District Court: polite, prepared and professional.

Sheila began yelling at Judge Francis Frasier during Brackett's arraignment. She began talking over the judge. Frasier asked Officer Bourque to remove her and he took her to a small room downstairs.

"I'm bleeding from the vagina and they won't help me!" she called out.

Emergency personnel were called to the courthouse. Sheila refused treatment from a Hampton FD paramedic. She told the paramedic that she was just having her period. A court employee offered her a maxi-pad, which this time she accepted.

Judge Frasier was not one for improvisation in his court. He ordered Sheila held for a psychological evaluation before she would be eligible for bail. LaBarre was taken from the district court and admitted to a mental health clinic.

Three days later, Sheila returned to face Judge Frasier. Her attorney presented the court with the psychological exam declaring Sheila was not a danger to herself or others and she could assist in her own defense. James Brackett spent his birthday alone and returned the following week to Exeter Hospital to have his four stitches removed.

Sheila LaBarre and James Brackett soon worked out their differences, and Sheila worked out more than that for him. She convinced Brackett to sign over power of attorney to her. With neither party willing to cooperate, prosecutors couldn't proceed with the assault charges. A few years later, Sheila petitioned the district court to have the assault charges against Brackett and her annulled. Judge Frasier signed off on the request.

Sheila had stayed in touch with her family in Alabama through the years. She telephoned her parents and her siblings, mostly her sister Lynn. She sent money home whenever she could, especially at Christmas. Aunt Sheila rarely missed one of the kids' birthdays, always sending a check in a card.

Visits to Fort Payne were uncommon, but when she did go, Dr. LaBarre drove her. The two visited with friends or family all day and then retired to a local hotel. Just as it had when she lived there, drama continued to follow Sheila whenever she returned to her hometown.

During one trip, the normally anxious Sheila telephoned a local drug store seeking a refill on her antidepressant prescription. It was already after 9:00 on a quiet Wednesday evening with little happening at the local drug store. Pharmacist Drew McDaniel explained he'd either have to see the written script or talk to the physician before filling the prescription.

Sheila telephoned her doctor's office in Epping, had her physician paged and explained the situation. The doctor called McDaniel and prescribed thirty 5 mg tablets of an antidepressant. Sheila called the pharmacy to make sure the medicine would be ready when she arrived. The woman went to the store, showed McDaniel her driver's license and paid $18.42 for the pills.

When she and Dr. LaBarre returned to his room at the motel, Sheila read the plastic bottle and had a conniption. The label said the prescription was for "Shirley Labar," and her physician's name was also misspelled. Sheila called the pharmacist back, adamant that the prescription was supposed to be completely accurate in all aspects. McDaniel told Sheila the prescription was fine and suggested she just take the pills. The woman insisted this was a serious error. It was already quarter after eleven and McDaniel didn't have the energy to talk anymore. He hung up on her.

Sheila would not stand for such an affront. She looked up the home phone number of the drug store's owner. She woke him and explained what happened with the label. The owner could hear the customer was nervous and distraught. He promised to call the pharmacist and square everything away.

Bill LaBarre listened quietly as Sheila made all these calls. He accompanied her to the drug store. Sheila strode in and marched to the pharmacist's counter with the mislabeled bottle of pills. McDaniel, who had been waiting for her, asked for her driver's license.

"Again?" she ejaculated. "I was just in here!"

The pharmacist said he hadn't checked it the last time. Sheila reminded him that he had, and after some jousting, he admitted he had seen it on the last visit. McDaniel grumbled something about verifying that the medicine was the same. Sheila's eyes grew wide. She dumped the tablets out and counted each pill. All thirty were still there; she hadn't swallowed a single one.

McDaniel grabbed the bottle of antidepressants from Sheila's hand, slammed an envelope on the counter and slid it to the customer. Sheila opened it. It contained $18.42.

"Now get out of my store," he said.

Sheila was nonplussed. She wanted those pills back. "Did the owner tell you to do that?"

"I told him you gave me a hard time, so he told me to fill it *if I could."* Gesturing with his thumb, McDaniel said, "Now get out."

Sheila went back to the hotel and tried to call the owner, but the line was busy. She called the police to file a complaint. Now after midnight, she called the owner's home two more times. Each time, the phone rang and rang and rang. After threatening to file a civil suit and filling out a police report, Sheila left for Baptist Medical Center at 1:30 A.M. to get treatment for her nerves.

Sheila returned to Fort Payne, Alabama, in July of 2000. Lynn Noojin threw a birthday party for her younger sister at her house. Bill LaBarre pulled up at Noojin's home in his car and gave hugs to all in the Bailey clan. Sheila was thrilled to have her sisters and her mother, now widowed, around her.

Noojin was surprised by a third person who got out of the car. James Brackett had come along for the ride, rounding out an unusual threesome. Certainly, Noojin knew of Brackett; Sheila maintained all her sisterly obligations when it came to disclosing details of her love life. But this was the first time Lynn had seen Brackett in person.

This guy is really slow, she thought. *There's something just not right about him.*

Sheila reveled in the attention showered on her by her family. She was the guest of honor, sitting on the front porch as she opened all her gifts. Her mother's "Little Firecracker" received presents all stuffed in red, white and blue bags. They weren't hard to find in Alabama around the Fourth of July.

It was hot, and Bill LaBarre relaxed with a large jug of ice water. He was comfortable (if not rightly fashionable) sitting in his dark shorts, black socks and white sneakers. A gold ring adorned his pinky finger. Jimmy Brackett, on the other hand, sat and watched the party while wearing long baggy jeans and a black tee.

No one among the family brought up why the couple had become a trio, why Sheila still went by Bill's last name even after her divorce from her third husband. Noojin kept an eye on Bill LaBarre though. He got around to drinking some bottles of beer and swatted mosquitoes while the assembled crowd waited for it to get dark enough for fireworks.

He seems happy though, Noojin thought of LaBarre. He was comfortable in his own skin, comfortable enough to drive Sheila and her latest boy-toy across the country just for her birthday.

Noojin couldn't recall how it all came up in conversation that day, but Bill LaBarre mentioned that when he died the farm in Epping would go to Sheila.

Wilfred "Bill" LaBarre died in his home in Epping, New Hampshire, on December 2, 2000. Sheila told his daughter that she found the chiropractor, the love of her life, on the floor in the kitchen. That he probably had a heart attack.

There was infinite sadness in the hearts of LaBarre's daughter and her husband. There was also the thought that with his passing, so would pass from their lives this woman who was living in their family home.

They were wrong.

The funeral arrangements for Bill LaBarre were a minefield of raw nerves and tried emotions.

There was more than one version of the obituary notice. The obit first appeared in the *Portsmouth Herald*. For survivors, it listed his two wives, children and blood relatives. When the obit reappeared in some of the smaller community papers also run by the *Herald*, Sheila's name appeared. The relation and hometown of each of the loved ones was included. For Sheila, the obit showed only her name.

A funeral home in Exeter handled the services for Wilfred "Bill" LaBarre. The event was not easy. There was tension between Sheila and Dr. LaBarre's children about the arrangements. Sheila got into an argument with the funeral director about the death certificate. She wanted to be listed as Bill's wife.

The funeral director, accustomed to highly emotional familial spats, remained calm. He knew Sheila and Bill had not been married. "Do you have a marriage license?" he asked.

"No," Sheila replied, "but I have a gun and I know how to use it."

The funeral director recoiled as if being bitten by a snake.

Kelly's husband tried to pull his wife's family together as best he could for the day. Leone, Bill's first wife, was there, but Bill's beloved cousin and partner, Ed Charron, had passed away only one year before. The LaBarre siblings found comfort in each other. Sheila brought James Brackett, who was shown courtesy and sympathy by LaBarre's blood relatives. Brackett was always quiet, always submissive. It was not lost on anyone that Bill had taken one last chance on romance almost fourteen years earlier with an Alabama in-génue, only to have gotten entangled in Sheila's diabolical clutches. She had never been afraid to show off a boy-toy to Bill or anyone else.

Among LaBarre's true family, there was an unspoken, unverifiable sense that Sheila had poisoned Dr. LaBarre.

At the funeral, Sheila stood before the assembled loved ones and announced she wanted to sing an original song for her departed love. She said she had written it a week before, when her cat died. "Bill loved it," she claimed.

Oh, Jesus Christ, one neighbor later admitted to thinking as she heard the self-proclaimed country music chanteuse sing for the first time. *Sheila was awful.* And the song warbled on and on, much to the discomfort of the gathered grieving. The neighbor had been to funerals where mourners had been inconsolable, had been drunk or had otherwise done something out of pain that would have embarrassed the person lying in the casket had they been alive. She had never seen anyone make a fool of themselves in such a way before.

Dr. LaBarre is finally free of this woman, this mourner thought.

The congregation was granted a reprieve when Sheila decided not to sing an encore. Then, Sheila told all those gathered at the Epping Community Church that the great love of her life, the chiropractor, had died snapping his own neck while giving himself an adjustment.

At Sheila's urgent insistence, Dr. LaBarre was cremated.

The next few nights on the Silver Leopard Farm were unsettling for Sheila. She thought she heard noises in the woods of Red Oak Lane and coming over the meadows. She was scared. Soon after Bill LaBarre's death she applied for a pistol permit, striking fear in Chief Greg Dodge about what the woman might do with a handgun.

Bizarre behavior was now what everyone expected from Sheila LaBarre. On December 7, two days before Dr. LaBarre's funeral, she paid the funeral home in cash for all of the expenses. The day before the funeral, Sheila went on a $1700 shopping spree at a discount store in Seabrook.

Before he died, LaBarre had his daughter over to the Epping farmhouse for a horse ride. The doctor conspiratorially pointed to a hiding spot in the house where he stashed some money for her and her brother for after he passed. After the funeral, Sheila called Kelly to tell her she found the hidden cash.

"Ha, ha. How does it feel to have nothing?" Sheila taunted her before hanging up.

The cold, sweeping end to the year 2000 on Red Oak Hill Lane was bitter. James Brackett was no comfort to Sheila. He instead became the recipient of more of her barbs.

A week after the funeral, an Epping police patrol car was sent to the farm by the Rockingham County Dispatcher. Sheila reported a saddle was missing from the barn. She showed the officer a photograph of the saddle, said to be less than a year old and worth about fifteen hundred dollars.

"It was Dr. LaBarre's favorite," she said, sniffling.

The officer noticed there were five other saddles in the barn next to where the missing one had been kept. Sheila said she had been feuding with Kelly since LaBarre's death and had discovered the doctor's daughter in her house without permission earlier in the week.

Seeing no financial gain from stealing one of the saddles but not the rest, the patrolman suspected the property had been taken because of some kind of emotional attachment. He recommended Epping police detectives speak to Kelly, who later denied taking the saddle.

Wilfred "Bill" LaBarre had not been a perfect romantic match for Sheila Kaye Bailey. She had gone far beyond "gold digging." It had been obvious the woman was dealing with some deep-seated paternal issues in seeking the affection of this much older man. But what he offered was more than money or the love she didn't get from her father. Bill offered a kind of structure that kept Sheila in check. He tried to set boundaries. It didn't matter that Sheila broke them; it was only important that they were there. She would yell, but he would yell back. He tried hard to maintain normalcy for himself during all the years they lived together. There was no one else in her orbit that had the ability to stand up to her.

When Dr. LaBarre died, that structure was gone. Now Sheila LaBarre was left alone to her own devices, to her own demons, to her own wicked intentions.

PART 4

MADNESS

"Though this be madness, yet there is method in't."
—William Shakespeare, *Hamlet*

CHAPTER 27

"IMALIVE"

Sheila had already been in a funk in the months leading up to Dr. LaBarre's death in December of 2000. Her father, who had loomed so large in her young life, died in February 2000. He had previously had three heart attacks and had battled lymphatic cancer. Her brother, Jimmy Bailey, died in May of 2000 of a heart attack, hours after a cardiologist in Chattanooga gave him a clean bill of health. He lived on Greenbriar Drive, but there was also a Greenbriar Road and a Briar Lane and a Green Avenue, which confused the ambulance drivers who'd been called when he fell ill. Later Sheila became very upset with Epping Police Chief Greg Dodge about the designation of her little road as "Red Oak Hill Lane," separating it from the main road "Red Oak Lane." She was utterly convinced first responders would not be able to find the farm because of the same kind of address snafu that killed her brother.

James Brackett had lived on the farm for nearly five years before Dr. LaBarre died. The chiropractor had been a calming influence on things. And though he had held a job or two, Brackett still depended on Sheila to take care of him.

Brackett met Sheila LaBarre in the winter of 1996 through a local man who took care of cars. Brackett had been living at a campground in Raymond. Their relationship became sexual within days and he moved in with her. They divided their time between the farm and the apartment above the clinic.

Though the only time he or Sheila were arrested was after the scissor-stabbing incident, Brackett's relationship with Sheila was filled with violence that continued to escalate after Dr. LaBarre's death.

Sheila smoked marijuana every day. She was also taking a tranquilizer. She had a habit of tape-recording everything that was happening around her. Brackett was careful not to fight with her, especially if she had the tape recorder handy.

Sheila began to subscribe to telephone sex chat lines. She spent hours listening to the men who responded to her postings, sometimes talking with them all day and night about their sexual fantasies. Brackett could only hear one end of the conversations, but knew that Sheila was going into some strange territory when he heard her questions.

"Do you ever fantasize about fucking another man?" "Did you ever want to have sex with your mother?" "Do you like little boys?"

Sheila recorded these calls and later played them back. They turned her on, worked her up. After a while she looked for Brackett in the house and worked out her frustrations by having sex with him. In the middle of their sweaty romps, she talked about her fantasies.

"You know what I want, Jimmy," she told Brackett, who already knew. "I want you to fuck another man while I watch." She thought the idea would be exciting to him.

On one occasion, Sheila took her boyfriend for a ride to the beach in her pickup. An argument began and Sheila pushed Brackett from the cab while the truck was still moving. He hit the asphalt hard, landing on his face. Sheila stopped the truck and climbed out. The sight of blood on Brackett's face seemed to dissipate the rage boiling in her.

"Shhh, it'll be okay," she murmured.

Sheila gently picked the man up and helped him back into the passenger seat. The incident kindled a kind of serenity about her. She drove Brackett back to the farm and patched up his face with bandages. She fancied that she was nurturing him, nursing him back to health.

One morning, the two of them were relaxing in the bathtub on the second floor of the farmhouse. Things were peaceful between them. Sheila stood up and showed Brackett her naked body, which was ample and arousing. Then she reached over, grabbed something resting on the sink and smashed him in the face with it.

"Argh!" Brackett was taken completely by surprise. She had struck him with a long barbeque marinating brush. There were stars in his eyes and blood in his mouth. The blow had broken two front teeth, left side, upper and lower.

Sheila only laughed. "I was aiming at your throat."

Some people described James Brackett as simple-minded, but he was sharp enough to know he was walking a razor's edge living with Sheila. He tried to move in with family, but Sheila did a marvelous job of locating him and pestering whoever gave him shelter. It wasn't long before Brackett was back on the farm.

Brackett tried not to piss Sheila off. It didn't always work. When she lost her temper, she scratched his face and tried to gouge his eyes out. She slapped him and punched him to the ground. In the months following Bill LaBarre's death, Sheila began to put on weight, which she used to her advantage in close combat.

One day a neighbor, Gordon Winslow, saw Sheila and Brackett make their way down Red Oak Hill Lane. But it wasn't like they were walking together. It was more like she was walking him, like a master would walk a dog. When the pair got close enough for Winslow and his wife to hear, Sheila stopped Brackett and pointed to some animal feces on the ground. The Winslows had a working dairy farm and a healthy dog. A pile of crap was not an unlikely discovery.

"That's *yours*!" Sheila said to Brackett. "Pick it up now."

Brackett obeyed, taking the feces in his bare hands. The Winslows were baffled, shocked by the abuse. The gangly man walked on with the crap in his hands. Sheila smiled triumphantly. She had demonstrated to the three of them exactly what she could get away with.

Sheila believed that Brackett was not without his own acts of rebellion. There were things that she perceived to be tiny acts of vandalism around the farm. For her, it was impossible to tell whether they were the collateral damage of sharing a home with a developmentally disabled adult or the premeditated actions of a plan to gaslight her.

Epping Police Detective Richard Cote was summoned to the farm in June of 2002. This was before the department established the two-man policy. Sheila told the officer that Brackett had chipped bricks and removed nails from her metal roof. Cote did a quick check but found no damage and filed no charges. The detective found the entire visit to be very strange.

Later that month, Sheila called Cote to report that Brackett had stolen her car keys. "I'm sure he took them," she said. The detective received a call from Sheila a few minutes later. "Never mind. I found them."

One day Sheila discovered a rabbit had died. It was one among a countless number of rabbits roaming free on the farm. She picked it up and began to weep for the animal. As Brackett crossed her path to see what was wrong, she turned on him.

"You killed him!" she said.

Brackett protested. "I didn't. He just died."

"You murdered my rabbit!"

The man had no idea how to answer. Sheila ran at him and scratched his face, bitterly despondent over the creature's death. Brackett ran away, hiding in a quiet corner of the barn until Sheila calmed down.

Afterwards Sheila disposed of the rabbit in the same manner that she disposed of all her dead animals. She built a pyre and incinerated the body.

More mischievous incidents aggravated her. One of Sheila's favorite horses, St. Serious, had been getting out of his stall at night. There were nicks and cracks on her antique salt shakers. A picture of Sheila's horses had been cracked. Her umbrella was broken. Then walls in the house were gouged, supporting beams damaged. Sheila was certain an attempt had been made to crack her safe. Whenever questioned by Sheila, Brackett denied responsibility.

A new line of questioning came and confused Brackett. Sheila accused him of having an affair with the wife of his boss at the garage he worked at. It came about after Sheila witnessed some benign act of civility toward Brackett on the woman's part.

"You're fucking her, aren't you?" Sheila demanded.

"No I'm not." His defensive response proved insufficient to suppress the building fire. It was an odd act of jealousy from a woman who spent her days engaged in dirty talk with other men.

Enraged, Sheila grabbed a kitchen knife and chased Brackett across the pasture. Since she had stabbed him in the head with the pair of scissors all those years ago, Brackett made it practice to run if she grabbed something sharp. He was generally faster and she would become winded.

After a late-night argument, Brackett decided to get off the farm for a while, but he didn't know where to go. He got in his car and crept down the tree-lined path of Red Oak Hill Lane. He parked the car on the dirt road and decided to sleep there in the back seat.

In his dreams he could hear the rumble of Sheila's pickup truck chasing him down, always behind him, always coming after him. In the nightmare he felt trapped, like he could never get away. But on this evening in Epping, it was no dream.

Suddenly the truck smashed his little two-door car from behind, throwing Brackett into the air. Sheila jammed the stick into reverse and then, spinning the wheels, fired the truck into the car for another wallop. Brackett's car skidded on the dirt path, pushed by the larger vehicle's strength. The pickup rear-ended the sedan a third time, pushing it into a tree and totaling it. Brackett crawled out of the car and ran into the woods to hide for the night.

Determined to put an end to the insurrection, Sheila hired a polygraph examiner to come to the farm and administer a lie detector test to Brackett. He told the examiner that he couldn't read the list of questions or the release form he offered him. The polygrapher asked if Brackett let St. Serious out, whether he damaged Sheila's saltshakers or tried to break into her safe. In addition to being quizzed about the list of property damages, Sheila gave the examiner a list of women's names. Four times they went through the list, asking, "Did you fuck" this girl or that girl?

Afterwards, the examiner provided Sheila with a dot-matrix printout of the lie detector test. A couple of the answers that Brackett gave indicated deceit, including one that had to do with a sexual liaison. The examiner suggested another test be administered and Sheila agreed to put Brackett through it again.

The incessant interrogations about Brackett's interest in his boss's wife grated on him so much that he moved out of the farmhouse and into the little camper parked in the carriage house. This is what Dr. LaBarre had done when he needed to get away from Sheila. It was cool and shady under the overhang where the white camper sat rusting. For a few moments, it was as quiet and still as possible on a property shared with Sheila LaBarre.

Brackett's daydreaming inside the camper was interrupted by a *ttthwump!* on the door.

"Get out! Get out!"

Sheila was outside screaming bloody murder. Another bang came and dented the locked camper door. Brackett had no idea what was going on. Then another blow landed and split the metal skin. He got a look at what just pierced the door: an ax blade.

"Sheila, what are you doing?!" he cried. She answered with another ax blow, this time to a different wall.

"You've been fucking her, haven't you!" she shrieked.

The edge of the ax poked through the wall at a new point. Through the holes, he could see Sheila moving around, setting up a new shot. It was like Nicholson's performance in *The Shining. I'm going to die here*, Brackett thought.

While Sheila continued swinging the ax, Brackett popped open the roof vent. He squeezed through the top, scampered across the roof and jumped to the ground.

"You son of a bitch! Come back here!" she yelled.

Brackett ran. He ran straight out of the carriage house and down into the pasture. He was making for the tree line. He was hyperventilating from both fear and physical exertion. He looked behind him. Sheila was chasing him with the ax. When he hit the woods, his footfalls on the decomposing leaves and fallen twigs seemed loud as clarions in his ears. The woods were thick and the main road was far, so Sheila could not keep up and Brackett got away.

In 2003, James Brackett made another attempt to leave the Silver Leopard Farm. He set off from the Epping farm on foot in the middle of a blizzard. He was able to hitchhike to Portsmouth, where he found his way to a homeless shelter. While there, he shared a room with a man about his age with long dark hair. The men talked about their lives and about how they got to be in this Portsmouth shelter on this winter day. Brackett's new friend explained that he had come to New Hampshire from Connecticut in search of work, but couldn't find any.

Suddenly there was a presence among them. They looked up and Sheila LaBarre was standing there.

"Come on Jimmy. Let's go home." Her voice was saccharine sweet. "Who's this handsome man you're talking to?"

The man extended a hand in greeting. "My name's Mike Deloge."

Sheila sized up the good-looking guy as if he were a chocolate piece. "Jimmy, why don't we invite your new friend over for dinner tonight?"

Sheila, Brackett and Deloge all went back to the farm. The night was uneventful by LaBarre standards. After dinner, the three of them ate popcorn and watched a movie. Sheila insisted Deloge spend the night, so she made up the couch while she took Brackett back to her bedroom. She made no sexual overtures to the guest. The next morning, she drove Deloge back to the shelter in Portsmouth, but James Brackett remained on the farm.

For a short period, Sheila and Brackett managed to get along, as they had over the years so many times. But then there was one last fight. Sheila came after him. There were slaps then punches. She gouged his face. Brackett put his hands around Sheila's throat and began choking her. He always was worried that it would come to this, that the violence that had been escalating for years would finally come to a fatal end.

I don't want to do this. I don't want to be a killer and I don't want to die here.

Brackett pushed back, throwing her off him. When Sheila got her balance, she didn't move back towards Brackett to reengage. Instead she scrambled into another room. Brackett knew what Sheila kept in there.

The man burst through the front door and into new-fallen snow. He ran for the wooden gate. It had been closed as part of Sheila's ongoing mindfuck with the town plow driver. She would be calling shortly to complain that the plow had stopped at the gate and did not continue on through to the courtyard.

Brackett ran as fast as his legs would take him. His feet were making the hard crunch on the snow that old-time radio sound effects artists would create squeezing boxes of cornstarch. It was, for a precious few more seconds, the only sound in the frozen pasture.

Sheila kicked open the front door with the rattle of wood. She grunted as she cocked the hammer, the only audible warning of what was coming. Then she yanked on the trigger and a flash exploded from the muzzle.

This was not the first time Sheila had fired her .38 revolver at him. It had happened on two other occasions. However, the shot was louder than Brackett remembered it. Its echo through the empty, barren trees and off the slick mounds of snow gave the report extra drama. This time, he could hear the bullet whiz by him through the dead branches. There was another shot. Brackett did not look back. He kept on running, just praying that Sheila would not come out of the farmhouse and chase after him.

Brackett headed back to the shelter, again sharing a bunk with Michael Deloge.

"That farm was beautiful," Deloge mused. He loved the roomy farmhouse with the wood paneling and the big barn. He imagined the horses roaming the grasslands in the springtime. And he fantasized about a rich woman taking care of him.

"You can have it!" Brackett spat back as if Deloge had challenged him to a fight. "I don't ever want to go back there. She's evil. I'd rather die than go back there."

It was not long before Sheila returned to the shelter in search of James Brackett. She came during the day when he was at work. Though she couldn't find Brackett, she did not go home alone. She took Michael Deloge back to the farm with her.

Though she had seemingly moved on, Sheila LaBarre was not through with James Brackett. The man had lived on the farm for about eight years. He probably would have stayed longer or been lured back if he didn't have family in the area that cared about him.

Years after his departure from Red Oak Hill Lane, Sheila would still rant to relatives about Brackett, about how he owed her money. She filed a civil lawsuit against him in March 2006 seeking to recoup her debt. Brackett did not want to face Sheila, in court or anywhere else for that matter. The only reason he didn't have to respond to the claim and appear in Hampton District Court for the hearing in April was the fact that Sheila LaBarre had been arraigned for first-degree murder earlier that same week.

Brackett was deeply shaken by all the news coverage of Kenneth Countie's death. Reporters trying to call him would instead get the number of his father, James Brackett Sr. His parents were protective of their son and his needs. They never made the only living man with the most knowledge about Sheila LaBarre available for public comment.

It had taken James Brackett many years and many scars before he could escape Sheila LaBarre's clutches. He knew better than most what a master snake charmer she was, how sinfully manipulative she could be. He knew better than most how violent she was. There had been beatings, stabbings, shootings. She had threatened him with all sorts of things, but he distinctly remembered three separate occasions when she told him she was going kill him and he had no doubt it was about to happen. Brackett knew that the fate of Kenneth Countie could very easily have been his.

James Brackett purchased a green pickup truck and vanity license plate. It read, "IMALIVE."

CHAPTER 28

LEGAL TROUBLES

On August 17, 2006, Sheila's attorneys went to court to ask that their client be released on bail. Though a judge at a hearing in April had found there was probable cause to hold her for first-degree murder, she had yet to be indicted for the crime. Generally the state is given 90 days to indict a suspect, and Sheila had been held for 130 days. During that time, defense attorneys Jeffrey Denner and Brad Bailey had not seen any of the evidence against Sheila for the murder of Kenneth Countie. They hadn't seen any crime-scene photos, witness statements or autopsy results. The only information the Attorney General's office had provided them was the same fifteen-page arrest warrant affidavit they gave the press. However, even this document was incomplete as several sections had been redacted before release. These deleted passages referred to evidence collected about Michael Deloge.

The trial of *State of New Hampshire* v. *Sheila LaBarre,* 06-S-2506, was to be heard by Rockingham Superior Court Judge Patricia Coffey.

Defense Attorney Jeffrey Denner was courteous and helpful to Assistant Attorney General Peter Odom when they settled in at their tables before Coffey entered the courtroom. Odom had always kept his cards extremely close to the vest and, although it was not his obligation to give the defense some indication of the government's intentions, Denner was surprised that the Assistant AG had not done so.

Odom's attention for much of the morning was with the Counties and the Lodges. His eyes scanned the room like a lion's, protective of its young. The prosecutor seemed to notice whenever someone passed the grieving family sitting in the front row or tried to make contact with them.

Sheila came into the courtroom wearing a tan prison uniform but looking slightly heavier than she had on the day of her arraignment. She had chains around her ankles and a sheriff's deputy standing almost directly behind her at the defense table. "You'll have to sit on her," the transporting deputies were told by corrections workers. "She's a live wire."

The strategic move of the hearing was to force the state to show some of what it was hiding. There was obvious frustration on the part of the defense, Massachusetts lawyers who were not accustomed to courtrooms outside of the Commonwealth. Legal analysts who followed the case said the state did not have to follow the ninety-day indictment guideline in extraordinary circumstances, but noted the LaBarre team did have grounds to push for more disclosure. The idea few people could fathom was that the hearing could result in Sheila LaBarre being released from jail that day.

The only person in New Hampshire who seemed to think Sheila stood a fighting chance of getting bail was Sheila herself. She talked on the phone to her sister, Lynn Noojin. None of her other siblings was taking her collect calls from Strafford County. Before the bail hearing, Sheila talked up a storm about how much work she had to do late in the summer to get the horse farm back in shape.

"My God," Noojin told her husband after hanging up. "She really thinks she's getting out of jail this week."

In Sheila's mind, she would walk out of court and return to the farm in Epping under some sort of house arrest. But the farm was no longer hers. The judge in the probate case had vacated Dr. LaBarre's will and turned the property over to receivership. If asked, no one could really give a straight answer as to whom the property belonged at that moment.

If Sheila were to roll back down the tree-lined path of Red Oak Hill Lane, she would pass by a display of flowers and sentimental knickknacks placed at a tree just outside the old gate. Carolynn Lodge had built a shrine to Kenny on the property where he died. The mother had never been given a body and, despite an emotional and completely conventional memorial service for Kenny, Lodge considered the farm a more suitable place to remember her son.

Each weekday for several months after Sheila's arrest, Lodge drove from Massachusetts to Epping and parked her car along the isolated, wooded road. She tended flowers, placed photographs or left bags of Kenny's favorite candy at the tree. There were hockey sticks and baseball caps, garden gnomes and Pez dispensers, and other trinkets of whimsy. Ceramic houses usually found beneath Christmas trees were there as well. There was also a beautiful white angel holding a bloom, consecrating the display. Dead flowers were never removed, taken back to the harsh world outside the quiet pasture. They were instead placed to one side of the tree and allowed to compost. It was a beautiful spot in plain view of the location where Kenneth Countie met his wicked ending. But it was in front of the tree, in that one place on earth, that Carolynn Lodge felt like she could truly commune with her son.

Lodge never commented publicly on the loss of her son. She never felt she had enough strength to get through such a performance. But she wrote out her eulogy of Kenny, laminated it and tacked the tribute to the tree for all to look into the pain in her soul:

Kenny, my son, my love. I wish you were here, so I could tell you how much I love you and what a wonderful son you are. You always amazed me, at all the challenges you took in your 24 yrs. My heart aches, for I know I'll never see your smiling face again or hear your voice calling to me. Be at peace my son & rest very gently. For there'll come a day when you and I are together again.

After holding conversations in the empty woods, Lodge often crossed her arms and shuddered. Then she walked the final two hundred feet to the rotting gate and walked along the property that had been the Silver Leopard Farm. Sprigs of new growth juxtaposed the ever-visible signs of neglect on the facades of the house and barn. Lodge did not go in the house (she had been told by authorities not to do so). The doors remained sealed with lengths of blue evidence tape signaling the interior had not been disturbed since NHSP crime technicians left the home in April.

In the passing months, Carolynn Lodge cut her trips back to three times a week, then weekly. They became less frequent, but never any less emotional.

When Sheila LaBarre was escorted into courtroom number six at 9:30 A.M., she fixed a cold gaze at Carolynn Lodge. Denner and his co-counsel, Brad Bailey, had explained her role to her: to sit and listen.

"The proof is not evident in this case," Denner argued before Judge Coffey. "The few details that have been made public indicate there was a death, but nothing of murder." He indicated, in what might have been a preview of a future defense argument, that there was only enough evidence to accuse LaBarre of the crime of illegally disposing of a body.

"We need extra time to get these things done," Assistant Attorney General Peter Odom replied. He listed what had been discovered during the first 130 days of the investigation. Bone fragments from the skull, legs and arm of a male in his mid-twenties had been found. DNA testing conducted on bloodstains found on the floor where a mattress had been proved the blood belonged to Kenneth Countie. And Odom reminded the judge of Sheila's shocking admission to Chief Dodge that Kenny was "in the bag."

Judge Coffey turned to the matter of unsealing a previously closed document. She called for a brief recess while she reviewed the file.

Carolynn Lodge sat in the first row, her husband Gerald at her right side. She had heard these details before, in private consultations, in open court, in media coverage. Each time Odom described another of the gruesome details, offered another piece of the hideous puzzle, she remained stoic. Now, two minutes into the silence of this recess, Lodge broke down.

"My son. My son." She was doubled over in the seat, heaving loudly. Gerald Lodge motioned to Kenneth Countie Sr., who embraced his ex-wife in comfort. "He would call me," she whimpered.

When the proceeding resumed, Denner pointed out the unusual delays. He told the judge an indictment surely could have been obtained by now and the discovery process could begin.

"Our experts don't have access to the same material that the government does. Our investigators don't have the same access," Denner argued. "So, literally, we are in limbo."

Denner made a mistake when speaking. He mispronounced Kenneth Countie's last name, calling him "coontee" instead of "count-ee." He did it more than once. Kenny's father growled, "Countie," from the gallery in response. Denner heard this and, thinking he was correcting himself, said "coon-tee" again. This time the Lodges and Counties all shouted out the right pronunciation.

Odom explained that the forensic evidence in the case had been compromised to such a point it was taking the state's experts a long time to conduct testing. And he said the defendant's actions were the reason the physical evidence was in such poor condition.

"And one other point I'd like to make for counsel," Odom said. He looked back at the grieving families then turned his own wicked gaze to Denner. He said pointedly, "The victim's name in this case is 'Countie,' not 'coon-tee.' "

The State argued against releasing Sheila on bail while

they awaited an indictment. Odom said the defendant was a flight risk, having been captured out of state with a new hairdo and tens of thousands of dollars in her purse. Denner tried to downplay it, saying Sheila took the money to get a lawyer.

"Your Honor, my client had every intention of returning to the state of New Hampshire to answer these charges once she had retained counsel," he said. "She did not want to leave her farm, her horses, her rabbits and her other animals."

Odom stood. "Your Honor, the defendant had no intention of coming back to New Hampshire. She had made arrangements with Pam Paquin of Manchester to sell those horses, to sell those rabbits . . ."

To the surprise of all, Sheila LaBarre stood up. "Your Honor . . ." she began.

Co-counsel Brad Bailey grabbed her arm and tried to get her under control. "Sheila, sit down," he loudly whispered, panic in his voice.

"Excuse me," she said to her attorney, brushing his hand away. Denner, who was already standing, was stunned to see this move. Sheila slowly flipped her hair while she addressed the court. "Your Honor . . ."

"Ms. LaBarre," Judge Coffey interrupted. "Your attorney appears to be advising you not to speak. And I would take his advice if I were you."

Sheila sat down, objecting no further. It seemed she could sit patiently through testimony that she had tortured, killed and dismembered a man, but she couldn't take accusations she was mean to her animals.

Judge Coffey asked the State when it might be ready to take the case to trial. Odom suggested that it would need perhaps two years to complete the forensic testing. Coffey was openly skeptical. She said the standard for New Hampshire was to bring a homicide case to a jury no later than one year.

When Judge Coffey dismissed the court, Denner walked across the room to the railing in front of the gallery. Very gently, he addressed Mrs. Lodge.

"I am sorry for mispronouncing the name. It wasn't anything intentional . . ."

"That's my son!" she spat back at him.

Denner remained diplomatic, unshaken. "I know. I know he is. It's something in my mind that I kept getting the names confused . . ."

Lodge would have nothing of the gesture. "He was my son."

From the prosecutor's table Odom watched the exchange, his eyes pinched with anger.

Jeffrey Denner's firm is located on the thirty-fifth floor of 4 Longfellow Place in downtown Boston. The view from his office is breathtaking. Virtually every historical and cultural landmark in the city can be viewed from the open-air deck or the picture windows behind his massive desk: Boston Harbor, Quincy Market, the Old North Church, the Aquarium, the North End and the runways of Logan Airport. When there's no haze, you'd swear you could see on the horizon Fort Revere at the tip of Nantucket. Virtually the only attraction not visible from this perch is Fenway Park, but the Back Bay and the Fens can be seen off in the distance from the windows of lesser associates on the opposite side of the building.

It had become clear early on that Sheila LaBarre was not the wealthy woman she presented herself as when Denner first agreed to take the case. The criminal defense team watched with concern as Sheila defaulted on the civil lawsuit filed against her by the Counties and Lodges. An examination of Sheila's finances discovered that, minus Wilfred LaBarre's property, the woman had only a couple of hundred dollars in stocks to her name. Even the roughly eighty-five thousand dollars she had withdrawn from her bank account for the purpose of obtaining a lawyer were no good to her. Despite a motion to release the money, the bank check and the cash were considered physical evidence in the murder case and were kept in state custody. The woman who paraded around Epping referring to herself as a millionaire and a land baroness was now indigent.

Denner knew Sheila would not be able to pay for another law firm if his dumped her as a client. "We made a promise to her to see her through this," Denner said. "We should stick to that promise."

The team returned to court with an unusual request. Rather than watch the LaBarre case file be turned over to another set of attorneys, Denner asked if the state would pay a portion of Sheila's legal bill. The court decided to reimburse Denner Pelligreno up to fifteen thousand dollars. That came out to about sixty dollars an hour for their services, as opposed to the five hundred dollars an hour they usually charged.

Denner was not only an able defense attorney, he also had a specialty: forensic psychology.

Meanwhile, when Judge Coffey stepped down from the bench, *State* v. *Sheila LaBarre* was passed to the Honorable Tina Nadeau.

Nadeau had made her reputation as a homicide prosecutor in the Attorney General's office, prosecuting thirty cases with a high conviction ratio. She had striking good looks and an easy temperament. In 1994, she left the AG's office in favor of the governor's office. She served as legal counsel to Governor Steve Merrill, a former AG himself. At the end of Merrill's second term, he nominated Nadeau, age thirty-three, for the judiciary.

Nadeau's grandfather had been a long-time member of the state Liquor Commission and had political clout. Her father, Joseph Nadeau, was the Chief Justice of the Superior Court when she was appointed to bench. Later, Joseph Nadeau went on to sit on the state Supreme Court.

In November 2007, the next-to-last chapter in the *State* v. *LaBarre* saga commenced at the Rockingham County Courthouse. The defense moved to have much of the evidence collected at the Silver Leopard Farm thrown out. For two days, Defense Attorney Brad Bailey grilled Epping police officers and NH State Troopers about their search of the property. He argued the search was unconstitutional, as Sergeant Gallagher and Detective Cote climbed through the closed wooden gate and kicked in Sheila's back door without a warrant. He further argued that Sheila had been intimidated into consenting to the search of her home because Officer Bradley Jardis was carrying an AR-15 rifle. The whole argument seemed like a long shot, but most observers agreed that the facts of the case were too damning and the defense had no choice but to seek the bone and blood evidence be barred as "fruit from the poisoned tree."

In January 2008, Judge Nadeau released a thirty-page decision denying all of the defense's motions to have evidence suppressed. Having done all the due diligence a criminal defense attorney in a homicide case can do, Denner prepared for what had always been his endgame.

The murder trial of Sheila LaBarre was slated to begin that March. The Attorney General's office had spent the better part of two years working on the forensics and trying to determine just what happened on that farm. One month before jury selection was to begin, the defense sprang a surprise.

Sheila LaBarre returned to the county courthouse in Brentwood and changed her plea to not guilty by reason of insanity. It essentially meant that Sheila was admitting she killed Kenneth Countie, but asserting that she wasn't legally responsible for her actions.

What stunned many in the courtroom was that Sheila also admitted she had killed Michael Deloge. The state seemed to be nowhere closer to bringing charges against her in Deloge's disappearance. The evidence had been compelling, but ultimately, circumstantial.

Carolynn Lodge, Countie's mother, was in the front row of the gallery as she had been for each hearing in the case. Also sitting there was Donna Boston, Deloge's mother. During the hearing, Sheila turned to them and glared, as if her current predicament had been their faults. At separate points in the proceedings, the mothers ran from the courtroom in tears, overcome as prosecutors again detailed the gruesome trail that led to their sons' deaths.

In New Hampshire, an insanity plea is an affirmative defense, putting the burden on the defense to make its case. Judge Nadeau addressed Sheila to ask her if she was fully aware of the implications of this action.

"This means that at trial, you and your lawyers will have to prove that at the time of the murders you were legally insane and therefore not criminally responsible for your actions," the judge stated. "Do you understand that?"

"I do," Sheila LaBarre said breathlessly, melodramatically. "Because I was."

CHAPTER 29

WAITING

Sheila LaBarre waited nearly two years in county jail before her trial began. There was no long-term co-ed facility in Rockingham County, so she was kept at the Strafford County House of Corrections in Dover. She waited for more than one year to have a visitor who wasn't a lawyer.

On a Wednesday in June 2007, Sheila ate breakfast in the mess hall as she normally did and remained on her best behavior through the morning. Since she got the letter requesting the social visit, she had been careful not to run afoul of anyone and lose her privileges.

At 10 A.M., she was summoned from the pod to come to the visitors' center. As she passed the guard desk and climbed the metal stairs to the room, a corrections officer barked a warning at her. She held her tongue and politely answered, "Yes sir," before continuing on.

Sitting down in a plastic chair, Sheila eyed her visitor through a thick glass window.

I was the visitor.

Her first Christmas in jail had been very lonely for Sheila LaBarre. She received a gift from her sister, but that was the only one. There were a couple of holiday cards from Alabama. But the only one that seemed to touch her was from me, a TV reporter. It simply wished her peace in the New Year.

Incarceration is, by its nature, supposed to be tough on an individual. Sheila found her thin skin and self-proclaimed delicate nature not suited for hard time, not suited for the burdens of being a celebrity inmate.

Worse for the woman who exhibited so much control over people was the sense of helplessness she felt behind bars. Within a matter of months Sheila, who had paraded around town in a mink coat, driving an expensive car and telling anyone who'd listen that she was a millionaire, was declared indigent.

Sheila's memories of her first few weeks in jail were erased by a pharmaceutical haze. She had numerous medical complaints. She felt groggy and out-of-sorts, then agitated and aggressive. When she was first brought to the House of Corrections, the staff physicians prescribed all kinds of medication to ease her anxiety and treat her depression.

Sheila said she remembered lying on a treatment table, surrounded by doctors and her lawyers. She thought one of the attorneys showed her a document that she viewed through slit eyes.

"It's a civil lawsuit filed by the Counties," she felt the lawyer told her. "Don't worry. We'll handle it."

A memory of the encounter, whether it was real or not, remained with Sheila, because her criminal attorneys never filed a response for the civil lawsuit. They said the civil proceeding was beyond the scope of their agreement to represent her. *Had she dreamt the whole thing?* It didn't matter, for Sheila immediately defaulted on the suit worth ten million dollars.

When Sheila LaBarre was introduced into the general population of A Unit at the HOC, there was a target on her back. Prisoners have little to do besides watch TV, and everyone in lockup knew who Sheila was. Whenever a story about her came on the news, and there were many, the women in the unit turned the volume on the set all the way up so Sheila could hear it in her cell. She could hear their laughs and taunts from down the hall.

Sheila turned to the corrections officers for intervention. She insisted, demanded punishment for all the inmates who wronged her. When she didn't get satisfaction, she went up the chain of command. It was the same pattern of behavior she exhibited at the Wal-Mart store.

By and large, the corrections officers at the Strafford County House of Corrections refused to suffer Sheila's unruly behavior and outbursts easily. She had to be broken in like every other inmate, learn the rules of the jail and follow them. Sheila did not surrender quietly to the ignominy of prison life. She didn't want to be told when to wake up; she didn't want to be told when to go to bed. In order to regain some control over her situation, Sheila barked back at the guards. Her defiance only brought more trouble for herself and further isolated her from the people who would surround her for the next two years.

One winter day, Sheila sat in a chair in the common area, her eyes glazed over from watching too much television and the side effects of a tranquilizer. Some female inmates had been whispering behind her, laughing at her stoned expression. One broke away from the pack, skipped over to Sheila and punched her square in the temple.

Sheila toppled over, grabbing the side of her head. Instead of getting up and giving some back, she curled up while the inmate followed up with more smacks. The woman shoved Sheila's head into a steel table and hit her with a stool. The joyous roar that exploded from A Unit immediately got the attention of the corrections officers. Sheila remembered being hit and toppling over, but she wasn't aware whether anyone else got a lick or two in while she was down.

Sheila could escape, of course.

In her dreams, she found herself back on the farm in Epping or back in Alabama. In her mind, she was surrounded by people who knew and understood her. When she dreamed, she felt at ease and at peace.

In one dream, Sheila was walking through the green grass of her farm looking for her horses. One lay in the middle of the field, dead. Sheila wept for the animal, then prayed to God to bring the horse back to life. She put her hands on the horse and was able to revive it.

Lights and the harsh shouts of corrections officers telling her to wake up often interrupted the dreams. Disturbances in B Unit, where the men were housed, meant no sleep for any of the prisoners. Medication made Sheila perpetually groggy and she never felt like she got enough rest.

Lynn Noojin's burden to be a support system for her increasingly erratic sister grew. Lynn carried her cordless phone around the house, even out to the pool, just in case Sheila called from prison. Noojin had no contact with Sheila's attorneys, so other than the newspapers, the only updates she got on the trial were from Sheila herself. Their conversations left her jittery and sleepless. A depression would linger after each phone call.

"How's your cellmate?" Noojin asked.

"She's horrible." Sheila said her bunkmate taunted and teased her when she tried to use the open-air toilet in the middle of the cell, but would revel in the rude noises and smells she herself produced.

"What's new with your case?"

Sheila complained that Boston's best criminal attorney was screwing up her case. There was real friction there.

"I read something," Noojin offered, "that said something about a plea bargain?"

"What?!" Sheila screeched. "In my case?"

"I read that there . . ."

"There will be no plea bargain in my case," Sheila shouted through the phone, "because I DIDN'T DO ANYTHING!"

As Noojin hung up the phone, she felt faint. She stumbled into the bathroom and vomited.

The LaBarre case was taking up more and more of my time. I pored over court documents, police reports. I created a very complex flowchart of figures in the case, reminiscent of the Mafioso power pyramids created by FBI agents in the movies.

During this period, I was growing distant from my wife. I began to drink on weeknights after work. It eased, for a short while, the never-ending machinations of the case passing through my mind hour after hour, day and night. *What really happened in that farmhouse? How will they prove Sheila killed Kenny? Did Michael die on the farm, too? What happened to Wayne Ennis?*

Finally, one of the mysteries of Sheila's missing third husband was cleared up. The Jamaican national had been deported in 2002 for overstaying his work permit. At the time of the Epping search, in which some wondered if Ennis might be scattered among the loam, the man was living comfortably in St. Elizabeth, Jamaica. Credit is owed to the *Union Leader* newspaper for spending several months tracking down Sheila's ex. After a week of calling around Jamaica with a lead on Ennis's new home address, I abandoned my hunt halfway through a ten-digit dial when a co-worker tossed a copy of that morning's paper on my desk.

I had been out to the farm on several occasions, just up to the wooden gate, to shoot B-roll and to record stand-up reports on the latest in the news case. I had examined every item placed by Carolynn Lodge at the tree memorial to Kenny. Now I knew I had to go farther.

A TV reporter rarely travels alone, requiring a videographer and his one hundred pounds of gear to accompany him. Occasionally, a sick day or scheduling snafu leaves the news staff short a cameraman. I drew the short straw and was given a videographer for half a day (perhaps it's more accurate to say the *videographer* drew the short straw, having to shoot two stories with two different reporters).

One day I went to the courthouse in Brentwood and looked up the latest reports filed in the LaBarre case. After ducking out of the clerk's office, I drove to the Epping farmhouse. It was not on the way or even close. It was several miles in the other direction.

Alone on Red Oak Hill Lane for the first time, I could feel the tension rise. Its silence was not peaceful; it was unsettling. I stood at the wooden gate, gazing at the farmhouse. Suddenly behind me, above me, I heard a *crack!*

I spun but could see no one coming down the tree-lined road toward me. The only noises were my breathing and the wind in the leaves. There was another hard crack in the branches above. An acorn falling?

There was no one around. I had to have a look at the farm.

I climbed through the crossbars of the wooden gate and walked toward the farmhouse. Crushed beer cans were left in the culvert; some teens had turned the "haunted house" into a place to party, probably daring each other to go inside.

The home was dilapidated. The white paint on the walls was chipping badly. *Had they always been that bad?* I could see now the black roof was made of metal and was beginning to rust.

It was quiet and desolate and I absolutely believed it was the creepiest place on the face of the earth.

I walked to the area of the courtyard where the fire pits had been. There was no sign of scorched earth from the previous spring. Grass and buds had reclaimed the land.

I noticed blue evidence tape on the door. I wasn't going to break into anyone's house, even if it was Sheila's. The evidence marker was all the inspiration I needed to fly the straight and narrow. The window was up high, but I managed to peek in. The room was a mess inside, with papers and furniture overturned.

Walking around, I found several rabbit hutches. They had been toppled or smashed. I imagined they had been built with skillful hands by Wilfred LaBarre and now they had been left to crumble.

I made my way toward the LaBarre barn, which was two stories tall with grand red sliding wooden doors in the front and back. They were open. I peered inside. Though the horses were gone there was still tack hanging and hay scattered in clumps. I imagined the NH State Police using the shelter of the barn to analyze evidence or even take a lunch break. I stood at the open door asking myself, *Should it be open? Shouldn't someone have closed it at one point?* Then I saw something that absolutely terrified me.

On the floor of the barn was a wooden crate filled with bones.

I could see they were long, clean white bones. Not burned or cut or crushed. On top was a skull. But it wasn't round like a human's. It was more of a cone shape. I am no expert, but I presumed they were the bones from a horse. Neighbors had said that Sheila cremated her animals. I couldn't imagine that, after nearly a month of forensic analysis of the property, they would have been left behind had they been perfectly preserved human bones. Just like that thing in the corner couldn't be . . .

I paused.

My knees knocked and I felt my legs quiver.

That can't be, I thought. Perhaps I said it out loud.

To my left, lying just inside the door, was a burnt mattress. There was nothing left but a twisted metal frame with blackened springs. It had been dragged into the barn and abandoned.

Who would leave this here? Whatever forensic evidence that could have been obtained from it certainly was sealed in a laboratory in Concord right now. Surely the mattress wasn't so bulky that it couldn't have been disposed of.

Next to the burnt mattress were two items. One was a charred newspaper dated a week before Kenny's murder. The other was the partially-burned DVD case for the movie *Saw*.

I got my first letter from Sheila LaBarre two months earlier, nearly a year after she had been arrested for the murder of Kenneth Countie. Though I continued writing to her, I had had no response since I received the hand-delivered letter from Pam Paquin. Occasionally Sheila wrote letters to a newspaper when it suited her. She wrote to the *Portsmouth Herald* until they sued to have her divorce file unsealed.

In addition to the first letter Sheila wrote for Pam Paquin to deliver, Sheila wrote once more to the television station for which I was a reporter. About two weeks after her arrest, she sent a new letter to Pam Paquin, asking her again to bring in the message. She made sure to coat the letter in honey in order to sweeten up its intended courier.

"I trust you, my beautiful redhead!" Sheila wrote. "You are great and strong and so good inside, a real Northern lady."

In the letter, Sheila proclaimed her innocence, complained about her health and tried to solicit information about her animals. This time, Pam was easily talked into going on camera and claimed to still be a supporter of Sheila LaBarre. After the gruesome details of the murder were revealed at the probable cause hearing, Pam publicly turned on Sheila, saying she was crazy and Pam no longer believed her claims of innocence.

The letters I wrote to Sheila had been the suggestion of one of the news executives. None of my earlier letters got a response. I tried playing sweet, playing dumb, playing skeptical. Nothing seemed to be working for me, then success.

As the Christmas season approached, all of the reporters were encouraged to send cards to their sources and contacts. Tasteful company Christmas cards with matching envelopes were printed. Many personal notes were scribbled inside and mailed to political leaders, decision-makers, police chiefs and government spokesmen. That year I wrote one card and it was to Sheila.

The first letter addressed to me from Sheila LaBarre came to the TV station in April of 2007. The envelope was clearly labeled "Personal and confidential," but a co-worker who saw LaBarre's name on the return address opened the letter and read it aloud during a meeting. I felt humiliated.

"How's your girlfriend Sheila?" people began asking me.

I made a deal with Sheila. I wouldn't ask her if she did it

and she wouldn't have to prove to me she was innocent. I was neither a prosecutor nor a judge.

Dear Kevin,

   Thank you for all the cards and your unique way to make me feel that you can be trusted. If I agree to be interviewed tell me the questions . . .

   This county jail should be sued by me and I am planning to do that when I am set free, God willing.

   I am innocent and I am being abused here, harassed by both inmates and certain employees, and discriminated against.

   If not for my beloved sister Lynn Noojin I would have already cried myself into Heaven . . .

In her first letter, Sheila complained about the guards and the inmate who had assaulted her. She asked that I go to Pam Paquin and check up on Sheila's three rabbits. There was no need, as I already had been in touch with the Paquins. Pam had told me that the pregnant rabbit, Sapphire, had died and she gave away the other two along with the hutch.

I wrote to Sheila, explaining what happened. She was terribly upset that Sapphire was dead and wanted to know where the other rabbits were. More so than Little Satin, she was mostly concerned about her alpha male Snooky, or as she formally referred to him, "Snookster Rydel LaBarre."

The letters continued. I had hoped for a television interview with the defendant, hoped her attorney made it clear he would not allow one before trial. But I could not, would not, give up. I had to learn the whole truth. Never had I been so embedded in investigating a case or studying the mind and motivation of an alleged killer. I strived to maintain a good relationship with Sheila so she would open up and tell me all she had hidden. It seemed to be working. In one letter she wrote, "I only trust you right now. Just you."

Sheila tried her flattery on me. Dozens of people told me she was a serpent, but I needed to learn it myself.

Dear Kevin,

I saw you on television recently. I want to tell you that you looked so polished, so professional . . . you should be the anchor . . .

I'm so depressed about Snooky and Little Satin . . . I'm begging you to get Snooky to someone loving who will keep him for me . . .

Now the day for our meeting had come. When Sheila sat down and picked up the phone on the other side of the glass, she flashed me a big smile. She was absolutely charming and seemed genuinely thrilled to have a visitor.

I was alone. No cameras were allowed, and this wasn't an on-the-record interview. One could say it was simply a visit, if there had been anything simple for me about it. I *had* to meet her face-to-face, this woman who indirectly turned my life upside-down.

I repeated that she didn't have to tell me she was innocent. That was bullshit; I *knew* she had killed. I knew she had butchered two men in an unimaginable way. Yet I was drawn to her. At the same time, I was afraid of her. Nevertheless, I needed to understand her. I was perversely fascinated by her.

She was coquettish as we spoke for one hour, mostly about Bill LaBarre, Lynn Noojin and the old farmer Dan Harvey. I'm sure whatever law enforcement official who listened in was bored to tears.

Sheila said she loved Bill LaBarre until the day he died. She laughed that he had made fun of her because she was one-eighth Indian and often asked her to do a rain dance when company visited. Only once in the conversation did she show any emotion. I brought up her horses and her voice cracked.

"I miss my rabbits."

"I bet you do," I told her.

"Do you think they're at the SPCA?"

"I don't know. Perhaps."

"You know I'm going to sue the SPCA to get my animals back. My horses."

"I can't give you legal advice," I said. "But you should wait until all this other stuff is complete. You don't have a home right now and a place to take care of the animals. Once your trial's over, you'll have better standing."

She demurred and smiled brightly. "Thank you."

She is *charming,* I concluded.

"You have to do me a favor," she said.

"What?"

"You must find my rabbits. You must track them down."

"Oh, I don't know if can find them."

"You must. You must."

I wondered if this would be the only time I'd ever speak to her. If I failed her, if I disappointed her like so many other men in her life had done, would she still write and allow me jailhouse visits? What was I willing to do to search out the truth?

"Please, Kevin."

I was left with one impression: *I can absolutely see how she could charm her way into someone's life and how she could use those charms to manipulate the weak-minded.*

I was not her lover. I was not developmentally disabled. I was not financially dependent on her. But, dammit, Sheila LaBarre always found a way to back a man into a corner.

CHAPTER 30

MAKING THE CASE

The trial for *State of New Hampshire* v. *Sheila LaBarre* was scheduled to begin in mid-May 2008 after more than a week of voir dire with potential jury members. More than two hundred people were brought in and lawyers on both sides were asked to sift through the potential jurors' backgrounds and mindsets to find people who were impartial and uninfluenced.

In New Hampshire, an insanity plea is an affirmative defense. That meant not only would the burden of proof be on the defense team, but they would also present their case first, followed by the State. For those who regularly follow murder trials, the structure seemed, in a word, crazy.

Jeffrey Denner warned potential jurors that the case would deal with "fairly ugly issues," such as "sadomasochistic sex, allegations of pedophilia and incest." On the first day, six jurors were chosen of the eighteen needed to make up the panel and alternates. The last person quizzed that day admitted to Brad Bailey that he didn't like defense attorneys.

"Why not?" the defense attorney asked.

"I don't know," he said. "I just know I don't like defense attorneys."

The line caused all the spectators to laugh. Even Sheila LaBarre laughed.

One attorney who would not be in the courtroom was Peter Odom. The Assistant Attorney General had done a lot of soul-searching in the months that followed the end of his marriage. Odom was a litigator on top of his game. There were only a half-dozen homicide prosecutors in the state and he had risen to the peak of their ranks. But the state pays horribly little for the services of such skillful attorneys. Odom wondered whether his kids would have to support him if his state pension didn't.

Odom took a job in the district attorney's office in Fulton County, Georgia. Atlanta seemed a long way from New England, but his teenagers liked making the trip and enjoyed the city. A musician himself, Odom found the nightlife was a bonus.

The hardest part of leaving the AG's office was telling Carolynn Lodge. Odom insisted on doing it himself. She was crushed; she always felt that Kenny was in good hands when Peter Odom entered the courtroom. He assured her that many of his colleagues had been working on the case and the prosecution was in good hands.

After Odom left, the LaBarre case was moved to Kirsten Wilson and finally to a trio of prosecutors. Among them was Jane Young, a senior assistant Attorney General for two decades. Young rose through the ranks prosecuting narcotics dealers as part of the AG's Drug Task Force and had great success doing it. For a brief time, she served as the interim Hillsborough County Attorney while she helped resolve a ballot dispute between the candidates.

Young was joined on the case by Anne Rice. She had great experience prosecuting murder cases, having handled such cases for two decades. Rice was also adept at arguing civil cases, representing the State in lawsuits in front of the State Supreme Court.

The junior prosecutor among them was James Boffetti. A Massachusetts native, Boffetti had been ordained a Roman Catholic priest. This man of the cloth continued his schooling and studied law. In 1993, Boffetti became a public defender and eventually headed up the office. Though he wore a suit and tie to court, Father Boffetti viewed his job as doing Christ's work, offering service to the needy and promoting social justice.

In subsequent years, Boffetti followed the well-worn path out of the ministry. He left his order, the Confraternity of Holy Fathers. Though he was never laicized, he is prohibited from performing the sacraments. Boffetti joined the AG's office after Sheila LaBarre had already been arrested, but was quickly up to speed on the case.

After six days of jury selection, the lawyers for both sides were ready to make their opening statements. The first order of business would occur later that day when the jury was to go on a viewing of certain sites, including the Epping Wal-Mart and the LaBarre property. The defendant said that she wanted to go with the jurors to see the farm. Instead of wearing shackles and chains, Judge Nadeau gave Sheila the option to wear a stun-belt. The idea both intrigued and disturbed her.

"Well, how would it work?"

Nadeau explained the belt would be worn under Sheila's jacket and would be inactive so long as she obeyed orders. But if she were to attempt to escape, the deputies could activate a charge to subdue her.

"Only as long as someone doesn't shock me arbitrarily," Sheila countered, to which the judge assured her no one would.

The Counties and Lodges were nearly late for court that morning. They had been at the farm removing the memorial to Kenny. The judge granted the defense's motion to have the items taken down, just for the day, so as not to prejudice the jurors who would be going there. Several cousins and friends joined the parents in court. There was one addition to the group, the mother of Michael Deloge.

A convoy of school buses and private cars queued up outside the Rockingham County Courthouse to make the trip from Brentwood up Route 125 to Epping. As the caravan made its way through the small town, several people gathered at the side of the road in anticipation of the jury's passing. The townsfolk pointed to a noose they had strung up to a mailbox as the defendant and her motorcade passed by.

When they got to the farm, the jurors were allowed to wander a bit in the front yard. No one was permitted in the farmhouse, as it had been condemned and deemed too dangerous to let anyone walk around inside. The prosecution wanted the panel to get a sense of isolation and seclusion the 115 acres provided.

Sheila did not wear the stun-belt. She was secured in shackles, but was not difficult for the deputies to handle. She mostly stood impassively, taking in the view. She was already aware that the house was in disrepair, that vandals had smashed all the windows on her vehicles, that no one was keeping up the place. When the view was over, Sheila seemed reluctant to go. Tears started to roll down her cheeks, the first time the defendant had shown any emotion in the case.

She knew, no matter what the verdict, that she would never see her beloved farm again.

The first opening statement was to be given by the defense and the job for setting the tone for the trial was thrown to Brad Bailey. A former homicide prosecutor in Manhattan and Massachusetts, Bailey had plenty of quality time at both tables. The chief criminal defense attorney of the firm Denner Pellegrino, he was tall, bearded and had the aura of an everyman. Sheila's relationship with her attorneys ran hot-and-cold, but she was tickled to have a lawyer who shared her maiden name.

Bailey began by reminding the jury that Sheila LaBarre was not contesting the two murders in the case. The sole question would be whether she was legally insane at the time of each murder.

"There is no legal definition of insanity in New Hampshire," he said. The law left it to the jury to decide for itself what "insane" was. Bailey said, "You will know it when you see it. And you will see it. It won't even be close. It will be staring right back at you, all you need to do is look."

Bailey painted a picture of a woman who spent the prior fifteen years tape-recording all of her conversations, who entered voraciously into relationships with the weak and debilitated. He asked the jury to think of her as a woman who thought all the men in her life were child molesters, who thought there were people living in her woods, who forced men to admit things that never happened. He asked them to imagine a woman who believed she died and was sent back to earth by God to fulfill a mission as "an avenging angel." That here was a woman who honestly believed her two victims came to her in a dream and thanked her for killing them.

Bailey described the first explanation from Sheila about the deaths of Countie and Deloge. He said Sheila had told psychologists she struck Michael Deloge in the head with a chain and that Kenneth Countie died after hitting his head on the bathtub during an argument. To further underline her lost grip on reality, Bailey said Sheila told them an alternate story about Countie's death: that she had smashed him in the head with a sledgehammer while he slept.

The defense also conceded that Sheila's claims that Countie and Deloge were child molesters had no basis in fact.

Prosecutor Anne Rice described the defendant differently. She said the State's position was that Sheila LaBarre had a personality disorder, that among the things she suffered from was paraphilia, or intense hypersexuality. They declared that she might have a mental illness, but she was far from insane. Rice said Sheila knew what she was doing and knew it was wrong.

"Violent, manipulative, seductive, controlling," was how Rice laid it out. "Witnesses will tell you she was always in control, intelligent and articulate, that she always knew what she was doing."

Almost on cue, Sheila interrupted the prosecutor by loudly ripping a piece of paper from a legal pad, making some notes, then sticking them in her pocket.

Although there was no burden on the State to prove the elements of either murder, Rice said Kenny Countie had been killed on either March 21 or 22 in 2006 and that Michael Deloge had been murdered sometime in the fall of 2005, only six months before Kenny.

The first witness was Lynn Noojin. Lynn had spent three days in New Hampshire in preparation for her trial testimony. We made dinner plans for the first night, but when I arrived at her hotel, she was still meeting with Denner and Bailey, revealing all the family secrets that had been buried for years. We rescheduled. I made a mental note of the fact that Sheila's legal team had put Lynn up in the same Manchester hotel that Sheila had been staying at when she gave the state police the slip and hitchhiked her way to Boston.

When Lynn walked into courtroom two, it was the first time in over three years that the sisters had seen each other. Noojin had begged the attorneys to let her visit with Sheila even briefly, but Denner and Bailey thought it would be far too emotional for their client.

Brad Bailey began the questioning by showing Noojin two photos of Sheila from the 1980s. "Aw, that's my baby girl Sheila," Noojin said, smiling, in what may have been the first and only true public expression of endearment for the defendant. Then Bailey offered another photo taken during Sheila's incarceration, showing how her youthful beauty had been ravaged. Looking at it, Noojin reached for a tissue and wiped her eyes.

Noojin said Sheila's personality took a drastic decline after Dr. LaBarre died. The last time they'd seen each other was in 2005 at the funeral of their brother Kenneth. Normally a very elegant dresser, Sheila arrived in blue jeans and bleached blonde hair. She had gained a lot of weight. At the graveside, her mother whispered something to her about the way she looked. Sheila yelled loudly and began an argument in front of her brother's casket, much to the dismay of the grieving.

At this point in her testimony, Noojin became tense, but

stiffened with resolve to discuss something she had never said aloud before. She said she recalled being four years old and entering her parents' bedroom in the middle of the day. Her memory was that Manuel and Ruby were lying there with infant Sheila between them. The father had done something with his hand that caused the mother to scoop the baby up and take her from the bed. "Aw, Man'yel!" Ruby shouted in disgust. According to her testimony, four-year-old Lynn presumed Daddy had done something sexual to the baby.

She knew, she said, because he had done those things to her, too.

Noojin also described times when her father had brought home strange men he called "uncles," who ran their hands up young Sheila's dresses. When this happened, Noojin fetched her mother, who would come out of the kitchen to rescue the child from the groping, but Ruby Bailey never did anything to stop it.

After her first day of testimony, with daylight fading, Lynn and her sister-in-law, who'd made the trip with Lynn for support, took their rented bright-yellow car to the Epping farm. Lynn said she needed to see things for herself. Just before they made it to the farm's wooden gate, Lynn noticed a group of people gathered at a tree re-assembling the monument to Kenny. "Stop, stop!" Lynn said to her sister-in-law who was behind the wheel. She warned Lynn not to get out of the car, but Lynn did anyway.

"Are you Mrs. Countie?" she asked one of the women.

"No, she is." She pointed to a woman kneeling down, arranging ceramic figurines. The woman stood and turned and looked into a face that looked eerily like her son's killer.

"Mrs. Countie, I'm Lynn Noojin." Carolynn Lodge froze, became ramrod-straight. It was the first day of the trial and she wasn't completely sure what the protocol on all this was. They'd recessed for the day with Lynn still on the stand, having just revealed the grotesque details of the childhood abuse she and Sheila had suffered at the hands of their father. Carolynn later said she had felt like a zombie.

Lynn pressed ahead. "I just want you to know . . . that I

am *so sorry.*" There was a bit more that trickled forth, but it seemed not to break the veneer of the grieving mother.

The women looked at each other in silence. No one in the crowd breathed. Feeling the incredible weight of the moment, Lynn stumbled back one step, her knees giving out. At that moment, Carolynn Lodge rushed forward and threw her arms around Sheila's sister and hugged her. The two rocked in the embrace and wept.

Afterwards, Lynn continued to the farm and—despite warnings from the police not to—opened the door of the farmhouse and went inside. She walked around looking for a set of pearls that had belonged to her grandmother that Sheila had taken to New Hampshire. She managed to find the empty box, but the necklace had been taken by vandals.

The only mementos she salvaged were photographs. She discovered many old pictures of Dr. LaBarre and his family. She even found the chiropractor's diploma. She left a message for Kelly Norris, told her what she had and urged her to get in touch. When her half-week in New Hampshire was over, she gave me the photos and asked if I would give them to the LaBarre children.

Going first gave the defense a strategic advantage in that they were able to present evidence before the State did. And as such, they were able to blunt its impact or to position it as further proof of their client's insanity.

State police had recovered over three hundred cassette tapes from the LaBarre farm. Totaling over one thousand hours of audio, a team of investigators listened to and catalogued it all. There were arguments, rants, songs and sex talk mixed in with hours of tedium. Ironically the tape they had originally been looking for, the one that Sheila played for Sergeant Gallagher, was never found.

A state police investigator testified that Sheila recorded her telephone calls to phone services and engaged men in all types of abhorrent sexual conversation. She asked them about homosexual fantasies, about whether they liked to sleep with children or whether they were abused themselves. She told

one man that she was a black widow and she could devour
him without mating. The defense said it demonstrated her
pattern of insane behavior.

On cross-examination by the State, prosecutors asked the
investigator about how Sheila had selected which men to
chat with. The investigator said Sheila would play back all
of the messages left for her. If the man sounded self-assured
or aggressive, Sheila deleted the call and dismissively said,
"Yeah, right." If the man sounded passive or insecure, she
listened to the entire message, then returned the call. It
seemed her telephone connection with someone like Kenny
Countie was by design, not by accident.

Defense Attorney Denner elected to play several hours of
Sheila's tapes with a live running commentary by defense
psychologist Malcolm Rogers. One of the first tapes played
was an interrogation of Michael Deloge by Sheila. Deloge
sounded hollow, giving stunted one-word answers to questions like whether his mother was a prostitute or whether he
abused Sheila's animals. At the end, Sheila made a speech
about how Deloge had killed some of her rabbits. Hearing
this in open court, the defendant leaned over the table and
collapsed. Judge Nadeau adjourned court for the day and
Sheila was escorted out of the courtroom to compose
herself.

The audiotapes went on for five days. In them, Sheila
hinted that the men she lived with were dangerous and she
might have to kill them in self-defense. She thought Countie
was trying to kill the President, at one point taking pains to
explain she had him at gunpoint and under citizen's arrest.

"He has tried to hurt me so many times," Sheila said of
Kenneth Countie on one tape. "God forgive me, but if he
touches me again, I will kill him in self-defense. God protect
me from this demon! He is evil and vile."

On one day, Sheila listened darkly to the tapes. The following day, she came to court with a frisky ponytail in her
hair and laughed when recordings of fights between her and
James Brackett were played.

"You're crazy, you know that!" Brackett shouted.

"Hot coffee! Hot coffee!" was Sheila's recorded response, apropos of nothing. The defendant heaved a pleasant sigh, as if the tape entertained her.

Four days into the tapes, Kenneth Countie's voice was finally heard. His mother steeled herself to listen; his father stepped outside the courtroom, unable to bear the pain. It was reminiscent of the frantic, vomiting interrogation that Sergeant Gallagher had heard.

"Are you a pedophile?" Sheila asked Kenny.

"Yes."

"Is Carolynn Lodge evil?"

"Yes."

Lodge, sitting dutifully in the front row, burst into tears when Sheila cajoled her son into saying he hated his mother. The defendant's rage at Carolynn Lodge was evidently brought on by Carolynn's repeated attempts to get police to check up on Kenny. Attorneys played tapes of Sheila rambling on to social workers in an attempt to report Lodge as a child molester. She went on about how she wished Kenny's mother would be murdered.

"Don't fuck with Sheila LaBarre!" she could be heard telling Kenny in a recording. "Your mother is going to learn real quick not to fuck with me. I will torture her."

Dr. Rogers testified that the tapes gave them a fifteen-year snapshot of Sheila's descent into madness. He said she projected her own childhood, her own traumas, her own rage on the people around her.

As the trial continued, things shifted from the dreadful theater-of-the-mind audio recordings to a large projection screen set up in court. The defense played videotapes of Sheila's interrogations. The aim was to demonstrate Sheila's disconnect with the reality around her.

Jurors avidly watched the first tape, seeing Sheila sitting in the small conference room at the Epping Police Department with a rabbit on her lap. For five hours, Sergeant Richard Mitchell and Trooper Jill Rockey quizzed Sheila about where "Adam" might be. On screen she was polite, but evasive. She spent more time stroking the bunny than giving answers. At one point, the rabbit urinated on her lap, but Sheila didn't pay it any mind. She simply brushed away the wetness and continued her conversation, cooing and laughing.

The defense offered a second video interrogation. This one took place the night that Pam and Sandy had led authorities to Sheila. On the tape, State Police Sergeant Bob Estabrook and Epping Chief Greg Dodge quizzed Sheila, providing the most dramatic evidence in the trial to date.

On this second tape, jurors saw Dodge and Estabrook calmly listening to Sheila's descriptions of life on her farm, the trouble with "Adam" and the mystery of how the boy disappeared from the farm. Unlike the dynamic when Rockey and Mitchell questioned Sheila, a good cop/bad cop technique, Dodge and Estabrook let Sheila talk herself into a corner, then pounced.

"I don't know where Adam is. That's the truth."

"You are a liar," Estabrook yelled at her. "It is not the truth!"

"It is the truth!" She slammed her hand down on the table.

"The chief asked you, 'Where's Kenny?' 'He's in that bag.' That's what you said. There's no way around it. You killed this kid!"

"I did not say . . ."

Estabrook pressed, his voice took on a razor's edge. "You killed this kid and you destroyed evidence by burning the bed. You destroyed evidence by burning his body in the pit!"

"No," Sheila calmly shook her head at Estabrook. "I didn't burn anybody."

"Who did?!" the sergeant snapped back.

"I don't know." She punctuated each word, as if to say her answer was final and would not change.

"Who did it? If you didn't do it, who did?"

"I don't know."

"Of course you know," Estabrook said. "You did it! Absolutely!"

"No."

"You're a liar."

"I am NOT a liar." Sheila pounded her fist.

"You absolutely are a liar."

Dodge sat with his arms folded across his chest, holding off getting his own licks in so as to not disrupt Estabrook's flow. Watching from an adjacent room, Peter Odom marveled at the sergeant's performance.

"Are we going to find blood in your house?" Estabrook asked.

"I don't know," Sheila responded.

"Are we going to find blood in the area where, oh I don't know, Adam, or Kenny . . ." By this time Estabrook had thrown his arms in the air in amazement, ". . . or all the different names you have for this poor kid . . . where he might have been lying down or sleeping? Are we going to find blood in the general area?"

"I don't know."

"Of course you know. You're a liar."

Sheila said nothing.

"You say you don't remember. That's a lie. You do remember! What you don't want to know is what drove you to that point to kill that kid?"

"I did not kill Kenny."

"Then what did you do with him?"

"He left the farm."

"That's a lie. You killed him."

"I did not kill Kenny!" Sheila pleaded.

"You killed Adam. You killed Kenny," Estabrook offered the semantics of the names. "Which one did you kill?"

Sheila unscrewed the cap on her diet soda bottle again. "I didn't kill anyone."

Chief Dodge let Estabrook do most of the interrogation, but when the state police detective grew tired of Sheila's denials, Dodge jumped in with a new line of reasoning.

"When we got to your house, you were packing your bags, putting your rabbits aside, your favorite rabbits put aside. All the rest were going to burn to the ground. You were taking the things that you like most with you." Dodge thought he had come up with the answer. "You were leaving, weren't you?"

Sheila laughed at this. She flung her head back and used two hands to flip her bleached blonde hair.

"No I wasn't."

"Yes you were," Dodge continued. "You were checking out. You had your bunny with you. The same bunny you brought in here. That's your child. You wanted it with you. And you got caught at the house before you could leave."

"'Shoot me, Chief. Shoot me,'" Estabrook repeated for her.

"None of this makes sense!" Frustrated, Dodge threw all of his papers on the floor.

"You wanted to die," Estabrook continued, anger heating his voice. "You know why you wanted to die? You killed him. He was in that bag."

"We were there to help you." Dodge stood up and pointed a finger in the suspect's face. "We got nothing from you. Except you tell us he's in the bag."

After a week of dramatic show-and-tells, prosecutor James Boffetti finally had a chance to cross-examine the defense psychologist. He asked why, if Sheila really thought of herself as an "avenging angel," wouldn't she have readily admitted her crimes? Why would she take so many steps to conceal her actions?

"Her mind is certainly very complicated," Dr. Rogers said.

Boffetti introduced a different audiotape, this one dating back to before Dr. LaBarre died and Sheila's mental decline supposedly began. On the recording, Sheila was in a stew over the clinic's secretary. She was screaming at the well-loved chiropractor. At one point, Ed Charron took the phone and suggested the police might get involved. Sheila went into a horrible rage.

"I suggest you talk to your cousin and let him know who exactly has the power," she shrieked at Dr. LaBarre. "If he goes and gets outside help, I'll burn everything!"

Dr. LaBarre stood firm and refused to yield. That sent Sheila into a screaming fit. "I'll cut your hands off!" she yelled at him. "Hey Bill! If you want to live, you better leave me alone! I'll come back tonight and kill a goddamn horse! You don't have the power you think you have! I want you to hold your hands up in front of you and look at them! And I want you to decide if you want to live or die!"

Even with the overwhelming evidence of past violence, the tape was jarring. Boffetti turned to the witness and asked if perhaps Sheila LaBarre wasn't insane. He suggested that instead, she just might be really mean.

CHAPTER 31

VENGEANCE IS MINE

I remember watching the scene in the movie *Capote* in which Truman Capote is drunk at the bar during the premier of Harper Lee's *To Kill a Mockingbird*. The author is so self-absorbed, so inconsolable about the Clutter case, that he can't enjoy his friend's success. When I watched that scene, I wondered if there would ever be a story so seductive that I would find myself in the same place.

By the time the Sheila LaBarre insanity case came to trial, I was no longer a television reporter. I had gone too far, done too much, found myself in places I never thought I'd be. My marriage was over. I had gained weight. My clean-cut TV look was replaced with facial hair and wrinkled shirts. I had lost my way.

Brad Bailey resumed control of the defense's case and called a series of Epping police officers to the stand. He questioned them about years' worth of contacts with Sheila LaBarre, more than one hundred calls dispatched to her property and why they never sought to have her committed. Didn't they find her actions "crazy"? It was the hardest thing *not* to use that word, a word that gets thrown around too often to describe people and actions we don't understand. In law enforcement it seems women are labeled "crazy" first and foremost. However, it takes a lot for a man to be described as crazy, disturbed, nuts or insane.

"I'd describe it as Sheila being Sheila," Chief Greg Dodge testified.

Bailey spent some extra time with Epping Detective Richard Cote. He was a big man, broad-shouldered, but had soft features. The defense attorney had the detective recount his encounter in Wal-Mart with Sheila and the sorely beaten Kenny Countie.

"Based on what you had heard, and based on what you had known . . . did you make any attempt to separate him from Ms. LaBarre?"

"No," Cote responded.

"Why not?" Bailey asked the question that had been on the minds of many people who were following the case.

Cote paused before answering. " 'Cause I didn't."

"Do you regret that decision, sir?"

Cote paused and looked down at his hands. The weight of that night, his own internal struggle about not saving Countie, was clear on his face. It was not the first time he had pondered the question. He said nothing, but nodded his head. *Yes, I do regret that decision.*

"Objection, Your Honor!" Senior Assistant Attorney General Anne Rice said.

Before Judge Nadeau could rule, Bailey dismissed the witness. "Nothing further. Thank you, Detective."

On May 29, 2008, Sheila LaBarre came to court with her hair in braids. She clearly was looking to make a good impression on someone. Perhaps it was on her former boyfriend James Brackett, who had been called in as a reluctant defense witness.

"I had to get out of there before she killed me," Brackett testified. "After I saw the news, I thought I was lucky to be alive. That could have been me." With that, the defendant laughed.

Bailey grilled Brackett about all of his and Sheila's violent encounters. He asked if Sheila ever threatened him. Brackett said that Sheila told him if she wanted to get rid of him, she'd put him in the swamp behind the house. Or she'd take him to Jamaica and throw him to the crocodiles. Or she'd put him in a snake pit in Alabama. Again, Sheila laughed while listening to Brackett repeat these threats.

"Didn't you think she was crazy?" Bailey asked.

"No, that's not what I thought," Brackett responded. "Evil, maybe."

On cross-examination by the State, Brackett was asked about the day he and Sheila had been arraigned in Hampton District Court for the scissor attack. Sheila had been removed from the courtroom, raving that she was "bleeding from the vagina." Brackett testified that Sheila later told him she was "playing the system."

Bailey struck back on redirect. "When did you remember that detail?"

"I remembered it last night before I came here," he said.

"Did the prosecution put you up to saying that?" Brackett didn't answer right away, his eyes darting around the courtroom. "Don't look at the prosecutor's table. Just answer my question."

Brackett denied that anyone put him up to saying that.

The defense brought in a series of people to relate tales of Sheila's odd behavior. One was a plumber who was escorted into the home by Michael Deloge. The plumber had to shuffle through a front room that was so full of rabbits he couldn't pick up his feet.

"The faucet is leaky," Sheila told the workman. He made his way to the kitchen sink and opened the cabinet. The plumber was shocked by what he saw underneath.

"I think I see the problem."

There were no pipes under the sink. It wasn't clear what happened to the plumbing, but it simply wasn't there. Any water that went down the drain poured into the cabinet below, spilling out onto the floor.

"No, no," Sheila insisted. "It's underneath. You have to

look way underneath." She was trying to convince the plumber that the sink had some other problem. She was standing over him, almost forcing him under the sink like a witch in a gingerbread house would force a child into an oven. The plumber, put off by her belligerent manner, decided he wanted to get out of there—and the fastest way any plumber gets thrown out of a house is to give an outrageous quote.

"It's going to cost twelve hundred dollars," he said.

"No, no. You'll do it for free."

The plumber said no, and that he was going to leave. Sheila insisted he stay and do it for free. She put her hand out to stop him.

"Please don't touch me," he said to Sheila.

She grabbed him again. "You're not going anywhere."

"I will go," he said. "And if you touch me again, I will kill you."

When the plumber got in his truck, he found that Sheila had ordered Deloge to close the wooden gate. The plumber turned the key and revved the engine. When it was clear he would drive right through the gate, Sheila yelled for Deloge to open it and let him pass.

The plumber testified that when he reported the incident to an Epping policeman, the officer laughed.

Several of Sheila's former tenants were called to testify. One said the furnace in the Somersworth apartment broke down in November of 2005, around the time prosecutors said Sheila murdered Michael Deloge. Sheila told them she had no money to fix it, so the tenants ran up their electric bill using space heaters. They refused to pay their rent unless Sheila split the difference on the power bill. Sheila refused, going on tirades, leaving screaming messages on their answering machine every day. She stopped by on Christmas Eve and Christmas Day, explaining she cared about the family's children, but resumed the harassment on December 26.

The family decided to move out. One afternoon, they came home to find all of their pet fish dead. Someone had poured bleach in the tank. All the burners on the stove had been turned on and the oven door left open. Furniture had been overturned and a glass door was broken. They discovered their new mattress upstairs smeared in blood, presumably from Sheila's menses.

Written on the wall was the phrase, "Vengeance is mine sayeth the Lord."

The final defense witness was Dr. Roger Gray, an expert in forensic psychology. Gray had worked with Jeffrey Denner on several other cases, although he rarely testified in them.

Gray had interviewed Sheila four times. He described her childhood as having been damaged by an alcoholic, abusive father and an indifferent mother.

"Her real world was populated with people who could use her however they wanted and wouldn't protect her. It was populated with a real threat of death."

At that piece of testimony, Sheila broke down in a fit of sobs. The judge ordered a recess and the defendant slumped against the wall on her way out of the courtroom.

When testimony resumed, Gray said, "The molestation, I don't think we know the extent of it. My hunch is that it was *very* extensive."

Gray was slightly unpolished, but it only made him more conversational, more powerful. He dutifully answered all of Denner's questions, but when he needed to make an important point, the doctor spun around, faced the jury panel and spoke to them directly. At times, he reclined in the chair, his back to Judge Nadeau and spoke casually to the men and women trying to decide whether LaBarre was legally crazy.

Dr. Gray reported that during his examination of the defendant, Sheila told him one of the good things about being in jail was that she was learning about her family. Lynn Noojin never told Sheila that she too had been molested, which Gray noted was not unusual in families when one of the parents is telling the children to keep the abuse a secret.

Gray said Sheila's delusional world was populated by the same people: people who would molest you, people who would rape you, homosexuals, pedophiles, people who would kill you. He said the defendant was screaming out for help in her own psychotic way. He said Sheila's trip to Wal-Mart with the battered and bruised Kenneth Countie was a cry for help, a plea for someone to stop her, a mental test to see how far she could push it.

Gray said Sheila never mastered trust.

As a child, no one paid attention to young Sheila. As an adult, she was looking for a loving father. "So she chooses a man thirty-two years her senior," Gray said. "And at least initially there's a good relationship. But she's delusional. She's psychotic. Her world is so populated with these demons. Everybody becomes tainted. Everybody becomes an actor in her internal play." So Sheila, the firecracker, discovered new ways to get attention.

When discussing her father, Sheila could speak about her own horror of running away in fear of Manuel Bailey, then revert to telling Dr. Gray what a wonderful man he had been.

The psychologist told the court that Sheila looked forward to meeting her father in Heaven. "They will not only be reconciled, but they will be totally happy. Because there will be no memory of the past. There will be no future. There will only be a wonderful, loving *now*."

At that point, attorney Brad Bailey, sitting next to this client at the defense table, noticed over the edge of his glasses that Sheila was again weeping and wiping her eyes.

Gray said Sheila had a vision that, after his death, Kenneth Countie returned to her and said, "It will all be fine." She had dreams that both Countie and Deloge came and thanked her for killing them, because they had been pedophiles.

"I think she is giving a phenomenal and horrible window into what it would be like to be totally crazy."

The courtroom was hushed and all eyes on Gray as he finished his testimony by telling the jury responsible for deciding whether or not she was crazy that Sheila LaBarre was the most profoundly disturbed individual he had ever met.

CHAPTER 32

SHEILA SPEAKS

The prosecution began their case on June 4, 2008. First they presented some of the bone evidence that technicians spent months trying to decipher. Dr. Marcella Sorg testified about the bone fragments recovered from Sheila's front yard pyre. Using an X-ray of an old fracture to Kenneth Countie's hand, Sorg was able to match fragments from the left index, middle and ring fingers.

Sorg estimated the fire must have gotten to 1,100°F to have done as much damage as it did, suggesting the fire had to have been tended to make it that hot.

The expert also offered that only the roots of the victim's teeth were ever recovered. The crowns had been destroyed. A forensic dentist who had identified plane crash victims through their teeth said he had never seen a case in which the crowns were shattered but the roots remained. It was Sorg's belief that the teeth were intentionally tampered with, though the effort involved in destroying each tooth would have been considerable.

The description of how thoroughly obliterated her son's remains were finally broke Carolynn Lodge's forced composure. After a month of stoic bravery, Lodge now let out a guttural sob. She ran from the courtroom, a victim's advocate from the Attorney General's office right behind her.

The emotional day continued as Kenneth Countie Sr. was called to testify. A hockey coach, he was still built like a player. His head was cleanly shorn, so those looking for physical resemblances to his dead son had to look into the man's eyes. His pain had been less overt than his ex-wife's, more introspective. Now, he struggled to hold his restraint together when describing his son.

"If you gave him the time of day, he would be your friend for life," Countie said. He fought back tears talking about their last night together at a college hockey game. "It was probably the best night of my life."

When asked, Countie said his son did not smoke. This was significant, because the evidence showed there had been a high concentration of nicotine in Kenny's blood.

Investigators said they recovered 310 items from the LaBarre property, including a blood-covered buck knife, partially burnt pruning sheers and over one hundred swabs of blood. There were ten VHS tapes taken from the farm. Messages from Michael Deloge were discovered on them.

On the video, Deloge appeared wearing a dark cap, looking directly into the camera. He had a scratch under his left eye.

"Mom," he began, "Who the hell is Tony? Why did you let him touch me? I cannot believe you let that happen. I'm really messed up about this. You really messed me up."

Deloge looked unsure of himself, like he was trying to remember what to say. It looked like the kind of video that terrorists forced hostages to make.

"If it weren't for Sheila, I wouldn't know half the things I know."

Not long after the video of Sheila's victim played, Donna Boston took the stand to explain how her son walked out of her life and into the darkest of homes.

In late spring of 2004, Donna Boston had been getting ready to leave for work when her son surprised her at her Somersworth apartment.

"There's someone I want you to meet," he said and introduced her to Sheila LaBarre. Right away, Boston didn't care for Sheila. She made Deloge fetch her purse or get her a drink and gave these orders with such attitude as to be repulsive.

"We should all get together at my farm for a cookout sometime," Sheila offered, but never followed through.

Michael Deloge and Donna Boston talked two or three times a week. When they greeted each other in person it was always with a hug and a kiss. This affection bothered Sheila, who told Deloge she would stop taking him to visit if he didn't knock it off.

At Christmas 2004, Sheila gave Boston many lavish gifts. Unlike at other times, Sheila showered Michael's mother with affection. The volume of gifts, from a person she didn't really care for, made Boston uncomfortable. Around the Christmas tree in the tiny apartment, Sheila seemed to take over the whole show, singing carols and acting as if she were the hostess.

Right after the holiday, Boston became sick and needed hospitalization. She tried to get in touch with Michael, whom she assumed was still living on Sheila's farm, but couldn't reach him. As a last resort, she called the Epping Police Department and asked them to go to the farm and tell her son that she would be in the hospital.

After the police visit, Boston tried to get hold of her son again, but no one picked up the phone at the farm when she called. It wasn't until July 2005 that she saw him again. Sheila and Michael came over to celebrate Boston's birthday.

That day, there was tension in the air. Everyone sat in silence at first. Then Sheila turned to Michael and prompted, "You've got something to say to your mother or I'm leaving."

Boston didn't know what this was about. Would this explain Michael's prolonged absence from her life?

"You raped me," the son said to his mother. "You assaulted me."

Boston was shocked. She knew nothing of what her son was saying. She became very angry with Sheila and Michael.

"Get out!" she said. "Get out! I don't want to have nothing

more to do with either of you!" Satisfied, Sheila picked up her purse and escorted Michael from the apartment.

From that day on, when someone asked about her son, Boston replied, "I don't know where Michael is and I don't care where Michael is."

In court, recalling these events brought tears to the witness. As prosecutor Jane Young showed the jury a photograph of Michael Deloge, members of the panel leaned forward to get a better look at the young man's face. Donna Boston wept directly into the microphone.

"Those accusations are 100 percent not true," said Boston. Then she completely lost hold of her emotions and began crying. Judge Nadeau ordered the jury out of the room, but each member took a long look at the suffering woman before he or she left.

Another witness was one of the handymen whom Sheila had working on her land. He had known Dr. LaBarre and knew Sheila when she came to town. He did odd jobs, like shoveled snow at the Somersworth apartments or split firewood on the farm. Sometimes Sheila paid him in cash, sometimes in beer or cigarettes, then drove him home.

The handyman had often worked alongside Michael Deloge on the farm. Deloge wouldn't make small talk, so the other man gave up trying. He had seen Sheila beat Deloge with a switch of red oak or throw him to the ground. He saw her accuse Deloge of killing her rabbits. One time, she accused Deloge of ripping the cloth cover on Dr. LaBarre's stagecoach. Deloge denied it, but after persistent nagging from the lady he admitted to the deed. Sheila beat him for it.

Sheila employed another farmhand, a local man of slow mind, and once beat him with a stick. After the man hit the ground Sheila spun around to Deloge and asked, "What are you grinning at?" The handyman had been watching Deloge and knew he had not been grinning, but Sheila struck him anyway.

The handyman noticed that Deloge often had gouges on his face and scabs that looked like they had been reopened.

Deloge had scars on his back. He had a green pallor to his skin and he seemed to be getting weaker.

Then one day, Michael Deloge was no longer on the farm.

The handyman testified that his wife and daughter had come to the farm at Halloween. While the adults were chatting, the handyman's daughter wandered into another room to make a cell phone call. Sheila stalked the girl and berated her. "Don't call people in my house!" The scene was so upsetting that the handyman ushered his family out.

Standing in the doorway, the handyman turned back to look at Sheila. This would be the moment for a cutting insult or a clever putdown. Instead, something else came to the handyman's lips.

"So Sheila," he asked. "Where did you say Michael went to?"

The woman moved in closer, her eyes burning.

"Where was it? Connecticut?"

"You think I killed Michael," she said. "You think I killed Michael, don't you?"

The handyman said nothing more and walked out of the house.

Investigators testified that when they drained the septic tank in Sheila's leach field they discovered the broken remains of a cell phone, three bullet casings and a wallet with Michael Deloge's birth certificate tucked in a protective plastic frame.

When Sheila LaBarre returned to the Silver Leopard farm on March 24, 2006 to find police kicking in her door looking for Kenneth Countie, she was not alone. A woman was waiting in a dark pickup truck. She inadvertently had seen more on the farm that week than she should have.

The woman, Brenda Cahill, had met the defendant after taking her child to the Silver Leopard Farm to look at Sheila's horses. The property owner was gracious to the child. She whistled to her horses in the field and said, "Come on, little babies," and they trotted into their stables. The woman had never seen anything like it.

The woman's twenty-ish child had learning disabilities, but was someone whom Sheila could count on for help at the farm. Soon both of Cahill's kids were making fifty dollars a day doing little chores around the place.

On Monday, March 20, 2006, Cahill returned to her home after work to find Sheila LaBarre in her kitchen talking with the kids. She had come to pay for some recent labor. Cahill noticed Sheila was dolled up. She had on a leopard-skin coat and the strong aroma of perfume permeated the air.

They chatted for about an hour. Cahill was completely stressed about her dog. He was going through kidney failure and she was a wreck about it. All the dog could eat was pizza from one particular restaurant. He'd eaten some Saturday but had nothing on Sunday. Sheila offered to drive to a little parlor the next town over.

The two bundled up and got into Sheila's car. As the woman opened the door, she was startled by the figure of a man sitting in the back seat.

"This is Kenneth. But we call him 'Adam.' We like 'Adam' better, don't we?" Sheila asked.

The man in the back said, "Yes."

Cahill didn't want to ask why Sheila called the man by a different name. It was twenty degrees outside and the temperature was falling. All this time they had been talking inside while a person had been waiting for them outside?

"Sheila! Why didn't you invite him in earlier?!" She was both embarrassed and confused.

Sheila replied, "I'd never bring a stranger into your home."

Cahill tried to get a better look at the passenger. He had some bruising on his face, but she could see little else. He wore a hat and an oversized coat, a coat that must have belonged to someone else. Sheila, not one to overlook the suffering of animals, offered to return to Cahill's house and give her dog a chiropractic adjustment.

At 5:40 P.M. early the next night, Sheila showed up with Dr. LaBarre's chiropractic table. It was much later than Cahill had anticipated and she needed to be at a school banquet at

6:00. Sheila quickly worked on the dog so that Cahill could get to the event on time.

The next morning, Wednesday, March 22, Cahill awoke to hear voices coming from her kitchen. Sheila and her dog, Demetrius, were visiting with the woman's son. Her son was thinking of buying a trailer and Sheila offered to evaluate it.

Later in the day, Brenda picked up Sheila at the farm. She noticed a horrible odor, unlike anything she had ever experienced before.

"Don't mind that smell," Sheila told her. "I'm burning my garbage."

Cahill took Sheila to the seacoast to check out the trailer. On the way there, Sheila complained about some employees at Wal-Mart, saying they accused her of being a suspicious person. Upon arriving, the women looked the trailer up and down and Sheila's advice was her son should not buy it. The two women went to dinner in Portsmouth, then stopped at the liquor store to buy some liquor.

Afterward, they went back to Cahill's house and Sheila poured shots. Cahill wasn't much of a drinker, certainly not on a Wednesday, but she drank a bit. Her kids were there and everyone was having fun.

Sheila downed another slug of lemon liqueur and slammed the shot glass on the table with such force it shattered. Everyone laughed. Sheila felt horrible when she learned the shot glass had been a gift to one of the woman's kids from a friend who had brought it back from Cancun. While the shards were taken away, Sheila said it reminded her of the broken glass in her tub that gave her the cuts on her hands.

The ladies moved into the kitchen and continued their laughter. Somehow, Sheila's conversation turned to how to kill someone.

"I know how," Sheila said.

"Oh yeah?"

"Like this . . ." Sheila made a little fist and pretended to hold a knife, then mimed stabbing someone repeatedly in the neck. Cahill said Sheila squealed with laughter while Cahill made the sound effects from *Psycho*.

"I did not!" Sheila LaBarre shouted across the courtroom at the witness stand, where Cahill had been testifying. After a brief admonishment to the defendant from her attorneys, Cahill continued to discuss the night of March 22.

Brenda said she drove Sheila home. On the way, Sheila offered to cremate Cahill's dog when it passed.

"How do you do it?" Cahill asked, knowing Sheila had cremated farm animals. "Put it on a spit?"

"No, you lay it on the ground and pile wood on top of it."

Inside the farmhouse, Cahill saw the couch was pulled out, the cushions were off. She could smell something foul coming from the basement.

Sheila took a pill and offered the woman half of another. The guest refused. The host turned on the oven, popped some pigs-in-a-blanket on a rack and did a few more lemon shots.

For the fourth day in a row, Sheila LaBarre turned up at Brenda Cahill's house. On Thursday, the woman left for a doctor's appointment. Sheila stayed behind and put the ailing dog on a mat so it could get some sun. She brought her portable stereo and played music for the sleeping dog. That night, the family got a pre-cooked chicken from a local supermarket and shared it with Sheila.

On Friday, March 24, Sheila came over to retrieve her boom box from the porch. Her demeanor was a little more frazzled, a little panicky. While Cahill was on the phone, she overheard Sheila telling her kids that Kenneth was a pedophile.

Sheila convinced the woman to come along with her on some errands. Sheila picked up food for the horses just before the feed store was closing for the weekend. After, they drove to a supermarket. Along the way, Sheila told the woman that Dr. LaBarre had married his cousin and his two children were the result of an incestuous relationship.

Cahill watched Sheila fill a whole cart of groceries. Brenda bought a turkey baster, the only thing she thought she needed. Sheila complained to the delicatessen manager that they didn't clean their slicers enough. She asked for all the items to be double-bagged, then placed them in the back of her pickup truck right next to two yellow diesel fuel containers.

When the women pulled up Red Oak Hill Lane, they spotted two police cars parked at the gate to Sheila's home. The truck stopped a short distance from the entrance.

"Wait here." Sheila walked up to the darkened house. The woman waited in the cab, Sheila's coat draped over her like a blanket. There was no heat, no light. Her cell phone wasn't charged. She was stuck in the cold pickup for a half an hour. From her position, she could see flashlights going from window to window, from room to room.

I just want to go home, she thought.

After the search, the police cars backed up and left, and Sheila walked to the truck.

"Why were the cops here?" Cahill asked.

"I don't know." Sheila put the key in the ignition and drove the truck up the road to empty her groceries. Sheila asked the woman to move a charred mattress on her front lawn so she could back the pickup to the door.

Cahill saw the splintered wood from where the police had broken in. Sheila began to feed the dog. Cahill noticed the odor was gone.

"What was that all about?"

"Hush up," Sheila said. "I have to think."

There was a worried silence. No doubt, enterprises of great pitch and moment were turning in her head. "What's happening?" the woman finally asked.

"My boyfriend is missing." Sheila turned to the woman and proclaimed the Epping police were trying to set her up. "If anything should happen to me, would you please take care of my dog?" she asked plaintively.

After they unloaded the rest of the groceries, she took Cahill home. Sheila said she thought a police car was following them. The woman looked back and the squad car was right behind them.

To wrap up the prosecution's case, the State presented videotape of twelve hours of psychological examinations by

Dr. Arthur Drukteinis. Because insanity is an affirmative defense, the exams are admissible in court.

Sheila met with the State's psychologist on three occasions in a holding room at the Dover Police Department. There were pleasantries in the beginning of the taped meeting. Acknowledging her upbringing, Drukteinis told Sheila that his son was about to graduate from the University of Alabama in Birmingham. Sheila said her niece went to UAB and would graduate too. Drukteinis commented that they might both be at the same graduation ceremony and they laughed.

Sheila complained about the tranquilizer she was taking and the pain in her pelvis. She said the single mattresses in jail weren't good for the left scoliosis in her spine.

As they continued talking, Sheila told Dr. Drukteinis that her daddy seemed like two people. He drank too much. One time he chased them with an ax. She thought if they hid under blankets, Daddy wouldn't find them.

Sheila said she had vague memories of sexual abuse at the hands of her father. She brought up the night during a thunderstorm when she was lying in her parents' bed. "No Daddy, don't," she said as he put his hand between her legs. Her mother woke up and yelled, "Stop." Sheila remembered Manuel kicking them both out of bed very hard.

Sheila talked of a dream she had in which her father was touching her left breast. She said she wanted to die in the dream, but she wasn't sure what the dream was suppose to symbolize.

Then Drukteinis asked about the death of Kenneth Countie. Sheila said it had been an accident. She said Kenny ran into the upstairs bathroom where they began to fight. Sheila thought Kenny was reaching into a hiding place behind the tub where she was keeping two thousand dollars. They struggled. He was strong and tried to choke her. Somehow the shower got turned on and the floor was slick. Kenny slipped and hit his head on the side of the tub.

On the videotape, Sheila LaBarre sobbed for two straight minutes. "It made the most awful sound." Sheila claimed she cremated the body, because she knew Kenny did not want his mother to ever touch his body again.

Her account didn't match the physical evidence. Arterial blood spatter from a live Kenneth Countie was discovered on the first floor, not the second. And judging by the physical condition Kenny was last seen in, it's unlikely he would have the strength to run or fight in the manner she described.

There was another version of Kenny's death Sheila told her attorneys: that she struck him in the head with a sledgehammer while he slept on the mattress on the floor. But the blood spatter did not match that version either; its position suggested the victim was not that close to the floor during the attack.

In the first interview, Sheila refused to discuss Michael Deloge with Drukteinis, as she had not been charged with this death. By the last interview, when she had changed her plea, she was ready to tell how Deloge died.

Sheila claimed Deloge harmed Snooky, her favorite rabbit, by burning his paw. Deloge looked at Sheila and said that he was going to hurt her next. In fear for her life, she reached for a four-foot chain and struck him repeatedly in the head. The blows knocked Deloge senseless. Sheila attended to Snooky, then turned her attention to Deloge.

She brought him inside and laid him on a couch, nursing his wounds. She offered to get medical help, but Michael trusted her nursing abilities. He lingered for several weeks. Before dying he confessed all of his animal abuse to Sheila.

"I deserved it. I know I deserved it," he told her.

Again, the physical evidence did not match this version. Deloge's blood was found in the upstairs bedroom in patterns not consistent with blunt-force trauma.

On the witness stand, Dr. Albert Drukteinis debunked the defense experts' findings about Sheila's mission to kill pedophiles as pseudo-science and psycho-babble. Though there had been men in her life who *were* pedophiles, Drukteinis said that was not, in his opinion, why she killed these lovers.

"It gave her an excuse to kill them because she's sadistic.

And that's what her aim was: to be sadistic." His voice was quiet but firm.

Drukteinis believed that Sheila did have a mental illness, but not one that compelled her to commit murder. At one point, he suggested that it might have been Sheila who had been abusing the rabbits instead of Deloge.

"I didn't harm my animals! I didn't kill any animals!" Sheila shouted from the defense table. "You're being paid to say that!" The deputies grabbed the defendant and dragged her from the courtroom.

CHAPTER 33

BLACK WIDOW

Closing arguments in *State* v. *Sheila LaBarre* were scheduled for the afternoon of June 18, 2008. A larger crowd packed the courtroom. Spectators were told that once the speeches began the doors to the courtroom would be shut and would not be reopened until the arguments were complete.

Epping Police Lieutenant Michael Wallace and Detective Richard Cote came to represent the town. NH State Police Sergeant Richard Mitchell and Trooper Jill Rockey sat in the back row with Wallace and Cote.

Two of the victims' mothers felt they badly needed closure. Donna Boston came into the courtroom before the proceedings and found Carolynn Lodge in the front row. While the Counties and Lodges had been surrounded as the trial wound on with loved ones, Boston had always come alone, sometimes needing to wait at the courthouse door for a ride home at the end of the day. Each day, the Counties figuratively put their arms around Boston and offered her what was her rightful place with the other parents in the front row. She had become stronger and seemed ready for this last fight.

When Boston reached Lodge, they embraced and exchanged warm glances. They recognized they had lived through this nightmare together and would always be bonded through the spirits of their sons.

I sat in the back row of the court among the journalists. They would all carry the story through broadcast or print, but not I. For a moment I felt like an elder statesman, offering little-known insights about the case or commiserating about some difficulty in doing the job.

Sheila came into the court, still dressed in prison clothes. I wondered why a woman of such self-professed taste did not choose a civilian wardrobe for these proceedings. Most likely, Denner didn't allow it. Jurors don't think of insane people as having any sense of style.

Sheila sat down and looked over her right shoulder at the media in the gallery. She had done this often during the trial. Sometimes she smiled and posed; other times she gave evil glares. At one point, Sheila made eye contact with Carolynn Lodge. At first, Kenny's mother seemed repelled by her stare. But, out of sight of the cameras and in plain view of the defendant, Lodge scratched the bridge of her nose with her middle finger. Realizing she had just been flipped the bird, Sheila made a sourpuss that got camera shutters clicking.

Neither the judge nor the jury had been seated yet, so things remained informal. I stood up so Sheila could see me. We locked eyes as we had a year earlier in the county jail. This time, Sheila's gaze was dark and unwelcoming. Her face was frozen, eyes narrowed, lips pinched. I understand she was feeling that now I was just another man who had let her down. Daggers shot forth toward me from her frozen expression. For a fleeting second, I saw in those eyes what Kenneth Countie and Michael Deloge had seen in them. Bile filled my mouth. I turned away and sat down; Sheila had won the staring contest.

The prosecution gave their closing statement first. James Boffetti offered it. His years as a defense attorney were a strength in this case, as he made the argument that LaBarre's lawyers had not met their burden of proof.

"At the very beginning of this trial, counsel for the defendant made certain promises. They said you would know insanity when you saw it, that it wouldn't even be close," Boffetti said. "I now stand before you and ask you to hold them to their promises, because those promises went unfulfilled. They have not met their burden of proof, because the evidence is so strong that this woman was and is indeed sane."

Boffetti retrieved the metal screen that Sheila had used to sift through the ashes in search of human remains. "She was in a panic. Burning, sifting, flushing everything in sight that could implicate her in the murder. She knew what she did in both murders was legally wrong. She made careful decisions to conceal her crimes and systematically destroy evidence.

"The killings of Kenneth Countie and Michael Deloge were the escalation of her pattern of choices to taunt, torment and ultimately torture those people whom she chose to ensnare in her life."

Echoing the testimony of Dr. Drukteinis, Boffetti called the avenging angel theory psycho-babble.

"Defense experts gave convoluted and confusing explanations; the truth is much simpler: those killings were the result of her perverse sexual desire and her uncontrolled violence gone too far.

"She taunted, tormented and tortured both men as part of her sexual perversion. She lost control of her anger and her sexual lust, which is combined for her, and she killed them," he said.

The jury appeared to be listening carefully as the prosecutor went on. To hear it from Boffetti, the former priest, it was like a homily on the evils of the world.

"She is a predator of vulnerable men. She is a black widow and she should be held criminally responsible for these murders." The rapid taps from reporters on laptops came quicker as Boffetti went on.

"Clear and convincing evidence of insanity? Folks, this isn't even close. This woman is not insane. She is evil, sadistic, violent and she is playing the system," the AAG said.

"Hold her responsible, because she is guilty."

* * *

Jeffrey Denner and the defense got the last word. His team took a moment to place around the courtroom poster-sized photos of the burn pit, of the farmland and of Kenneth Countie being wheeled through Wal-Mart. The exhibits caused a stir in the front row where the victims' families sat.

"Sheila LaBarre is crazy," Denner began. "Sheila LaBarre is utterly crazy. Sheila LaBarre is a severely disturbed woman. Sheila LaBarre is nuts. Whether you call it crazy, whether you call it nuts, fruitcake, fruit loop, it basically gets to the same place. She is a deeply troubled human being and has been deeply troubled for a long time. Almost everyone who has met her knows that." Denner's voice was soft and even. Tension built in the courtroom as he went on.

"Why did these murders happen if she's not crazy, if she's not insane? If she's not suffering from an actual deluded psychotic illness? You cannot identify any other rational motive for why she's done what she's done."

The attorney tried to get jurors into the tortured mindset of Sheila. "On the one hand, you have bunnies running around and ponies and horses, and there's love. And on the other hand, you've got hate and pedophiles and everything that's inconsistent with the first world."

"She wants revenge," Denner continued. "And, at the same time, there's a part of her that's a decent human being. She wants to be liked. She wants to be loved. She wants to be protected. You see an absolutely tortured soul whose inner torture is regularly played out in the external world."

Denner also planted the seed that the true culprits in the deaths of Michael Deloge and Kenneth Countie were the authorities who ignored and laughed off Sheila's violent behavior for years. He said someone (meaning the victims' families) would have the right to sue the police for their inaction.

"If the police admitted on the stand that they made a mistake, they could be held liable," Denner suggested. "That it was not 'just Sheila being Sheila.'"

Finally, Denner concluded the defense's case quietly,

firmly stating, "I'm happy to look you all in the face and say we have met our burden."

After giving the jury instructions, Judge Tina Nadeau drew four names from a cup to determine which of the jurors were the alternates. One juror had been removed in week five, cryptically telling a reporter it was because he "knew too much." The trial had gone two weeks longer than anticipated and should deliberations continue past the weekend, it would have messed with another juror's summer vacation, so she volunteered to step aside. The four other jurors chosen as alternates accepted the news, but disappointment was on their faces. They had just spent six weeks listening to grueling, gruesome testimony and now they were not going to be part of the decision. All the jurors filed out at the end of the day, prepared to return Thursday morning and begin deliberations.

Before leaving the bench, Judge Nadeau addressed those remaining in the courtroom.

"I don't want anyone on either side to think these attorneys left something on the table," she said. "In my fifteen years on the bench, this was the best tried case I have ever seen." Everyone nodded his or her head. There was mutual respect on both sides.

The bailiff ordered all to rise as Nadeau left the room, but there isn't a judicial equivalent of "at ease" or "as you were." There was only the alien feeling of being alone in court with nothing left to do. The attorneys stood around for a moment, then mingled with some handshakes passed back and forth. The reporters stood with notepads open and nothing to write.

The prosecutors turned to the gallery and spoke to the families. Soon the relatives were passing out hugs to the attorney who had asked the court for justice for their sons.

Brad Bailey moved ever so cautiously towards the families. Over the weeks, he had been unable to make conversation with them. There was something he wanted to say to Carolynn Lodge, but she wouldn't let him. Instead, the stick-thin woman hugged the bear of a man who had defended her son's killer. The embrace wasn't born from admiration, but from an acknowledgment that they had all gone through this ordeal together.

Sheila LaBarre got up quietly from her chair, waiting for direction from a deputy. Jeffrey Denner came over to the woman and shook her hand. She smiled softly at him and he spoke.

"The most anyone can do is the best they can. And we've done the best we can for you. And now the chips will fall where they fall."

Sheila seemed to take some comfort in that. She and Denner hugged, then she left the courtroom. All they, and those of us who hoped for justice, could do was wait.

One hundred and fifteen years earlier to the day, another New England jury returned a verdict in that century's most violent and puzzling crime. On June 20, 1893, twelve Massachusetts men found Lizzy Borden not guilty of the ax murders of her father and stepmother.

Two days of deliberation passed. On the afternoon of Friday, June 20, 2008, word came from the jury of equal parts men and women that they had reached a verdict.

All the parties had about fifteen minutes to prepare to hear the verdict. Jeffrey Denner and his team had been camped out in an adjacent courtroom given to them by the judge to use as a temporary office. It was much too far to travel to Epping from Boston, even with an hour's notice. The city was a wreck anyway. On Tuesday night, the Boston Celtics had won their first NBA title since 1986. (That last championship had come around the same time Sheila Bailey Jennings moved to Epping to live on the farm.) Denner's law office shared a parking garage with the Garden and the area around North Station had been a madhouse.

"All rise for the jury."

The panel filed in, waited for Judge Nadeau, then everyone sat en masse. No one sat all the way back in their seat. Anticipation and tension filled the air.

"Has the jury reached a verdict?"

"Yes," the foreman answered.

"On both charges?"

"Yes."

"On the case of 08-S-517, the first-degree murder of Michael Deloge, how say you? Is the defendant sane and guilty or is the defendant not guilty by reason of insanity?"

"Sane and guilty," the foreman said.

Sheila stood between her attorneys, her hands folded neatly in front of her, her hair pulled back in a ponytail. She offered no reaction to the verdict.

"So say you all, ladies and gentlemen of the jury?" The members of the panel gave an affirmation in unison.

"As to the charge of 06-S-2506, the first-degree murder of Kenneth Countie, how say you? Is the defendant sane and guilty or is the defendant not guilty by reason of insanity?"

"Sane and guilty."

There was an excited gasp from Kenneth Countie's mother and the others in the front row tried to steady themselves and their emotions. Tears began to pour freely.

A brief recess was called before sentencing. James Boffetti, Jane Young and Anne Rice all turned to the families of the victims reaching out to hold them. Their frames were weak and the wrenching pain of the past two years was evident, from their fingernails in tight clutches, from the full weight of their bodies that seemed unable to stand any longer. The prosecutors wiped away their own tears.

Donna Boston grabbed on to Carolynn Lodge. "We got it," Boston said.

Lodge responded with a sigh, saying, "It's over."

It truly was over. The thing that motivated them to get out of bed, to put food in their mouths, to keep on living, they had finally heard and seen it. *Guilty.* They had lived to see only that. "I'm worried about you," Boffetti later told Carolynn Lodge. Her single wish of a conviction was obtained. With that, what was left to wake up for, to eat for, to breathe for? Only now would life without her son truly begin.

Donna Boston was too emotional to make a victim impact statement. Kenny's stepmother began by telling the judge Sheila was "the most evil villain this country has ever witnessed." A friend of the family read an original poem, in which the last line predicted Sheila would go to hell, much to the cheers of the victims' families.

Carolynn Lodge finally spoke in public about her son. She read from notes that had been prepared days earlier, leaning on Jane Young while she gripped the podium.

"Sheila LaBarre took advantage of my son, who was a kind, caring, gentle young man who could not socially defend himself," Lodge said. "She was a master of evil. Sheila LaBarre stripped my son of all his dignity and self-worth, and in the end, she murdered him."

The mother who had seemed so mighty for the six weeks of the trial, who had grown so strong since that first court appearance in Massachusetts, showed not only her anger but also her own frailty. She told the judge she was haunted by the idea she could have done more to save Kenny's life.

"Oh, Kenny, my love, I did everything in my power to save you. You were at my fingertips, and I could not reach you. Kenny, I was so close. I am so sorry."

Lodge said she dared not sleep, for when she closed her eyes she could see Kenny calling out to her. Each day, she waited for him to come through the door. It seems for a mother, two years is not nearly enough time to be ready to move on.

The sentencing was swift and simple. There was only one remedy the state of New Hampshire allowed. Nadeau made no speech. She simply laid down the law.

"I hereby sentence you to two life-without-the-possibility-of-parole sentences at the New Hampshire State Prison."

There was a look of relief on Sheila LaBarre's face.

She told her legal team, "I never wanted anyone to think I was crazy."

Denner couldn't believe she seemed relieved, even happy, about the verdict. *That has to be,* he thought, *the greatest indicator of the depths of her insanity.*

EPILOGUE

JULY 4, 2008

This week, Peter Odom handed in his resignation to the Fulton County District Attorney. The man who loved to argue found the job in Atlanta was not what he thought it would be. He told me on the phone that I was the first in New Hampshire to learn that he was starting his own private practice. He did not follow Sheila's trial from Georgia, but he still keeps a photo of Kenny Countie on his bulletin board.

Aside from the lawyers and law enforcement officials involved, I believe I am the one person in the world who knows the most about the Sheila LaBarre case. But Pete Odom told me something I didn't know, something that completely blew my mind. It was something I'm not sure he was supposed to tell me.

Sheila had pointed to the blue Wal-Mart bag and said of Kenneth Countie, "He's in the bag."

Investigators sifted through it, but later discovered the human remains inside that plastic bag did *not* belong to Kenneth Countie or to Michael Deloge.

Immediately following the verdict, Sheila was taken to Concord for some kind of evaluation. Whatever took place there didn't change her fate. Her handlers did *not* decide to spin her around and point her down the hallway to the Secure Psychiatric Unit after her evaluation. They stuck her in the van and shipped her back to the New Hampshire Prison for Women in Goffstown, the facility that biker Steve Martello thought the eccentric hitchhiker might have escaped from. Today is Sheila's fiftieth birthday.

Once Sheila settled in prison, she wrote to Lynn Noojin. The sisters had had one last conversation before the verdict. Lynn sent me an e-mail the next day:

> Well, I ratted you out to Sheila!!!!! I told her you were writing a book. She was like happy happy. . . . said is he portraying me in a good way? I said well, don't know, it's about what happened up there. Then I told her the title and she laughed a little laugh and very comically said "well, let me see, uh no I would say NOT!"

After the verdict, Sheila called Lynn and forbade her to ever talk to me again. And then she asked Lynn for money.

Only God knows the pain that went through Carolynn Lodge's heart each day of the trial. Yet over the two years of the legal prosecution, she changed. She had been so frail at first, not eating and torturing herself with all those trips to the farm. I've come to have great respect and affection for her, but sadly, I feel she is not ready to move on.

Carolynn has tried. She has tried to find Kenny wherever she can. The month before he died, Kenny was supposed to start in a hockey league. As a tribute, the former figure skater joined a female hockey team. She admitted she was horrible. *Come on, Kenny,* she muttered to herself, completely aware that the whole team must have thought she was "daft." *What am I doing wrong here? How am I supposed to hold this stick?* The experiment ended when Carolynn fell backwards on the ice and broke her wrist.

"I don't *feel* him," she told me, concerned, because she believed she was supposed to. She was resentful of those well-meaning people who told her things would get better and she would get through it. "They haven't walked a mile in me shoes," she said.

On Kenny's first birthday after his death, Carolynn brought a cake and a candle to his memorial tree. She sang to him then lit the candle.

"Come on, Kenny. If you're here, show me a sign." Just then a breeze kicked up and blew out the candle. It was life-affirming for her.

The following year, Carolynn returned on his birthday. Again she brought another candle.

"Come on, Kenny. It's your mum. Show me you're here with me." She waited and waited but nothing happened.

I decided to wait a week before I contacted Kelly Norris's husband, Timothy, to follow up about the photos Lynn Noojin recovered. The couple was greatly suspicious of the phone call from one of Sheila's relatives, fearing yet another scheme orchestrated from behind bars. Only after I vouched for Lynn's sincerity, her need to make an act of contrition on behalf of her sister, did Norris entertain the thought that this wasn't some sort of trick. LaBarre's son had passed away, and the last I heard from Leona LaBarre, she had declined a request to discuss the case. Kelly was all that was left of the "LaBarre Estate." Though the children had won a victory when the probate court vacated the will, by that time there was a line of litigators ready to pounce on the property. The Counties and Lodges, the State, even Sheila's own attorneys were rumored to have their eyes on what was the only tangible asset belonging (maybe) to Sheila LaBarre. On previous occasions, Timothy Norris said the potential legal battles over the 115 acres in Epping were so numerous that they were likely to walk away from it.

Jeffrey Denner surely could have put a mortgage on the farm to recoup some of his legal expenses from defending Sheila. The State agreed to reimburse Denner Pellegrino $15,000 for its costs. Denner told me that had they billed their normal rate, the defense of Sheila LaBarre would have been close to $700,000.

Denner invited me up to his high-rise office overlooking Boston, the Cradle of Democracy, where patriots like John

Adams and Samuel Adams roamed the cobbled streets below and dreamed of a new rule of law. The entire thirty-fifth floor was under renovation, upgrades I presumed. Denner still had many compelling cases on his desk. Most recently he won a settlement on behalf of the family of Melina Del Valle, a woman killed when a ninety-ton slab of concrete fell from the ceiling of a tunnel that was part of Boston's infamous "Big Dig." The makers of the epoxy anchor bolts that held the slab in place settled for six million dollars. Other companies, all with pockets allegedly fattened by working on the transportation boondoggle, are still on the hook.

Denner told me he was heartbroken over the LaBarre verdict. His assertion that Sheila was insane was not a convenient legal strategy, nor a "defense of last resort." He and his staff honestly believed Sheila was insane and they felt compelled to work as hard as possible to get her the appropriate care. He had no illusions about actually winning; he felt the standard to prove insanity in New Hampshire was nearly impossible to achieve. During voir dire, many potential jurors expressed concern about finding the defendant "insane" if it meant she might get out some day. At best, Denner and Bailey had hoped to get a hung jury and seek some sort of agreement with the State for criminal psychiatric confinement.

"In many ways, the trial was academic," he said. Once placed in the custody of the Corrections Department, authorities examined Sheila to determine where best to house her and how to meet her needs. Denner maintained there was no way a personality as severely deranged as Sheila's would properly function in prison, that regardless of what the jury said, in his opinion, she was likely to end up in the Secure Psychiatric Unit anyway.

Sheila did not last long at the Prison for Women in Goffstown, NH. In December 2008, a corrections official announced that Sheila had been transferred to a facility in Massachusetts. No reason for the change was given. An inmate who was in Goffstown at the same time said Sheila was threatening the other prisoners. She claims Sheila, fully aware of her legend and reputation, was threatening to "charcoal" them.

There was one important piece of evidence that was never introduced at trial. Paperwork filed by an FBI profiler (who was later barred from testifying in the case) indicated that among the remains found on the farm was an unidentified set of human toes. It has never been made public where they came from or to whom they belonged.

One might ask, More than two years and hundreds of hours of audiotapes, thousands of documents later . . . do we even know what happened on that farm?

It's not right that there is no answer to that simple question, I keep thinking. Dark questions revolve in my mind. *What happened to cause blood from two murdered lovers to be scattered all over that farmhouse? How did they die?* Based on forensic evidence alone, investigators can offer a solution to part of the puzzle. But no one except Sheila can say with any certainty what actually happened to those men.

What do I think happened? I don't know, but on these remaining pages I'm going to hazard a guess. I often meditate and drift back to those places, those confrontations. What do I imagine happened? How do I think those men lost their lives? If I close my eyes, I can almost travel back in time to those days on that farm. That paint is not chipped. The grounds are well-tended. However, inside the house a storm is brewing . . .

It was autumn and the leaves were changing colors on the farm. Michael Deloge was hobbled. He was physically exhausted from the crushed cigarettes she had been feeding him, giving his skin a green pallor. He could do little but lie in their bed in the second-floor bedroom.

He slept topless, because the shirts irritated his skin. His torso was covered with scratches and scars. He had a mark on his forehead where she had delivered a nonfatal blow with a metal chain. He had limped away from the farm that day, bleeding from the head, stumbling past the neighbors who did nothing, said nothing.

Michael wanted nothing more than to get better. Perhaps if he got back on his feet, he would be of some use to Sheila again. He could work hard on the farm for her, if only she'd give him the chance.

Sheila darkened the doorframe, wearing a smart barn coat suitable for outside chores. There were tears in her eyes. She looked genuinely sad. Michael rolled over. "What is it?" he asked.

"You killed her."

"What?"

The tears continued down her face. "My rabbit. I just found her outside, dead." The grieving pout turned to gritted teeth. "You murdered her!"

"Sheila, I've been up here the whole time . . ."

The woman removed her .38 from the pocket of the coat. "You did it."

Adrenaline started to pump through Michael's veins. She stood between him and the doorway. He stood and held both hands out.

"Sheila. Don't do this."

"You killed my sweet babies. My sweet, sweet babies."

"Sheila, Jesus Christ, no. I didn't kill your babies."

Her face was beet red, dripping with tears and spit and snot. "They were innocent! They did nothing to you! Why would you hurt them?! WHY?"

Michael, plaintive and crying, said, "I didn't hurt your rabbits, Sheila. Please, please don't kill me. Don't kill me, Sheila."

"I'm supposed to protect them, the little babies!"

"Sheila, don't."

"Never again. Never again!"

"Sheila, I have a son . . ."

Sheila fired three shots into Deloge. One slug passed through him and lodged into the wall. The impact caused a thin mist of blood to spray around the hole it made there.

She dragged his body into the second floor bathroom and began to dismember it in the tub with garden tools. In the process, she got blood all over the ceramic tiles, the wall, the ceiling. She was clumsy as she carried the remains from the second floor; in doing so, she smeared blood on the walls of the stairwell.

In an area away from the house, she built a pyre like the ones she'd made to cremate her horses. She placed Michael Deloge's body parts—along with the remains of the dead rabbit—in the fire pit with the mattress from the bed and watched it all burn. There was a cleansing calm that settled over her now that the deed was done. She walked away, leaving it all for a dog named Clancy to find months later.

Sheila pried the bullet out of the wall and got rid of it, probably by tossing it in the swamp or burying it in the woods. She took the ashes and flushed them down the toilet. She did the same thing with the spent casings from the .38. She gathered some of Deloge's papers, including his wallet and birth certificate, and flushed those too.

Sheila had known what to do, because she had written of all this in her journal. In July she'd sketched the outline of a body into her diary and drew cut lines through the limbs. Then she wrote about Daniel 3 in the Old Testament and the "fiery furnace" that would purify Michael when he walked out of the flames.

When Sheila took Kenneth Countie to bed, it wasn't in the upstairs room where she murdered Michael Deloge. By late March 2006, the house smelled ruinous. Kenny was constantly sick from nicotine poisoning. It kept him passive, controllable. Sheila had beaten him, scalded him with hot water. Now he was continuously vomiting from the cigarettes she crushed into his food. He had thrown up all over the leopard skin comforter that covered the mattress.

"Stop faking that," Sheila yelled at him. She was content to watch him suffer. "Kenneth Countie is faking vomiting," she announced for the benefit of the tape recorder. Sheila had just finished grilling him about all the children she *imagined he had molested. Now, physically spent, he was on the floor vomiting into the heat register.*

"Get up!" *Sheila, with the tape-recorder still in her hand, ordered the sick man to his feet. When he stood, Sheila slapped him. He began to back up.*

"You are an evil pedophile, aren't you!?"

"Yes," *he responded robotically.*

"You like to fuck little children, don't you?" *With each question she stepped forward, pushing him farther back into the corner.*

"Yes."

"You get off on it, don't you?"

"Yes." *Kenny's back was literally against the wood-paneled wall.*

"You hate your mother, don't you?"

"Y-yes . . ."

"You want to, don't you? You want to fuck your mother?"

Kenny hesitated. "N-no."

Sheila, with the tape-recorder running in her other hand, exploded. "No? Don't fucking say no to me! You want to! You want to fuck your mother! You want to fuck your mother!"

Instinct and disorder took over. Kenny, whose manner included tactile-defensiveness, felt smothered. He may not even have known at this point that Sheila was slowly killing him. But backed up with nowhere to move, her hands on his neck, he flinched, just as he had flinched in Wal-Mart when Sheila suddenly grabbed his shirt. Kenny, now trapped, fought back.

He flailed in a tantrum, swinging his arms, attempting to swat Sheila away. The ungraceful but powerful movements knocked Sheila back. He shouldn't be this strong! Sheila probably thought. He's been throwing up all day!

The wiring in Kenny's head was such that even now he wouldn't have been aware he was in a fight for his life. Sheila dropped the running tape-recorder so she could come back at him. Swinging, punching, clawing, they brutalized each other. Kenny gave her a wallop on the arm that would leave a bruise.

Sheila went into a death scream. There was rage in her eyes. She went to the kitchen and grabbed a buck knife from a cabinet and pulled the sheath off. As she approached him, he put his hands up in defense. Her first cuts were to his arms. As she sliced the skin, he gave a high-pitched "Ah!" a reflex consistent with any wound to the arms or neck. They struggled briefly with the blade and Sheila cut the outside of her hand.

Kenny ran into the kitchen. There she plunged the knife into him twice, leaving two medium-impact stains on the cabinets. He stumbled away, pressing his hands against the wounds.

He made his way into the dining room and steadied himself on a chair, dripping blood on the cushion. Sheila was coming quickly from behind. Kenny summoned all of the strength he had left and ran for the living room.

He tripped on the mattress on the floor and fell onto it. He was weak from blood loss and the poisoning. He couldn't get up.

Sheila ran in and climbed on top of him. In her eyes, she didn't see Kenneth Countie. She saw all the people responsible for her unhappiness, for her guilt, for her anger. In that moment, Sheila only saw who it was she was really trying to kill.

Sheila drove the buck knife into Kenny's chest, through the ribs, and into his heart.

"Daddy," she said as she pulled the blade out, reared it back and drove it in again, creating an arc of blood drops along the wall.

"Daddy!"

Kenneth Countie looked up at her, the light fading from his eyes.

"Mommy," he whispered. His last thoughts going to the one in life he truly loved the most.

Covered in blood, Sheila calmed down. She looked over the body on the mattress. Then, she slumped down next to it to think. She found the cassette recorder and played back the whole fatal attack. The police were already on to her; his mother wasn't going to stop calling. She had to get rid of the body, but also this tape. But the cassette also contained Kenny's "confession." It would exonerate her. No one would care about the death of a pedophile.

Sheila thought she had a way of preserving only the important portion of the tape, so she could get rid of the rest. She'd play it over the phone for the police. They record their phone calls. They'll have a copy of his confession. Then I can destroy the original. *She didn't know Epping PD did not record their calls.*

She began a process that was all too familiar at this point. She used hedge clippers and trimmers to cut up the body in the tub. This was tedious, exhausting work. She went around the house and washed all the blood she could see, using rags and sponges that were already tinged with blood-soaked water.

Sheila dragged Kenny's destroyed remains outside on a mattress still sopping in brownish-red fluid. She brought out a barrel in which to throw additional material. To improve her burn method, she had decided to use diesel fuel to get the fire going very hot. She filled the same yellow cans she made Kenny carry out of Wal-Mart days earlier. Murder had always been her intention, but she hadn't planned on killing him this soon. Sheila was like a cat playing with a mouse, but she'd lost control before the game was through.

Over the coming days, Sheila ran about town, running errands with Brenda Cahill and playing amateur chiropractor to her dying dog. But she also added fuel to her fire, continued to stoke it so that it burned every piece of what she'd placed there. She brought out a chair and placed the Indian chief photo to watch over the whole mess. When things cooled down, she sifted through the ash in search of bones to remove and dispose of. Larger bits she smashed with a rock, pulverizing the crowns of teeth.

But with the scrutiny of the police this time, Sheila knew she could not simply go back to life as normal on the farm. She began to pack mementos, including the crucifixes that were family heirlooms. She planned to take her things and run, run far from Epping. Perhaps she'd go back to Alabama where she could see her mother one last time. Perhaps to the tropical island she dreamed about as a child. But first she had to cover her own trail and write a suicide note to throw them off the scent.

There were just a few more hours to go before the fires would have completed their duty. Covered in dirt and sweat and ash, she continued to run about the yard when she noticed Chief Dodge and Lieutenant Wallace approaching her.

No, I'm not done. They're here too soon and I'm not done. *A few more hours and there would have been nothing left.*

In March 2009, the relatives of Kenneth Countie filed a lawsuit against the town of Epping. The suit alleged the police department caused or contributed to his death. The documents specifically pointed to the incident at Wal-Mart in which Sergeant Sean Gallagher and Detective Richard Cote failed to act to protect the injured and clearly suffering Countie. It asked for unspecified monetary damages.

On May 28, 2009, the circa-1777 Cape-style farmhouse at the end of Red Oak Hill Lane was sold at auction. The winner would be responsible for $7,500 in back taxes. A crowd of about 50 people, well more than the number that had registered to bid on the property, showed up in the rain to watch the proceedings—among them, Carolynn Lodge and her attorney. Dan Harvey, the man who had sold the property to Dr. LaBarre all those years ago, contemplated buying the land back. After four minutes of vigorous bidding, the parcel sold to an anonymous bidder for $600,000.

The new owners of the former Silver Leopard Farm began to clean up the debris that had been left by vandals and nature alike. They began to gut the interior of the farmhouse, a measure that would allow them to both modernize and sanitize the home.

Unsure of what would become of the shrine erected to Kenny at the end of the road, Carolynn Lodge was pleased to learn that the new owners would allow her to keep the flowers and other knickknacks. In June 2009, Carolynn invited me to come to the farm for a memorial service for Kenny. I was touched to know she thought enough of me to include me in the small guest list. The day of the event, it rained like mad. I, now a single father, thought asking my 8-year-old daughter to travel with me to Epping for a memorial service while standing in a rainy wood was more than I could expect of her, and was forced to miss it. Later that week I contacted Carolynn, who said there had been a small group of attendees. One of them was a priest who, at the family's request, performed an exorcism on the house.

I believe Sheila LaBarre symbolizes the absolute worst in humanity. Her depravity is deeper and more shocking than these pages can convey. She also represents an opportunity lost, a waste of what could have been an extraordinary life. She had raw talent, remarkable intelligence, ravishing beauty and spirited drive. She had the makings of a compelling celebrity, the kind of person whom childhood friends tell biographers they all knew would overcome, persevere and become famous some day. Instead, her rage and disappointment ate away at her star quality, channeling her power in a methodically diabolical fashion.

There is a scene in an episode of *The X-Files* called "Clyde Bruckman's Final Repose" about an apathetic psychic whose only power is that he can see how people will die. The character, played by Peter Boyle, is being hunted by a man who is killing psychics and fortune tellers, because they're unable to divine for him why he does what he does. Finally, the killer corners Bruckman and asks him why he's done these terrible deeds. Bruckman turns and says, "Don't you understand yet, son? Don't you get it? You do the things you do because . . . you're a homicidal maniac!"

I feel the answer to how Sheila LaBarre became a homicidal maniac is probably as simple as the fact that she just *is* one. Never have I encountered one person who has destroyed so many lives, bewitched so many people. Yet I'll always have some sympathy for her, knowing exactly how much pain fuels her own fiery furnace of hate and violence.

My trip down Red Oak Hill Lane doesn't look the same. All the trees lining the road leading to the edge of the La-Barre property have been cut down. It's brought light and warmth to a path that had been plucked from a horror movie.

I draw closer. The farm still sits there, rusting, slowly melting into the landscape where all the evil done still rests in microscopic pieces.

These days I live in a small New Hampshire town, one even smaller than Epping. There are no Wal-Marts or Star-bucks in this town. Perhaps it's small enough that a neighbor would take notice of a bleeding stranger stumbling along and step in to do something.

At dusk, the sun sets over rolling yellow fields and the green mountaintops that cradle my town in the valley they create between them. The smell of horses from distant prop-erties wafts in as neighbors pass by, taking their dogs for one last long daily stroll. Before the mosquitoes arrive I take one last look at what was, for at least one day longer, another Eden.

I stand in silence as I hold a rabbit in my arms, scratch him behind the ears and think of simpler times.

ACKNOWLEDGMENTS

I would like to thank the many investigators, attorneys and journalists who assisted in the creation of this book. I want to give special recognition to the families of both the accused and the victims, in particular Lynn Noojin, Joy Storer, Donna Boston and Carolynn Lodge. The grace, strength and gentle spirit they exhibited when thrust into these horrible events was truly remarkable.

I would like to thank my agent, Sharlene Martin, for shepherding this project in good times and bad. Also, Dr. Joan Dunphy of New Horizon Press, and her staff, Ron, JoAnne, Justin and Joanna, thanks for putting this tale on the page. Not to mention Charlie Spicer and the talented Allison Caplin at St. Martin's Paperbacks, and proofreader Richard Onley—thanks for making me part of the True Crime Library.

I want to recognize my family and the small circle of secret readers who helped with suggestions and encouragement. You kept me going. Lastly, I want to thank my editor and dear friend, Rebecca Lavoie, who makes both my books and my life infinitely better.